"Beginner's heartmind is the true standard for embodying boundless intimacy and ungraspable enlightenment in the sacred and pristine ordinariness of everyday life."

Shugyo Daijo-roshi
(Dr. Bonnici)

BOUNDLESS INTIMACY
The Eye And Treasury Of Core-Self

ANDREW SHUGYO DAIJO BONNICI, PH.D.
Doctor Of Humanistic Psychology
Practicing Zen Buddhist Roshi

ISBN: 978-145753-592-5

This Edition Published by Dog Ear Publishing,
4011 Vincennes Road Indianapolis, IN 46268
www.dogearpublishing.net

This book is printed in the
United States of America on acid-free paper.

A BRIEF NOTE

All the teachings in this book were written to facilitate and advance intrapersonal growth, interpersonal integrity, and transpersonal fulfillment. They are not intended to replace the services of your physician, clinical psychologist, psychotherapist, or psychiatrist. If you are taking prescribed medications or are currently receiving medical or psychological treatment, please inform your general practitioner or mental health care provider that you are practicing or beginning to practice the embodiment of these teachings.

Andrew Shugyo Daijo Bonnici, Ph.D.

DEDICATION

This book is dedicated in loving memory to my mom and dad, to Diana who is my eternal lover and soul mate, to Tony and Eric who are my treasured sons, to Amber who is daughter in my heart, and to my four precious grandchildren, Meira, Sage, Portia, and Bodhi.

無私親切
Boundless Intimacy

Art Work And Photos

Kannon, the female figure on the front cover, is the Zen archetype of infinite compassion. She is painted on an old Japanese scroll that has been hanging above the training altar of our Zen home temple for twenty-five years. The artist signed his name"Tetsuro." I used my photo of this Kannon because she reflects the total dynamic functioning of core-Self that is the tender embodiment of stillness, peace, intimacy, sensuality, and deep caring even in the midst of vast impermanence.

I wish to express my gratitude to Kanouro sensei who shared with me the four Japanese Kanji that mean "Boundless Intimacy." The script on the left of Kannon is my beginner's Way of brushing Boundless Intimacy in the loose Sosho style of Japanese calligraphy.

The ink paintings, Japanese Kanji, and reflective poetry that introduce each chapter were created by me in the summer of 1996. I also brushed the crooked pine on the title page in the same year. The meaning of each Kanji in the order that they appear is as follows: Infant, Breath, Zen Circle, Love, Faith, Wanderer, Flower, The Way, and Peace.

The black and white sketches that emphasize simplicity and naturalness throughout the book are public domain images. The photographs that introduce the epilogue and the five major sections of this written work are part of my personal collection. The training snapshots of my wife and two sons that appear in the last chapter were taken in the Zen meditation dojo of our temple home.

• CONTENT •

To Study Human Completion

"To study what is human completion, what is boundless intimacy, what is vast Oneness, and what is ungraspable enlightenment is to study the functioning of your ego-self. To study your ego-self functioning is to abide in the still composure of core-Self that silently illuminates the surface and depth of total reality. To abide in the still composure of core-Self is to effortlessly molt off your ego-self identity without fear of loosing yourself or your existence.

When you molt off ego-self in this gentle Way, you will recover the pristine nobility of your beginner's heartmind, continuously romance vast Oneness as the ever fresh impermanence of total reality, passionately extend tenderness and deep caring to yourself and others, and wholly realize your completion and fulfillment as a radical human being with not one thing lacking. This is how we live as core-Self in boundless intimacy with total reality. This is the Way we live in vast Oneness while gratefully blooming in ungraspable enlightenment with all beings and things."

Dr. Bonnici
(Shugyo Daijo-roshi)

"The most beautiful thing we can experience is the mysterious. It is the source of all true art and all science. Whoever does not know it and can no longer wonder, no longer stand rapt in awe, is as good as dead, a snuffed-out candle. To know that what is impenetrable for us really exists and manifests itself as the highest wisdom and the most radiant beauty, whose gross forms alone are intelligible to our poor faculties - this knowing, this feeling ... is the core of the true religious sentiment. In this sense, and in this sense alone, I rank myself among profoundly religious men."

Albert Einstein
1879-1955

• PREFACE •

Writing From My Body Core

I have been eagerly anticipating this moment with great excitement. The time has intimately arrived where I can passionately clarify how the embodiment of Zen enlightens the surface and depth of our everyday life while instantly manifesting the healing transformation of our global future. After forty-eight years of investigating and living the Way of Zen meditation, thirty-six years of postdoctoral research into the spiritual evolution of humanity, and twenty-five years of teaching others how to embody beginner's heartmind from the still brilliance of their core-Self, I am able to confidently share with you the Way to live in boundless intimacy and ungraspable enlightenment far beneath your figuring and thinking. The book itself took me seven years and thousands of hours to write, edit, and artistically design. Although it is for the benefit of all human beings, I have written it just for you. This may seem odd and strange to your thinking mind. However, your gut-core intelligence will come to accept this truth as you continue to read this book.

The teachings I share with you here were not written exclusively from my cerebral thinking. Every time I sat down to wholeheartedly write this book especially for you. I anchored all my thinking and writing within the gut-core intelligence of my whole body. Throughout this book, I refer to this gut-core intelligence as our core-Self. I wrote from the integrity of core-Self and the authenticity of my beginner's heartmind to somatically encourage the felt credibility and trustworthiness of these teachings.

However, even as you experience this felt credibility and trustworthiness, I encourage you to question these teachings with the genuine curiosity of your beginner's heartmind, somatically study how they enhance and improve your experience of everyday life, and confidently investigate their trustworthiness by applying the gut-intelligence of your core-Self.

Anchoring While Reading

This is not a book that you will read quickly. Keep in mind that this book teaches you how to live as a radical human being who openly lives in vast Oneness and boundless intimacy with all beings and things. Sometimes, you will have to reread sentences, phrases, and paragraphs several times. Do not try to understand the meaning only through your thinking mind. Before you begin to read this book, I encourage you to anchor your embodied awareness within the center of your lower abdomen. Do not read this book as if it is just verbal information. Do not think that you are only reading about written things. What I share with you is more than knowledge or bright ideas. Here, I have created an illuminating tapestry of words, phrases, and images that will viscerally resonate with the still vibrancy of your core-Self and the brilliant clarity of your beginner's heartmind.

About This Book

This book is a personal invitation to cultivate a Zen garden of boundless intimacy while enjoying the fragrant blooming of ungraspable enlightenment within the simplicity and complexity of your everyday life. In this book, I will teach you how to nourish your health, healing, and longevity, how to experience compassion, wisdom, and composure in your everyday life, how to refine the wholesome functioning of your ego-self and thinking mind, how to practice loving and being loved beyond resistance and fear, how to optimize your sports endurance and peak performance, how to naturally sustain your mental ease and emotional balance during work and business activities, how to socially express your individuality and personality from the still integrity of core-Self, how to advance the limitless nature of your creativity, empathy, and intuition, how to recover the exuberance and authenticity of beginner's heartmind, how to viscerally realize the completion and total fulfillment of your radical humanness, and how to lucidly and brilliantly actualize all your dreams far beyond your desiring and expecting.

All the chapters in this book are based on evening talks that I gave between 2005 and 2007. These were extemporaneous talks given to my Zen students in Hawaii. Each talk was given after two half hour periods of Zen meditation. The unfolding of each talk emerged spontaneously through the gut-intelligence of my core-Self before any planning or thinking. After transcribing the talks, I expanded, refined, and edited their original content into nine interweaving chapters that teach the visceral Way to live an authentic Zen life of vast Oneness and boundless intimacy.

Chapter Summaries

The book begins with a prologue that heralds a profound and exquisite Way of living in boundless intimacy, vast Oneness, and limitless interdependency during the passage of everyday life. I have divided the book into five major parts.

Part 1, entitled "Practice," has four chapters. The first chapter teaches you how to naturally and organically embody your core-Self; the second chapter tells you how to passionately live from your core-Self integrity; the third chapter unveils core-Self as the taproot of your radical humanness; and the fourth chapter discloses your core-Self as the still paradox of total reality.

Part 2, entitled "Illumination," consists of two chapters. The fifth chapter turns the light inward to reveal the total dynamic functioning of core-Self inside of just sitting; and the sixth chapter clarifies how core-Self unfolds the Way of ungraspable enlightenment while just living.

Part 3, entitled "Transmission," includes the seventh chapter. This chapter acquaints you with the three roots of Zen life, kindles the lamp of ancient buddhas, illuminates core-Self as the original seed of Zen transmission, advances your awakening to the power of lucid dreaming, and shows you how to respectfully actualize all your dreams within the vast Oneness of being dreamed with all beings and things.

Part 4, entitled "Cultivation," contains the eighth chapter. This chapter describes how to embody your life as a surprising journey, how to live beyond a fixed identity, how to satiate the root of desire, how to continuously refine the healthy functioning of ego-self, and how to practice a beginner's Way-seeking heartmind that heeds the vast Oneness and boundless intimacy of total reality.

Part 5, entitled "Instruction," presents the ninth and final chapter. This chapter teaches you how to create and somatically sustain a Zen dojo in your own home, how to set up a Zen meditation training altar, how to sensually and precisely embody Zen meditation far beyond mental concentration, and how to viscerally realize the brilliance of your core-Self in both activity and stillness.

The Epilogue, entitled "This Only Moment," is my final encouragement to live ungraspable enlightenment by tenderly loving others as your Self, by wholeheartedly practicing deep caring for all sentient beings, by passionately living and dying beyond regret, and by enjoying your boundless intimacy and limitless interdependency with total reality.

Rhythm And Repetition

While reading this book, you will notice that I use pivotal words and phrases in a repetitive and rhythmical manner. This verbal rhythm and repetition will help you to effortlessly recall how to embody boundless intimacy and ungraspable enlightenment far beneath the functioning of your ego-self and thinking mind. Each time you read my pivotal words and phrases, do so with the freshness and openness of your beginner's heartmind. Just remember how a true beginner wholeheartedly enjoys the pitter-patter of rhythmical raindrops that simply illuminate the treasured Way of being alive before talking and thinking.

IMPORTANT PHRASES

Bright Wisdoming

Throughout this book, I use the phrase "bright wisdoming" to refer to the original nature of material reality itself. As most people are not familiar with the way that I use this phrase, I want to clarify its true meaning that is viscerally realized and somatically verified in Zen meditation.

When we hear the word "wisdom," we usually think of all the spiritual and practical insights that have been acquired by our human ancestors throughout the ages. We associate the acquisition or gathering of wisdom with our study of spiritual books and religious scriptures, with our reflection on the teachings of ancient sages, or with our honest and open examination of life experiences. However, this view of "wisdom" is not what I am referring to in this book.

When I use the phrase, "bright wisdoming," I am referring to the Way that all matter and energy reflect a coherent and dynamic informational process that is happening everywhere without obstruction or hinderance. What I am saying here is that the structural organization and interdependent functioning of all matter and energy is inherently a lawful and dynamic informational state or condition arising as matter and energy itself. This is why we call all matter and energy the bright wisdoming of total reality. When scientists investigate the bright wisdoming of all matter and energy, they create verbal knowledge and mathematical formulas to understand the vast informational process that is total reality itself. However, all matter and energy as total reality is inherently a lawful and dynamic informational process that is brilliantly wisdoming before we label it, think about it, or analyze it.

Vast Oneness

When I speak of "the bright wisdoming of vast Oneness," I am referring to the total dynamic functioning of a process, state, or condition that binds and integrates the deep informational nature of all matter and energy without coming or going. The total dynamic functioning of vast Oneness is not yet incorporated into any comprehensive scientific paradigm that describes the interdependent functioning of matter, chemistry, and energy throughout the whole universe. One way to understand the great functioning of vast Oneness is to imagine a deep wisdoming process that is flashing everywhere at infinite speed throughout the surface and depth of total reality. As vast Oneness is flashing everywhere at infinite speed without coming or going, we can only comprehend IT as an absolute stillness that binds the informational nature of total reality. This speed of absolute stillness exists far beyond the speed of light and deep within the quantum depth of total reality. As the absolute stillness of vast Oneness integrates the deep informational structure of the whole universe, we are able to investigate the bright wisdoming of matter and energy and extract a mathematical understanding of universal laws that operate everywhere.

The bright wisdoming of vast Oneness is the basis for the inherent structural integrity of all beings and things as they function individually and interdependently to manifest the wholeness of the universe from the smallest (like energy quanta and atoms) to the largest (like galaxies and black holes). When we use our ego-self, our thinking mind, and the language of mathematics to objectively examine the bright wisdoming of vast Oneness, we naturally speak of the laws of chemistry, the laws of classical mechanics, and the laws of quantum physics. These operative laws that pervade the entire universe are intertwined and upheld in boundless intimacy by the vast Oneness of total reality.

As the bright wisdoming of vast Oneness is expressed everywhere in life and the totality of existence, we call IT the bright wisdoming of all that is inherently birthing into infinite forms, all that is touched by the truth of impermanence, and all that is constantly functioning in interdependency. As the bright wisdoming of vast Oneness is expressed everywhere in death and the totality of nonexistence, we call IT the bright wisdoming of all that dwells in formlessness, all that resides in the womb of emptiness, and all that inhabits the unborn and the undying.

Ungraspable Enlightenment

Many times in this book, I refer to "ungraspable enlightenment." By "ungraspable enlightenment," I am referring to the ancient Way of being in boundless intimacy, vast Oneness, and limitless interdependency with all beings and things. The embodiment of ungraspable enlightenment is the birthright of all human beings who viscerally live through their core-Self far beneath the drivenness and grasping of ego-self functioning. I speak of enlightenment as "ungraspable," because our ego-self cannot objectively know it, gain it, own it, think about it, or manipulate it. Although ungraspable enlightenment cannot be objectively known by our ego-self and thinking mind, it can be viscerally realized and somatically verified through the still composure of our core-Self that is in boundless intimacy with the vast Oneness of total reality.

Beginner's Heartmind

From the very start, I introduce you to the magnanimous openness of beginner's heartmind. By beginner's heartmind, I mean your "originally unified heartmind" that preceded the cerebral development of your ego-self functioning. We embodied profound wonder and lived with bright exuberance from our beginner's heartmind before we knew our name or learned to talk and think with words and ideas. This means that our beginner's heartmind is before the mental dawning of language and the cerebral genesis of "I, me, and mine." We recover our beginner's heartmind when we simply embody the still brilliance of our core-Self that silently illuminates this boundless moment of everyday life far beyond figuring and thinking.

"As we live from our body's still center
point of gravity, we feel more at home in our body
and in our daily life with others. We embody a deep joy,
peace, composure, and sensuality by simply allowing our heady
awareness to sink into our visceral core-Self that is the body's true center
point of gravity. We do not have to rely on any external stimulation to make
us feel more vital, alert, fully alive, at ease, and passionately engaged in our
everyday life. Our grounding in the innocent and pleasureful sensuality of
our body's center point of gravity naturally softens our attachment to
ego-self, thinking mind, and the ever momentary passage of
thoughts and desires. We experience our true fulfillment
as radical human beings when we freely and openly
embody our still center point of gravity that
is exactly the bright wisdoming of vast
Oneness within all beings and
things at the surface and
depth of total
reality."

Dr. Bonnici
(Shugyo Daijo-roshi)

• INTRODUCTION •

"To accept some idea of truth without experiencing it, is
like painting a cake on paper which you cannot eat."

"The most important point is to accept yourself
and stand on your own two feet'"

Shunryu Suzuki-roshi

The Journey

I was born in 1944 on the island of Malta. Malta is located between Sicily and Africa, right in the middle of the Mediterranean Sea. My family immigrated to the United States in 1950 and settled down in San Francisco, California. I am forever grateful to my mom and dad for bringing us to the United States of America. They provided my brother and two sisters with a stable and loving family life. As I remember them right here and now, my heart still feels the loss of their physical presence in my life.

The journey I am going to share with you began just two weeks after I married my wife Diana. Diana was then nineteen and I was twenty-one. I had just bought a motorcycle and decided to share it with a good friend who was also newly married. He hopped on the back seat for a short ride around the block. A car speeding through an intersection hit us broadside. We were very fortunate that we did not die. This motorcycle accident was the crucial event that shook my life "to the core." I ended up in the hospital for two and a half months. My right calve muscle was totally crushed. My right femur was broken just above my knee. I had to have six surgeries on several fractures to my right leg and hip. At the time, I didn't know if my calve muscle would restore itself or whether I would be able to walk naturally again. My

friend remained in a coma for a whole week before he regained consciousness. I remember being so grateful that he was released shortly afterwards in good health.

While at the hospital, my right leg was in constant traction. I had to stay completely on my back until I was released. At night I worried about Diana being alone, whether I would recover completely from my injuries, and how we would meet the difficulties and challenges to come. Although our life was turned upside down, the one thing that did not change for Diana and I was our deep love for each other. We both thought that if we could make it through this critical time early in our marriage, we could make it through anything.

While I was in the hospital, Diana went to a Catholic church in the early morning to pray for my healing. She visited me daily after work and stayed by my bedside until night visiting hours were over. While alone in my bed at night, I began to question all that I had been taught. I began to doubt the integrity of my way of knowing. I doubted all that I had come to know to be true and real during the development of my ego-self and thinking mind. Turning the light of my awareness inward, I realized that I knew nothing for certain. Everything that I thought I knew firsthand had really come from my family, my education, my religion, my peer groups, and my culture. I felt that I knew nothing by firsthand experience.

Before the accident, I had been a devout Catholic who cherished the practice of a religious life and deeply valued intimacy, passion, tender caring, and authenticity in married life. Diana, originally a devout Lutheran, felt the same way about living a religious life while practicing a loving, intimate, and passionate relationship together. Although Diana and I fell in love and married each other for many reasons, our devotion to live a religious and spiritual life together was very important to both of us. However, after I came home from the hospital, I completely changed. I gave up my Catholic faith and asked Diana not to become a Catholic. However, Catholicism was her true refuge while I was in the hospital, so she decided to become Catholic anyway.

I realized that I no longer trusted Catholicism to tell me who I was as a human being and if there was a spiritual reality in the total dynamic functioning of everyday life. I became skeptical of all the social, cultural, and religious ways of knowing about our life and our world. I felt that they were all perceptually biased and negated all of them. I mistrusted all that I had assimilated while growing up. I did not even trust my logic, reason, or analysis to investigate the true nature of humanness and the pristine nature of total reality. I intuitively knew that logic and reason would only separate me further from my firsthand experience. I questioned the very presumption of objectivity and doubted the scientific way of investigating, knowing, and thinking about reality. This all pervasive negation and skepticism toward my familiar ways of knowing left me with no mental ground to stand on. I realized that I had to find a Way to confidently embody the pristine nature of total reality, the original nature of humanness, and my true Self beyond the functioning of ego-self and thinking mind.

Several weeks after leaving the hospital, I began to experience a transpersonal or spiritual crisis that included a debilitating paranoia, an emotional fragmentation, and an ever deepening fear that I was loosing touch with my physical and social reality. My behaviors were being driven by an overwhelming dread of each moment that had no basis in reality. I remember thinking that my sanity was hanging on by one very fine thread. I felt that if that thread would break, I would lose all contact with reality and my ability to function in society. I consciously knew, by one sane thread of clarity, that I was teetering on the edge of an inner darkness that I may never be able to come back from. This was my overwhelming fear, my greatest despair, and the "darkest night of my soul."

When I watched everyday social interactions, all I saw was dishonesty, inauthenticity, and incongruity. People were saying one thing with their mouths while simultaneously thinking something completely opposite or different in their minds. No one seemed to express a truthfulness or genuineness in the way that they talked and shared together. I saw this dishonesty and incongruity as an obstruction to authentic human communications and a hinderance to realizing felt intimacy in everyday social interactions. I could see that everyone was always at the crossroads of life and death, but they constantly avoided awareness of this truth. I started visiting cemeteries because the truth of impermanence and the ever intimate arrival of death could not be hidden or denied there.

During this time of my journey, Diana stood by my side, took more responsibility for the business of our everyday life, and continued to love me as I struggled with the inner darkness that almost overwhelmed me. I did not know how to liberate myself from the fear of insanity, how to recover a dependable way of knowing and being, or how to confidently meet the challenges of living. However, through my thin thread of clarity, I knew exactly what I needed. I had to experientially realize and verify the true nature of total reality, intimately recover the pristine Way of being human beyond all cultural, racial, and religious differences, and recover a true emotional balance that would bring the dawn of illumination to the darkest night of my soul.

Although I knew that I had to somehow recover an illuminating sanity within myself, outside myself, and in my relationship to others, I did not know where to start or how to begin to examine, realize, and intimately verify the pristine nature of humanness and the Way of being total reality just as it is. I felt that I would never experience a deep confidence that I was being total reality as a true human being unless I intimately investigated the truth from the deep visceral core of my body. I made a conscious decision that I would remain completely independent of any scientific views, religious beliefs, spiritual scriptures, and verbal wisdom passed down through the ages. I realized that if I was going to intimately experience the truth before anyone's interpretation of it, I would have to trust my visceral body core and go through this difficult psychological crisis on my own. This is why I also decided not to have any psychotherapeutic or psychiatric intervention.

Investigating Reality

When I realized that I needed to independently embody the true nature of total reality and experientially verify the radical root nature of humanness before anyone's interpretation of it, I recollected the story of the historical Buddha who investigated reality and attained enlightenment in Zen meditation. It was then that I experienced an instant gut-certainty that Buddha's seated Way of Zen meditation was a reliable and trustworthy empirical method for realizing and verifying the radical root nature of humanity and the integrity of being total reality from the deep visceral core of my body. This is why I began diligently sitting as Buddha did in the upright posture of Zen meditation.

While sitting in Zen meditation, I practiced in the wholehearted Way of a childlike beginner by trusting the deep wisdoming of my breath, the pristine functioning of my five senses, and the visceral knowing of my gut-core intelligence. I did not try to stop my thinking, silence my mind, transcend my daily life, or become a buddha. I just sat in Zen meditation to be somatically intimate with the original nature of all human beings and the deepest nature of physical reality. As I sat in Zen meditation, I continued to experience a deep confidence in my gut-core intelligence and its visceral Way of knowing. I somatically knew far beneath my cerebral thinking that my gut-core intelligence would truthfully guide me as I investigated the pristine Way of being fully human at the surface and depth of total reality.

I passionately sat every day before dawn, practiced sitting during the day whenever I could, and sat before going to bed at night. I sat in Zen meditation with an urgency like someone facing death in the last moment of their life. This encouraged me to remain ever alert and wakeful within the easeful and upright posture of Zen meditation. This is the Way I embodied my gut-core intelligence at the crossroads of life and death far beneath my ego-self identity, my passing thoughts, my fears and doubts, and the functioning of my thinking mind. I practiced by myself and did not reach out to a Zen teacher or Zen group for support. I just sat alone in the silence and stillness of Zen meditation to investigate the foundation of total reality and the true nature of all human beings before the dawning of languages, cultures, and religious beliefs.

It took me four years to gradually pass through the darkest night of my soul and finally experience the dawning of a silent visceral illumination that enlightened my life and liberated the wholeness of my spirit. This silent illumination showed me that the radical root of all human beings and the vast Oneness of total reality are both viscerally realized and somatically verified far beyond doubt through the still discernment of our core-Self. My silent visceral illumination of core-Self somatically verified the true Way to live in boundless intimacy and limitless interdependency with all beings and things. Over time, the still discernment of my core-Self healed my debilitating social anxiety, my emotional fragmentation, and my deepest fear of plunging into the abyss of insanity. It was the dawning visceral illumination of my core-Self that transformed my daily experience of fear, hopelessness, depression, and despair into the embodied practice of courage, wonder, clarity, and endless gratitude. This is how I viscerally awakened to the still brilliance of core-Self, somatically realized the radical taproot of all human beings, joyfully recovered the playful authenticity and wild exuberance of a childlike beginner, started to live the Way of loving and being loved beyond resistance and fear, and gratefully began to embody boundless intimacy, vast Oneness, and ungraspable enlightenment within the ordinariness of everyday life.

Meeting the Swans

For the next eleven years, I continued to just sit alone as core-Self inside of Zen meditation while practicing and unfolding the Way of vast Oneness and boundless intimacy in the practical matters, affairs, and relationships of everyday life. In 1974 Diana started going to a Lutheran church that encouraged the practice of meditation. Three years later, while still at the Lutheran church, Diana took a Sonoma State University course in Zen Buddhism. This course was taught by Jakusho Kwong-roshi who was a practicing Soto Zen Buddhist priest that had studied and trained at San Francisco Zen Center with Shunryu Suzuki-roshi. Kwong-roshi invited Diana's class to visit and practice Zen meditation at Genjo-ji, the Zen Mountain temple that he founded.

While sharing her experiences at the Zen Center, Diana kept encouraging me to visit Genjo-ji. She said that I would feel totally at home in the Soto Zen tradition. She was right. The first time I visited Genjo-ji I saw myself and my practice intimately reflected in the teacher and the community of Zen practitioners. I looked deeply into the still and mirrored lake of a traditional Zen community, and there I saw the reflection of a Zen swan that had been practicing alone for fifteen years. This is how I became aware that the swans of Zen had intimately arrived on the lake of everyday life to fully investigate the radical root nature of humanness, realize ungraspable enlightenment, and openly embody the pristine Way of being total reality beneath the functioning of ego-self and thinking mind. This is why Diana and I began to sit in meditation with the Zen community. We started practicing at Genjo-ji in late 1977. We practiced twice a week with our sangha or Zen community while continuing to practice daily in our own home. I was very grateful that Diana had found Genjo-ji because it brought our spiritual practices closer together and provided us with a true foundation for living Zen in our everyday life.

Doctoral Research

On February 28, 1978, I received my Doctorate in Humanistic Psychology (Ph.D.) from Saybrook University in San Francisco, California. My doctoral method of research is rooted in the "modern science of experience" called Phenomenology, pronounced (feh-nom-in-ol-ogy). Phenomenology is a Western scientific field of inquiry that gathers empirical knowledge from an investigator's inherent ability to purely witness, intuitively comprehend, and meticulously describe the total dynamic functioning of intelligent human embodiment and the pristine experience of total reality before the interference of ego-self and thinking mind. The domain of Phenomenology is the full range of our human embodiment including dreaming, imagining, perceiving, thinking, emoting, desiring, needing, feeling, willing, creating, and behaving. In my doctoral dissertation, I introduced Zen meditation as a valid Eastern methodology that investigates the pristine nature of total reality and the holistic functioning of human embodiment similar to the field of Phenomenology. I rationally established Zen as a valid empirical Way for investigating and actualizing the farther reaches of our somatic and emotional intelligence, our cerebral thinking and quantum consciousness, and our empathic intimacy, visceral compassion, and behavioral wisdom. I also postulated a quantum model of human nervous system functioning that explained the still arising of core-Self at the surface and depth of total reality. Upon completion of my Ph.D, I began introducing the general public to the ancient wisdom and modern insights of Applied Meditation Psychology while promoting the healthy embodiment of Applied Meditation Therapy in everyday life.

Jukai Ceremony

In June of 1986, Kwong-roshi officiated my Jukai ceremony. When I received Jukai, I publicly vowed to embody the Zen precepts of everyday life. This is how I became ordained as a lay-monastic Zen practitioner in the Buddha Way. At my Jukai ceremony, Kwong-roshi gave me the Zen name "Hoden," which means "The Field of Truth" or "The Field of Total Reality." It was Kwong-roshi who introduced me to the ancient lineage of Zen, to the teachings of Shunryu Suzuki-roshi, to the Heart Sutra of Perfect Wisdom, and to the thirteenth-century Zen monk, Eihei Dogen, who founded our Soto Zen school in Japan. It is our Soto Zen tradition that practices the Way of living in boundless intimacy and ungraspable enlightenment within the ordinariness of everyday life.

Visceral Calling

After my Jukai ceremony, Diana and I continued to practice at Genjo-ji until 1988. When we left Genjo-ji, I responded to the visceral calling of vast Oneness within my core-Self and immediately established our home as a Zen temple. After establishing our home as a Zen temple, I gave it the Japanese name "Jotoku-ji," which means "Quiet Virtue Temple." My visceral calling made it absolutely clear that the time had intimately arrived to confidently teach Soto Zen as the Way of living in boundless intimacy and vast Oneness with all beings and things.

Expressing deep faith in my core-Self and the visceral calling of vast Oneness, I officiated my formal Tokudo ceremony at Jotoku-ji. Tokudo is the Zen ceremony that marks a lay-practitioner's ordination as a Zen priest. Diana and my two sons participated in the Tokudo ceremony and intimately witnessed my early dawn ordination. It was then that I took formal vows as a Soto Zen priest and viscerally accepted my core-Self transmission as a Zen teacher in the Buddha Way. At the time of my ordination, I chose the transmitted name "Shugyo Daijo," which means "Great Way of Continuous Practice."

In my Tokudo ordination ceremony, I vowed to passionately teach and honorably exemplify the Zen embodiment of boundless intimacy that was viscerally transmitted beyond intending by Shakyamuni Buddha, Eihei Dogen-zenji, Shunryu Suzuki-roshi, and Jakusho Kwong-roshi. I also vowed to hold myself intimately accountable to vast Oneness as I sincerely embodied and honestly shared the Way of living and dying in zazen-only. Over the last twenty-five years, I have taught, trained, ordained, and continue to guide two Zen sanghas while professionally educating, mentoring, and counseling people of all ages to fully embody the still brilliance of their core-Self and the magnanimous nobility of their beginner's heartmind.

Counseling Practice

In 1990, two years after my Tokudo ordination ceremony at Jotoku-ji, I established a private counseling practice in Applied Meditation Therapy®. I defined Applied Meditation Therapy as a "somatic core-Self based therapy" that promotes and sustains personal health, mental clarity, emotional balance, intuitive intelligence, visceral empathy, behavioral wisdom, life transformation, and compassionate action in daily affairs and relationships. For the last twenty-four years I have taught, trained, and mentored individuals, couples, athletes, business leaders, and managerial teams to viscerally embody the still brilliance of their core-Self and actualize peak states of consciousness, performance, intimacy, leadership, creativity, productivity, efficiency, and interpersonal synergy.

In 1996, I taught myself how to design a website and created the Internet portal that is now known as *ZenDoctor.Com*. Through Skype and Facebook video, I am able to extend my professional training, counseling, and mentoring worldwide. In January 2005, Diana and I moved from California to the Big Island of Hawaii. Just before leaving for Hawaii, I performed a public Jukai ceremony for the California sangha and officially ordained them in the Buddha Way. While still teaching and guiding the Jotoku-ji sangha in California, I am counseling and training new Zen practitioners at Jotoku-ji temple of Hawaii.

As I continue to enjoy the simple blessings of everyday life with Diana and our growing family in Hawaii, I still provide counseling and mentoring, conduct professional workshops, creatively maintain my four Internet websites, give talks on the practice of shikantaza and zazen-only, write Zen poetry and publish articles on living a healthy, loving, creative, and compassionate life, develop future books for publication, promote the field of Applied Meditation Psychology, and globally teach human beings how to passionately live from the still brilliance of their core-Self.

Our Way

Throughout this book you will read about the embodiment of "our Way." By "our Way," I mean the Buddha Way of vast Oneness and boundless intimacy that has been passed down with visceral integrity and somatic impeccability within the Chinese Cáo-dòng Zen lineage of "silent illumination" and the Japanese Soto Zen lineage of "wholehearted sitting." As a Self-ordained Zen priest and teacher in "our Way," I emphasize that the still essence of core-Self is key to understanding the seed transmission and awakening of Shakyamuni Buddha, the vital composure of Suzuki-roshi who lived everyday life with beginner's heartmind, and the brilliance of Dogen Zenji who expounded a lucid dream within a dream while living ungraspable enlightenment as this only moment of vast impermanence with all beings and things.

A Radical Shift

To live through our visceral core-Self is to experience the three marks of human embodiment as fulfillment, vast Oneness, and boundless intimacy. To live through our heady ego-self awareness is to experience the three marks of human embodiment as dissatisfaction, duality, and separation. In this book, I will show you that these two ways of experiencing human embodiment are not mutually exclusive or contradictory within the Zen practice of everyday life.

This book represents a radical shift in our understanding of how to continuously romance the embodiment of Zen, how to somatically realize the visceral root of our humanness, how to live in boundless intimacy and vast Oneness with total reality, and how to unfold ungraspable enlightenment in the ordinariness of our everyday life. I offer this book as a fresh experiential perspective on living the body of Zen with a beginner's sincerity, humility, and exuberant passion. It is my hope that this work will encourage and inspire you to faithfully embody your core-Self, to openly share the nobility and humility of your beginner's heartmind, and to daily take refuge in the Buddha Way of living and dying within the boundless intimacy and vast Oneness of total reality.

Endless Gratitude

I am forever grateful to Shakyamuni Buddha who first inspired me to just sit as core-Self inside of just sitting, to Zen Master Dogen who revitalized the ancient seal of zazen-only, to Shunryu Suzuki-roshi who continues to encourage my beginner's heartmind even in death, and to Jakusho Kwong-roshi for diligently exemplifying the body of Zen in everyday life. It is with this deep feeling of gratitude that I share a future world where all radical human beings compassionately embody their core-Self while living together in boundless intimacy, vast Oneness, and limitless interdependency. This book is my passionate way of telling you that this future world is always arriving in this only moment right here and Now.

"As Mother Earth is my witness, the Deep Valley is my true home.
As this Only Moment is my whole body, my lineage comes from Being-Time.
As I wholeheartedly dwell in the still brilliance and silent illumination of core-Self,
I treasure the vital freshness of beginner's heartmind and the Way of ancient buddhas.
Deeply rooted in the truth of suffering, I live a vital, exuberant, and simple life.
Embodying boundless intimacy amidst everyday affairs and relationships,
I teach the ancient Way of Zen with the sincerity of moonlight,
the pristine exuberance of mountain streams, and
the healing constancy of ocean waves."

Shugyo Daijo-roshi
(Dr. Bonnici)

Be as Drifting Clouds
and Flowing Water~
Return To Nature as
an Infant To its Mother.

"When timelessness is realized, you are empowered.
When timelessness is realized, you are alive. How long
have you awaited timelessness? This auspicious day
knows the increasing light of opportunity."

Dogen Zenji
(1200 AD - 1253 AD)
Eihei Koroku: Informal Talk

ZAZEN-ONLY

There is a timeless, wondrous, and exquisite Way to live in boundless intimacy, vast Oneness, limitless interdependency, and immeasurable gratitude. It is the ever fresh Way of just sitting as core-Self inside of "zazen-only." Zazen is pronounced "zaah-zen" with equal emphasis on each syllable. "Za" is viscerally sitting within the still vibrancy of core-Self inside of just sitting. "Zen" is living from your core-Self that silently illuminates the surface and depth of total reality. To viscerally embody the still vibrancy of core-Self inside of zazen-only is to brilliantly arrive in boundless intimacy and ungraspable enlightenment beyond attaining, gaining, owning, and knowing.

When I use the term "only," as in zazen-only, I mean to say that the embodiment of zazen is peerless and beyond comparison. Zazen-only is peerless because it is not a mentally designed method, belief, or technique for gaining, grasping, or attaining anything. Zazen-only is the wholehearted Way of living as a radical human being from our visceral core-Self. Zazen-only is the ancient practice of embodying the true nature of total reality, living in sacred entanglement with life and death, and joyfully abiding in boundless intimacy with all beings and things. When we just sit as core-Self inside of zazen-only, we viscerally realize our total completion and fulfillment as a radical human being with not one thing lacking.

Our Way of intimately realizing and experientially verifying core-Self inside of zazen-only does not have anything to do with attaining the bliss of nirvana, gaining moral merit for a heavenly salvation, preparing the way for a better reincarnation, practicing the body of Zen exclusively as a Buddhist, or worshiping the historical Buddha as a deity. This ancient Way of embodying core-Self inside of zazen-only precedes the development of world languages, the emergence of cultures and traditional religions, and is before all written scriptures and spiritual beliefs.

When we just sit as core-Self inside of zazen-only, we viscerally recover our basic goodness, our original human integrity, and our inherent moral compass. This visceral recovery of our basic goodness, our original human integrity, and our inherent moral compass are intimately transmitted inside of zazen-only without the interface of priests, shamans, ministers, mullahs, rabbis, scriptural writings, and religious views.

Our timeless and peerless Way of zazen-only includes just sitting as core-Self inside of just sitting and just sitting as core-Self inside of just living. We call just sitting as core-Self inside of just living "shikantaza" (pronounced she-cahhn-taah-za). "Shikan" means "just this" or "only this." "Ta" means "hitting the mark." "Za" is the same as in zazen-only, "viscerally being seated as core-Self." Thus, shikantaza is hitting the visceral mark of core-Self while just living, loving, working, playing, doing, caring, and being. Shikantaza is viscerally sitting as core-Self in this Only Moment Body while wholeheartedly enjoying and passionately living in boundless intimacy with all beings and things.

We viscerally realize boundless intimacy and somatically verify the effortless flight of ungraspable enlightenment by continuously spreading the wings of shikantaza and zazen-only.   Although shikantaza is all of zazen-only and zazen-only is all of shikantaza, they are entirely not one; and yet, they are wholly not two. Zazen-only is core-Self transmitting the still vibrancy of core-Self beyond the seated stillness of zazen-only. Shikantaza is engaging our everyday life from the still vibrancy of core-Self that was originally transmitted within and beyond zazen-only. In our Way, the daily practice of zazen-only precedes the continuous embodiment of shikantaza. Without the daily practice of just sitting inside of just sitting that is zazen-only, there can be no somatically verified practice of shikantaza that is just sitting inside of just living.

We treasure the pristine embodiment of core-Self inside of zazen-only that liberates the wondrous freshness, magnanimous openness, and profound wholeness of our beginner's heartmind. We bow to all beginners who fervently sit as core-Self inside of zazen-only because every beginner's zazen-only is entirely the ever fresh embodiment of a radical human being who is continuously arriving in boundless intimacy and ungraspable enlightenment itself.

Our Zen practice is the ancient Way of viscerally being core-Self with beginner's heartmind. To sit down in zazen-only and embody core-Self with beginner's heartmind is not mentally focusing on the present while excluding the past and the future. Zen is not the practice of willfully minding each moment during the activities and relationships of everyday life. Zen, as the Way of beginner's heartmind, is not mentally arousing a mindfulness of what you are doing. This is not our Way. Zen is to viscerally embody core-Self inside of shikantaza and zazen-only with the wondrous humility, effortless grace, fervent exuberance, and confident freshness of beginner's heartmind.

"You must not cling to
the words of the ancient
sages; they, too, may not be
right. Even if you believe them,
you should be alert so that, in the
event that something superior
comes along, you may
practice that."

Dogen Zenji
1238 A.D.

"Do not believe in anything just
because you have heard it. Do not
believe in anything simply because it
is spoken and rumored by many. Do not
believe in spiritual traditions just because
they have been honored and handed down by
many generations. Do not believe in anything
simply because it is written in holy scriptures.
Do not believe in anything merely on the
authority of your teachers and priests.
But after careful study and diligent
examination, believe in what
you have found to be true,
wholesome, and conducive
to the good and benefit
of all beings; then,
simply accept it
and live
by it."

Shakyamuni Buddha
(563-483 B.C.)

• PART I •

PRACTICE

"Zazen practice is the direct expression
of our True Nature. Strictly speaking, for a
human being, there is no other practice than
this practice; there is no other way of
life than this Way of life."

Shunryu Suzuki
1904-1971

CHAPTER 1

Abiding In Core-Self

Breathing into the
Belly of Silence—
Nourishing Dignity,
Integrity, and Vitality.

One day Dogen said, " I can remember monk Yunmen asked
Zen Master Caoshan, "Why don't we know that there is a place
of great intimacy?" Master Caoshan said, "Just because it
is greatly intimate, we do not know it is there."

Eihei Koroku
(Dogen's Extensive Record)

The Hara

When we embody Zen in our everyday life, we practice deep intimacy with three somatic experiences. These three somatic experiences include the natural flow of our breath, the expansion and contraction of our belly breathing, and the sensation of being in the visceral core of our lower abdomen. These three somatic experiences establish the traditional Zen foundation for viscerally realizing core-Self inside of just sitting while embodying the visceral seal of core-Self inside of just living.

In our traditional Way of Zen, we call the lower abdominal area of the human body the "hara" (pronounced hah-rah). Your "hara" is an oval shaped area just below your belly button. The hara is six inches across your lower abdomen. It is about two and a half inches wide at the very center. Although the Japanese word "hara" is translated as "lower belly," this does not give us any indication of its profound spiritual meaning, its inherent capacity to manifest an honorable human being, or its deep interconnectedness with the dynamic functioning of total reality. Nor does it reveal the hara's awesome power to stabilize, regulate, and enhance our daily experience of health, vitality, wellness, and aliveness. The hara contains the bio-energetic reservoir for our whole body, the somatic integrity of our radical humanness, and the visceral center-point that promotes physical health, mental clarity, emotional balance, and confidence in our intuitive gut-core Way of knowing. When you dwell in the deep bio-energetic core of your hara rather than your heady ego-self, people intimately sense your authentic visceral presence as a trustworthy and honorable human being. To faithfully embody the visceral bio-energetic core of your hara in everyday life is to openly and effortlessly communicate the integrity, soundness, and dependability of your humanity and your character.

Our True Home

We take refuge in the bright wisdoming of our hara that nourishes our daily well-being and our felt completion as a radical human being. We take refuge by letting go of our heady mental experience of being alive while allowing our total somatic awareness to naturally sink into the sensual vitality of our hara and the vibrancy of its bio-energetic core. As we take refuge and ground our total somatic awareness in the sensual vitality of our hara, we become intimately aware of meaningful sensations that arise within the deep bio-energetic core of our lower abdomen.

In our Way, we sink into the bio-energetic core of our hara whether we are seated in the body of zazen-only or actively living in the body of shikantaza during the activities and affairs of everyday life. We cultivate sensual intimacy with our hara by always breathing, relaxing, energizing, grounding, moving, and responding from the bio-energetic core of our lower abdomen. When we wholly embody our bio-energetic core, we speak from the deep somatic integrity of our hara. Our hara is where breath, flesh, energy, mind, heart, and intuition become One. Hara is where acceptance of each moment meets the bright wisdoming of change and impermanence. Our hara is where visceral relaxation and bright wakefulness translate into an ever confident readiness to instantly meet the challenges of everyday life with caring, compassion, creativity, and wisdom. Hara is not only our deep refuge, it is our true home in this Only Moment Body. Hara is the radical root of our visceral humanness that exists far beneath the functioning of our ego-self and thinking mind. As human beings, we feel confidently grounded in each moment when we somatically rest with ease and joy in the sensual vitality of our hara and our visceral gut-core Way of knowing.

Earth Dwellers

To embody the integrity of Zen life is to passionately live from the vitality of our hara and the vibrancy of our bio-energetic core. In our Way, we practice felt intimacy with our hara and our bio-energetic core by daily sitting in zazen-only. When we just sit in zazen-only, we simply linger with ease and joy in the sensuality of our hara and the vibrant wakefulness of our visceral core. To linger in the hara and the bio-energetic core of our lower abdomen is to embody a brilliant stillness, a silent illumination, a deep composure, and a grounded integrity that is far beyond the seated form of zazen-only. All of living Zen and embodying zazen-only is viscerally realized when you dwell within the sensual vitality and vibrancy of your hara. To embody zazen-only is to begin each inhalation and exhalation from the hara while enjoying the pristine wakefulness of the bio-energetic core that always exists far beyond thinking. As you dwell in the vibrancy of your visceral core and the ever fresh sensuality of your hara, the flow of your breathing will feel like the vital freshness of a spring breeze. This is the Way we daily nourish an ever deepening intimacy with the bright wisdoming of hara and the core of our lower abdomen in zazen-only.

When we practice zazen-only and linger in the visceral and sensual vitality of our hara, we experience the vast wisdoming of Nature itself. What I am talking about here is how all earth dwellers experience the bright wisdoming of their lower abdomen far beyond thoughts and thinking. As earth dwellers embody the visceral core of their hara, they experience a sensual, vibratory, and energetic quality within the center of their lower abdomen. Right there, in the visceral core shared by all true earth dwellers, each one of us intimately experiences our gut-core Way of knowing. Right there, in the visceral center of our whole body, we realize our boundless intimacy with total reality and verify our interdependency with all beings and things. Right there, we recover our visceral connection to the continuity and vast Oneness of life and death.

In our Way, we flow with each inhalation into the visceral center of our lower abdomen. Right there, we continuously meet a true earth dweller who diligently embodies a gut-core Way of knowing. When we embody our gut-core Way of knowing, we sense that Nature is not just outside of us. We come to intimately realize that the vast wisdoming of Nature is deeply felt and fully expressed within our hara. When we live from our hara and our visceral core, we experience our true belonging within the larger context of Nature. We come to viscerally know that we are not separate from the wholeness and sacredness of total reality. Just as hara is the true home of all earth dwellers, so too each moment of vital aliveness is where all earth dwellers truly belong.

The Tanden

When earth dwellers sink into the bio-energetic core of their hara, they naturally live and move from their body's center-point of gravity. To consciously live and move from the body's center-point of gravity is to be intimate with the visceral gut-core intelligence of all true earth dwellers. In our traditional Way of Zen, we call the body's center-point of gravity the "tanden," pronounced "tahn-den." Your tanden is located three inches below your navel. It is in the middle of your hara, an inch and a half under your skin. The tanden is where your visceral gut-core intelligence is experientially felt within the body. This is why we refer to the tanden as the true visceral center-point of our gut-core intelligence.

The tanden is where our total somatic awareness and our vital bio-energy reserves are viscerally merged and concentrated to provide us with an easeful alertness, an ever fresh aliveness, and a vibrant wellness during the activities, affairs, and relationships of everyday life. This natural concentration of somatic awareness and bio-energy reserves within our visceral gut-core intelligence is not dependent on our heady cerebral power to focus or concentrate our mind. This means that the brain's capacity to generate and sustain an intensely focused awareness or deep mental concentration has nothing to do with the inherent capacity of all earth dwellers to naturally sink and linger within the viscerally concentrated power of their gut-core intelligence.

When earth dwellers naturally sink into the viscerally concentrated power of their gut-core intelligence, they experience a sensual warmth and a pleasant heaviness within the hara. To linger in the sensual warmth that pervades your hara in zazen-only is to become somatically aware of a deep stillness that arises from the tanden center-point of your gut-core intelligence. To viscerally sense the arising of this deep stillness within the tanden center-point of your gut-core intelligence is to intimately experience that peace and tranquility pervades your whole body. Here, I am not talking about mind or mental things. Rather, I am speaking about felt visceral sensations and deep somatic experiences that naturally arise when you faithfully embody the tanden center-point of your lower abdomen in zazen-only.

Our Core-Self

When earth dwellers sit in zazen-only and experience the still center-point of their gut-core intelligence, they viscerally realize that the stillness they are experiencing is a vast and unownable stillness that penetrates all beings and things. To intimately realize that you cannot own the still center-point of your gut-core intelligence in zazen-only is to viscerally confirm that vast stillness has been timelessly existing at the surface and depth of total reality. To viscerally meet the vast and timeless stillness of total reality in zazen-only is to confidently live beyond fear. To confidently know life and death beyond fear is to embody boundless intimacy within the unownable stillness of your gut-core intelligence. To sincerely embody the stillness of your gut-core intelligence in this Way is to instantly awaken to your core-Self beyond thinking. To awaken to core-Self in zazen-only is to naturally express the awesome power of core-Self that silently illuminates and compassionately refines the functioning of your ego-self and your thinking mind from the still center-point of total reality.

This Way of embodying the awakened power of core-Self is very different from living exclusively through our heady ego-self and thinking mind. When we live exclusively from our ego-self and thinking mind, we view the body as an object to be shaped, manipulated and controlled. On the other hand, core-Self does not view the body as an object. When we are faithfully being our core-Self inside of zazen-only, we do not separate our core-Self from this Only Moment Body. This means that core-Self is exactly the ever fresh aliveness of this Only Moment Body far beneath thinking. This is how we compassionately dwell as core-Self inside this Only Moment Body of zazen-only.

The Practice Of Clarity

When we cherish the flow of each passing breath inside of zazen-only, we naturally begin to dis-identify with our passing thoughts, our ego-self, our unique personality, and our mental way of knowing and gaining knowledge about reality. This allows our total somatic awareness to naturally sink into the sensual vitality of our hara and the vibrant stillness of our visceral core-Self. To wholly embody the vibrant stillness of core-Self is to be the brilliant intelligence of core-Self beyond thinking. To be the brilliant intelligence of core-Self beyond thinking is to silently illuminate your ego-self and thinking mind. To silently illuminate the functioning of your ego-self and thinking mind is to compassionately witness your prejudicial way of thinking, your biased and exclusive perceptions, your drivenness and your grasping desires, your denials, projections, and rationalizations, your attachment to an illusory and reactive life of drama, your defensive, aggressive, and greedy way of being, your bondage to mental, emotional, and behavioral automaticity, and your constant resistance to accepting the truth and embracing total reality just as IT is. To compassionately witness your ego-self and thinking mind in this Way is to constantly refine and develop their healthy functioning in everyday life and relationships.

As we participate in society and family life, we ground the total dynamic functioning of our ego-self, our personality, and our thinking mind within the still brilliance of our core-Self. To ground the functioning of ego-self and thinking mind within the still brilliance of core-Self is to see the virtual and insubstantial nature of our heady ego-self and thinking mind. When I ask people to nourish clarity in everyday life, I am asking them to somatically anchor their ego-self and thinking mind within the brilliant stillness of their core-Self. This Way of engaging everyday life and relationships from the still brilliance of core-Self is called, "The Practice Of Clarity." The practice of clarity is compassionately seeing all beings, things, and events just as they are while respectfully engaging and responding to them just as IT is. To compassionately see all beings, things, and events just as they are is to see them before we instantly name, objectify, judge, control, and manipulate them. When we acknowledge that the still center-point of total reality penetrates all beings, things, and events just as they are, we respectfully respond to them from the vast Oneness and interdependency of total reality, just as IT is. This is why we openly bow to all beings, things, and events that intimately come forth to engage our core-Self in the still dance of boundless intimacy at the surface and depth of everyday life.

The practice of clarity always begins with core-Self just sitting as core-Self inside of zazen-only. Our daily embodiment of zazen-only helps us to somatically distinguish the still brilliance of core-Self from the heady virtual functioning of ego-self and thinking mind. Once we somatically discern the still brilliance of core-Self, we can clearly see and openly respond to all beings, things, and events from the still center-point of total reality. As we become viscerally intimate with the still brilliance of core-Self inside of zazen-only, we somatically establish the true Way to silently illuminate and intuitively refine the healthy functioning of ego-self and thinking mind. This is how we embody and sustain the practice of clarity, compassion, and wisdom in our everyday life and relationships.

The Cosmic Mudra

When we just sit as core-Self inside of zazen-only, we form an oval gesture with our two hands. Our hand gesture emphasizes the middle of our lower abdomen and the still center point of our gut-core intelligence. We call this oval hand gesture, "The cosmic mudra of zazen-only." We form the cosmic mudra by overlapping the fingers of both hands while gently putting our two thumbs together. If you go to photo twenty-two in the last chapter, you will see a visual example of the cosmic mudra.

The oval hand mudra of zazen-only reminds us to always live from our hara and the still center point of our gut-core intelligence. As this reminder is wholly visceral in nature, it does not depend on the recollecting power of our ego-self and thinking mind. When we heed the visceral reminder of our cosmic mudra, we somatically sink into the still brilliance of our core-Self with each inhalation. To somatically sink into the still brilliance of core-Self with each inhalation is to viscerally realize our boundless intimacy with all beings and things. To viscerally realize boundless intimacy in shikantaza and zazen-only is to somatically verify the vast Oneness of total reality. When we viscerally comprehend all of this by gently holding the cosmic mudra in zazen-only, we wholly liberate the noble completion, wondrous humility, and pristine authenticity of our beginner's heartmind.

The cosmic mudra speaks to us beyond thinking. It wants us to generate and contain our life force and not deplete it. It wants us to be completely at ease beyond our behavioral drivenness and emotional frenzy. It asks us to gently rest our mental chatter and courageously stretch beyond the thinking and knowing of our ego-self. It asks us to drop our total somatic awareness into the sensual warmth of our lower abdomen. However, it intimately assures us that this resting, stretching, and dropping cannot be forced or pushed. The cosmic mudra wants us to naturally flow into our hara and experience the vibrant stillness of our core-Self. When we allow ourselves to flow downward in this effortless Way, we become less attracted to experiencing life from our detached and heady ego-self identity. This flowing downward is far beyond willfulness and choosing. Just like water flows effortlessly downward without intending, we flow into the sensuality of our hara and the vibrancy of our core-Self beyond pushing, grasping, practicing, and training. To be sensually alive from our hara and the still vibrancy of our core-Self is to be deeply relaxed and totally composed even as we see the emptiness and insubstantiality of our ego-self and thinking mind.

Body Of Mindfulness

When we flow into the viscerally concentrated awareness of our hara and the still brilliance of our core-Self, we experience the original somatic nature of mindfulness that precedes the cerebral arousal of mindfulness itself. When we practice shikantaza and zazen-only, we do not cerebrally focus the mind to be more mindful of our living, loving, being, and doing. To live from our hara and the vibrant stillness of our core-Self is to be somatically mindful in everyday life without the cerebral intensification of our conscious mind. To embody the sensuality of our hara and the still brilliance of our core-Self is to passionately engage our everyday life from a visceral composure, a somatic mindfulness, and a boundless intimacy that is far beneath the power of our mental concentration. Just resting in the embodied sensuality of our hara and enjoying the vibrant stillness of our core-Self is exactly the pristine embodiment of mindfulness without any interference of ego-self and thinking mind.

Mindfulness is not focusing the mind on each moment. It is not remembering the existence of Now. The essence of mindfulness is the total embodiment of our visceral gut-core presence beyond thinking. The pristine nature of mindfulness is not mental. It is wholly visceral and originally somatic. To embody the still center-point of core-Self is to instantly experience a viscerally concentrated awareness and a somatically grounded mindfulness that silently illuminates the surface and depth of total reality. To experience the still center-point of core-Self is to be the whole body of mindfulness beyond the mental arousal of mindfulness itself. To be the whole body of mindfulness from the still center-point of total reality is to confidently live as core-Self in boundless intimacy with all beings and things. This is a very important point to study, investigate, and comprehend beyond thinking.

Autonomic Balancing

When we experience the original somatic nature of mindfulness through our hara and the visceral center-point of our core-Self, we naturally stimulate the harmonious functioning of our autonomic nervous system. The autonomic nervous system functions beneath our cerebrally generated mental awareness and is largely beyond the control of our ego-self and thinking mind. Our autonomic nervous system regulates digestion, respiration, metabolism, blood pressure, heart-rate, and glandular secretions. The total dynamic functioning of our autonomic nervous system is responsible for our felt embodiment of stress, hypertension, relaxation, edginess, alertness, fatigue, agitation, calmness, mental clarity, and emotional stability.

Our autonomic nervous system has two major subsystems: the sympathetic system and the parasympathetic system. The sympathetic nervous system is stimulated when we instinctively engage in a "fight or flight" response to the stress of everyday life. The "fight or flight response" is our body's primitive physiological reaction to perceived threats or attacks against our physical, mental, or emotional survival as a real and substantial ego-self. The sympathetic system is the "arousal, readiness, and high alertness" branch of our autonomic nervous system. The sympathetic system speeds up our heartbeat, increases shallow breathing, raises our blood pressure, suppresses our immune system, restrains our digestion, inhibits tissue rejuvenation, and releases adrenalin into our bloodstream. The parasympathetic nervous system is stimulated when we begin to relax, slow down our drivenness, take time to rest, and establish a deep sense of ease in our body. It is the "calming, renewing, and rejuvenating" branch of our autonomic nervous system. The parasympathetic system slows down our breathing and heart rate, decreases our blood pressure, enhances tissue rejuvenation, conserves our overall somatic resources, and promotes healing, easefulness, and deep relaxation throughout the body. The harmonious functioning between these two branches of our autonomic nervous system is crucial in sustaining our daily health, healing, wellness, and longevity.

The sympathetic and parasympathetic branches of our autonomic nervous system constantly seek a balanced state of interdependent complementarity as they function together during the challenges of everyday life. However, we tend to disrupt their inherent tendency toward balance, harmony, interdependency, and complementarity by the way we adapt to our stress filled environments. When faced with the difficulties and challenges of our everyday life, many of us continue to karmically relive the same dysfunctional behaviors, emotional dramas, and reactive mental prejudices that reinforce the over stimulation of our sympathetic nervous system. This sympathetic over stimulation can become so chronic or continuous that it creates a constant state of imbalance in our autonomic nervous system. To embody chronic stress and continuous autonomic imbalance is to feel persistently driven, irritable, anxious, fearful, overwhelmed, worried, depressed, isolated, angry, panicked, resentful, depressed, helpless, and powerless. Chronic stress and its related feelings and emotions have been medically linked with diminished immunity, high blood pressure, heart disease, recurring headaches, insomnia, cognitive impairment, Alzheimer's disease, tension backaches, gastrointestinal problems, and accelerated aging.

A continuous state of stress and autonomic imbalance can creep up on anyone. Most people are not aware of how the dynamic functioning of their ego-self tends to reinforce the unhealthy embodiment of stress. They are so identified with their ego-self that they cannot discern the inner causal links that perpetuate stress. They cannot see how they are karmically reinforcing their own chronic state of autonomic imbalance by the way that they think, perceive, emote, believe, and behave as an ego-self. They are not aware of how their attachment to egoself-centricity keeps them in karmic bondage to heightened levels of stress, prolongs their unhealthy autonomic imbalance, and obstructs their ability to deeply experience the sensual vitality of their hara and the vibrant stillness of their core-Self.

When we remain entrenched in a heady and substantial ego-self while ignoring or denying the inner causal factors that perpetuate our bondage to stress, we are automatically driven to seek instant relief. This instant, impermanent, and dysfunctional relief usually takes the form of drugs, alcohol, food, sex, and other forms of stimulation that suppress, numb, or push away our painful feelings, thoughts, sensations, and emotions. This way of living in karmic bondage to stress while remaining chained to our maladaptive coping behaviors tends to reinforce an antagonistic and unhealthy relationship between the sympathetic and parasympathetic nervous systems. This antagonistic relationship hinders our natural ability to nourish and sustain the ever fresh embodiment of our vital wellness, our emotional zest, and our passionate aliveness during the ordinary activities, affairs, and relationships of everyday life. On the other hand, when we sink our total somatic awareness into the sensual vitality of our hara and the still vibrancy of our core-Self, we effortlessly molt off our egoself-centricity, liberate ourselves from bondage to chronic stress, and naturally stimulate the balanced and healthy functioning of our autonomic nervous system. To experience the healthy functioning of our autonomic nervous system is to embody the vibrant alertness, refreshing calmness, and easeful exuberance of our visceral core-Self.

Ocean Of Ki Energy

When we viscerally abide in the vibrant alertness of our core-Self in shikantaza and zazen-only, we become somatically intimate with the vital bio-energy that upholds and sustains the total dynamic functioning of this Only Moment Body. The ancient Chinese sages (5000 B.C.) called this vital bio-energy "Chi" or "Qi" (pronounced as "chee" and "key.") In our Japanese Soto Way of Zen, we call this vital bio-energy "Ki" (also pronounced "key"). Ki is a universal form of bio-energy that upholds the life of all plants, animals, creatures, and beings on our planet. In shikantaza and zazen-only, we experience Ki as the life force that penetrates the surface and depth of this Only Moment Body. The total dynamic functioning of our biochemistry, our neurobiology, our somatic mindfulness, our gut-core intelligence, our cerebrally generated ego-self consciousness, our logical and rational thinking mind, our emotional way of being with ourselves and others, and our daily intending, goal setting, and behaving are all expressions and transformations of Ki.

According to the ancient model of Chinese medicine, peak experiential states of health, healing, and longevity are nurtured and sustained by the continuous generation, conservation, and unobstructed flow of Ki energy within the human body. Since time immemorial, Chinese sages have spoken of an intimate relationship that exists between the simple act of breathing and the inherent core-Self power to generate Ki within the lower abdomen. To breathe deeply into the center of your lower abdomen while silently abiding as core-Self in shikantaza and zazen-only is to viscerally generate Ki throughout the full extent of your hara. When we inhale and generate Ki within our hara, we sense the vitality, warmth, and vibrancy of Ki flowing throughout our whole body.

To become somatically aware of Ki being viscerally generated within your lower abdomen is to intimately experience the sensuality of your hara. To experience the vital sensuality of your hara is to allow each inhalation to take you deeply into the still vibrancy of your core-Self beyond thinking. To breathe into the visceral center-point of your hara and abide in the still vibrancy of your core-Self is to generate and conserve a reservoir of Ki within your lower abdomen. The Japanese martial and aesthetic arts refer to this reservoir of Ki as the "Kikai" or "The Ocean of Ki Energy." In our Way, we just sit as core-Self inside of shikantaza and zazen-only, breath into the sensual center-point of our hara, viscerally generate Ki within our lower abdomen, conserve Ki energy within our Kikai, somatically sense the flow of Ki energy throughout our whole body, and extend Ki into our everyday life to express tenderness, compassion, and deep caring for all beings and things.

As we expend our Ki to think, sense, emote, feel, and behave in this Only Moment Body of shikantaza, we remain viscerally anchored in our core-Self. To be viscerally anchored in our core-Self is to be somatically mindful of how much Ki we are generating, how much Ki we are conserving in our Kikai, and how much Ki we are extending from our hara at any given moment. When we somatically abide as core-Self within our lower abdomen while consciously generating, conserving, and extending appropriate quantities of Ki within our everyday life, we naturally promote the balanced functioning of our autonomic nervous system, optimize our immunity to illness, and nourish health, healing, and wellness throughout our whole body.

Extending Ki In Zazen-Only

In our Way, we embody shikantaza by living from the still vibrancy of core-Self while being somatically mindful of the great functioning of Ki in our everyday life. This somatic mindfulness of Ki is viscerally transmitted in our daily embodiment of core-Self inside of zazen-only. It is in zazen-only that core-Self viscerally comprehends the vital functioning of Ki in this Only Moment Body. To viscerally comprehend the vital functioning of Ki through your core-Self in zazen-only is to somatically realize how to generate Ki in your hara, how to viscerally contain Ki in your Kikai, and how to viscerally extend a sensory field of Ki energy into your immediate surroundings.

When we viscerally generate Ki as core-Self inside of zazen-only, eighty percent of our generated Ki is contained and conserved within our lower abdomen. To viscerally conserve eighty percent of your generated Ki within the lower abdomen is to cultivate an abundant Kikai reservoir within your hara. To cultivate an abundant Kikai reservoir is to fully appreciate the sensual Ki of your hara while resting in the still vibrancy of your core-Self. To fully appreciate the vital sensuality of your hara and anchor into the still vibrancy of your core-Self is to viscerally realize that twenty percent of your generated Ki is naturally being extended into the great functioning of your five senses. To viscerally realize that Ki is naturally being extended into the great functioning of your five senses is to be somatically mindful that a spherical Ki field of sensory awareness is surrounding your whole body. This spherical Ki field of reflective sensory awareness is the extension of your core-Self that silently mirrors the still essence of total reality. To be somatically mindful of the great round mirror of core-Self while remaining anchored in the sensual vitality of your hara is to intimately arrive as a radical human being who embodies the awakened eye and treasury of zazen-only.

As core-Self shines outward through the five senses while viscerally cultivating an abundant Kikai reservoir within the hara, Ki does not leak into our headiness to energize thinking or to perpetuate the fleeting life of passing thoughts. To not leak Ki into your headiness is to enjoy the vibrant sensuality of your hara in zazen-only. To be the great round mirror of core-Self while viscerally enjoying the sensual Ki of your hara is to effortlessly shine all five senses outward beyond thinking, willing, measuring, or intending. To shine all your senses outward beyond thinking and measuring is to liberate the pristine wonder of your beginner's heartmind and viscerally realize that core-Self is brilliantly illuminating the stillness of total reality.

As we cultivate an abundant Ki reservoir within the hara and extend Ki into the vital functioning of our five senses, we confidently experience the pristine nature of total reality just as IT is. Just as IT is means that sensory information is not being mentally filtered by an ego-self that seeks to preserve its virtual existence, to substantiate its biased and selective view of reality, and to perpetuate its endless grasping and pushing away. As our five senses silently illuminate the pristine nature of total reality in zazen-only, they reflect all beings and things just as they are. To reflect all beings and things just as they are is to simply embody the great round mirror of core-Self far beyond labeling, thinking, and figuring. To simply embody the great round mirror of core-Self while enjoying the vital sensuality of our hara is to liberate our beginner's heartmind and arrive as a radical human being in zazen-only.

Extending Ki In Shikantaza

Our somatic Way of zazen-only teaches us how to embody shikantaza while just living, loving, playing, working, and being. We embody shikantaza by continuously sensing the vital sensuality of our hara, by remaining viscerally anchored in our core-Self, by constantly generating and conserving Ki within our lower abdomen, by shining all our senses outward beyond thinking, and by consciously extending healthy quantities of Ki into the activities and affairs of everyday life. This is the Way we practice living as core-Self in this Only Moment Body of shikantaza.

As we arise from zazen-only to consciously extend Ki into the matters and affairs of our daily life, we do so from the visceral confidence and somatic easefulness of our core-Self. We practice living with ease and joy in the body of shikantaza by constantly abiding in our core-Self beyond thinking. We do this from the moment we wake-up until the moment we fall asleep at night. We embody shikantaza by cultivating and conserving our Ki beyond labeling, measuring, and thinking. However, as we practice living as core-Self in the body of shikantaza, we increase our extended Ki to forty percent while containing and conserving sixty percent within our hara. This increase in the extension of Ki allows us to conscientiously take care of the business of everyday life while meeting all beings, things, and events with the openness, clarity, and compassion of our core-Self.

To extend forty percent of our generated Ki does not mean that we withhold giving one hundred percent of our core-Self within the affairs and relationships of everyday life. It does not mean that we show up with forty percent of our core-Self while living, loving, working, playing, and being. As we generate and conserve a substantial amount of Ki in our hara, we meet all beings, things, and events with the total wakefulness, caring, acceptance, clarity, and attentiveness of our core-Self. To be core-Self in shikantaza is to be all of core-Self passionately engaged in the appropriate and healthy extension of Ki for the benefit of all sentient beings.

To conserve sixty percent of your Ki within the hara is to wholeheartedly entangle in your daily activities and relationships without losing visceral intimacy with your core-Self. You could not give one hundred percent of your core-Self if you did not cultivate and conserve a substantial quantity of visceral Ki within your lower abdomen. To be viscerally anchored in the vibrant Ki of your core-Self during daily activities, affairs, and events is to faithfully embody the ancient Way of shikantaza. To embody the ancient Way of shikantaza by cultivating, conserving, and extending healthy quantities of Ki in your everyday life is to passionately live as core-Self with vitality, exuberance, vigor, and discerning wisdom.

Caring For Core-Self Ki

When I speak about nourishing the visceral Ki of your core-Self inside of shikantaza and zazen-only, I am speaking of a Way that promotes the balanced functioning of your autonomic nervous system, increases your immunity to illness, contributes to your overall well-being, and enhances your spiritual development and compassion as a human being who lives in community with others. This means that shikantaza and zazen-only are ancient Ways of tenderly caring for your physical health, emotional vitality, mental stamina, and spiritual well-being. When we take good care of ourselves by nourishing the visceral Ki of core-Self in shikantaza and zazen-only, we benefit ourselves, our loved ones, our friends, our fellow workers, and all the beings and things that we meet in the passage of our everyday life.

Nourishing the visceral Ki of core-Self in shikantaza and zazen-only is not narcissistic, selfish, egotistical, or hedonistic. When you are somatically mindful of the visceral Ki of core-Self while cultivating, conserving, and extending healthy quantities of Ki from your hara, your ordinary everyday life becomes experientially richer, authentically fulfilling, relationally enjoyable, and refreshingly intimate in each moment. To wholeheartedly practice shikantaza and zazen-only is to somatically comprehend a balanced Way to passionately care for all beings and things while nourishing and sustaining the visceral Ki of your core-Self moment by moment.

Most people do not know about the great functioning of Ki. They do not know that they can generate and conserve Ki in their body. They are unaware that their Ki reservoir is constantly being depleted in stressful and challenging environments. They do not know that somatic mindfulness of Ki and visceral mindfulness of core-Self are both crucial to promoting their embodied health, their mental stamina, their emotional vitality, their overall wellness, and their functional longevity.

Many of us are so focused on taking care of others at home, at work, at school, and at social events that we end up feeling fatigued, exhausted, resentful, hostile, fragmented, overwhelmed, and physically sick. We see individuals everyday who are not aware of the significance of Ki or the importance of nourishing the visceral Ki of their gut-core intelligence. They do not know how to take time to be intimate with the sensual Ki of their hara and the vibrant Ki of their core-Self. This is why they do not practice generating or conserving Ki within their body. This is why they continue to think, emote, and behave in dysfunctional ways that quickly uses up their Ki reservoir before they know it.

In our Way, we practice being somatically mindful of the great functioning of Ki while wholeheartedly meeting all beings and things that intimately come forth to engage the visceral Ki of our core-Self in the dance of everyday life. We place a high priority on generating and sustaining a vibrant Kikai reservoir within our hara. We are always somatically mindful of nourishing the visceral Ki of our core-Self. We are tenderly attentive to cultivating, conserving, and extending healthy quantities of KI to sustain our felt wellness throughout the day. This is how we are able to continuously express deep caring and compassion for all beings and things beyond exhaustion, hostility, resentment, and fatigue.

Speaking From Core-Self

When we embody core-Self in shikantaza, we extend our spherical field of Ki energy to include everyone we meet. We wholeheartedly reach-out and speak honestly to others from the felt visceral Ki of our core-Self. While speaking with others, we continue to cultivate and conserve Ki within our hara. This is the Way that we remain viscerally present within our lower abdomen while being true to others from the integrity of our core-Self.

We practice speaking with words that are viscerally grounded, emotionally meaningful, and intellectually accurate beyond the prejudices, biases, fears, and defensive postures of our ego-self and thinking mind. This means that we speak to others while remaining somatically grounded in the sensual Ki of our hara and the visceral Ki of our core-Self. When we practice speaking in this Way, we are in a constant state of relaxed alertness and vital readiness to verbalize our feelings and experiences, to listen wholeheartedly beyond thinking, to empathically accept others just as they are, to spontaneously share our true feelings and emotions, and behaviorally respond with sincerity from our "true home."

As we anchor within our hara and our core-Self while speaking, people who are not familiar with our Way may interpret this as Zen detachment. However, what they interpret as Zen detachment is really our passionate Way of living as core-Self while earnestly generating, conserving, and extending healthy quantities of Ki into our everyday life. To generate and conserve Ki within our lower abdomen while speaking from our core-Self is to be viscerally mindful of the abundant ocean of Ki within our hara. When we embody the visceral Ki of core-Self and the abundant ocean of Ki within our hara, we remain true to ourselves and others beyond the mental drama and fabricated abstractions of ego-self and thinking mind.

Although we use words and ideas to speak and communicate with others, we do not dwell in the mental functions of ego-self and thinking mind. We dwell in the sensuality of our hara and the still center-point of our visceral gut-core intelligence. When we do just this, people somatically experience the embodied truth and sincere emotional texture of our words that come directly from the visceral integrity of our core-Self. This is very different from dwelling in our headiness, generating words and ideas from our ego-self and thinking mind, and then moving our mouth and our tongue to speak from our egoself-centricity.

To always dwell in our headiness is to be detached from our embodied visceral experience. To be detached from our embodied visceral experience is to mentally objectify all beings and things while expressing our intelligence solely with our word thinking mind. To be detached from your visceral experience of core-Self is to manipulate the truth, speak with a hidden and ulterior motive, indulge in your myopic egoself-centricity, and rigidify your dogmatic view of an exclusive reality. To be ego-self and think with words while talking words about words is to spin a partial truth into a delusion and weave virtual reality into an illusion. When people talk only from their ego-self and thinking mind, we feel that they are disconnected or detached from their true visceral humanity. We sense that they are not fully embodied as they speak. They may seem sincere while speaking and facially emoting, but they are really being egoself-serving while deceitfully catering to the ego-self biases and prejudices of others.

When we dwell in the sensuality of our hara and let words spontaneously flow from the visceral integrity of our core-Self, people somatically realize beyond thinking that our speaking is trustworthy and completely congruent to who we are in each passing moment. Our Way is to speak to others from our core-Self with candor, generosity, clarity, tenderness, and compassion. This is very much like a gracious host who is always ready to welcome people into his true home and share the simplicity of his everyday life with heartfelt caring, hospitality, sincerity, and gratitude.

Listening In Non-Thinking

The practice of shikantaza and zazen-only is the Way of being total reality from the visceral refuge of our core-Self. Whether we are practicing just sitting as core-Self inside of zazen-only or living from core-Self inside of shikantaza, we are just being this Only Moment Body with each breath. To be this Only Moment Body with each breath is to be core-Self before thinking. To be core-Self before thinking is to realize that felt intimacy with daily life is entirely visceral and wholly somatic. Our training in zazen-only prepares us to live as core-Self in this Only Moment Body while being in boundless intimacy with total reality. This is why we passionately embody shikantaza as the pristine Way of being viscerally and somatically intimate with all beings and things during the passage of our everyday life. In our Way, we embody boundless intimacy with all beings and things by continuously abiding in the sensual Ki of our hara while living from the vibrant Ki of our core-Self beneath thinking.

When we viscerally anchor into our core-Self beneath thinking, we recover an organic and unfabricated Way of "being listening" as this Only Moment Body. In our Way of shikantaza, we always practice "being listening" as this Only Moment Body before employing the cerebral functions of our ego-self and thinking mind. To continuously "be listening" as this Only Moment Body is to compassionately meet our daily life from the silent illumination, still composure, and boundless intimacy of our core-Self. All of "being listening" as this Only Moment Body is viscerally transmitted inside of zazen-only. That which is viscerally transmitted inside of zazen-only is fully embodied in the practice of shikantaza. To faithfully embody the transmitted integrity of core-Self in the practice of shikantaza is to continuously be listening in non-thinking. To continuously be listening in non-thinking is to embody core-Self beneath the daily passage of I, me, and mine.

All of somatic and visceral listening inside of zazen-only is far beyond the power of your cerebral thinking. To viscerally grasp that the brilliant listening of your whole body is far beyond the power of your cerebral thinking is to confidently be your core-Self in the brilliance of non-thinking. To confidently be core-Self in the brilliance of non-thinking is to be deeply listening with the whole body far beyond ego-self and the function of thinking. To viscerally embody core-Self in the brilliance of non-thinking is to somatically realize that core-Self is always listening at the surface and depth of total reality.

In our Way, we entrust our whole life to the still brilliance of core-Self in non-thinking. To entrust our whole life to the still brilliance of core-Self in non-thinking is to always be listening as this Only Moment Body before thinking. When we viscerally embody the still brilliance of core-Self in non-thinking, we realize that there is no need to still our passing thoughts or silence our thinking mind. We simply sink into the birthless stillness and unborn silence of our core-Self that is far beneath the inner chatter of ego-self and the natural function of our thinking.

As we are continuously attracted to the felt sensuality of our hara and the still vibrancy of our core-Self, we are not distracted from viscerally "being listening" in non-thinking even as thoughts are endlessly arising and passing away inside of zazen-only. This is how we embody listening through core-Self in non-thinking without pushing away the passage of thinking or grasping at the brilliance of non-thinking. Just like this, in our daily practice of shikantaza, we do not let the functioning of our ego-self or thinking mind distract us from enjoying the sensuality of our hara and embodying the still listening of core-Self in non-thinking. This Way that core-Self listens in non-thinking is exactly a beginner's Way of being deep listening in shikantaza and zazen-only.

Being The Still Essence

When we abide in the still brilliance of core-Self inside of shikantaza and zazen-only, we are somatically being a timeless moment that flashes everywhere without coming or going. This "Only Moment" that flashes everywhere without coming or going is the vast Oneness and boundless intimacy of total reality. As our whole body is being this "Only Moment" of boundless intimacy, our core-Self is viscerally listening to the vast Oneness of total reality far beyond thinking. As this "Only Moment" of vast Oneness and boundless intimacy flashes everywhere without coming or going, we call IT, "The still essence of total reality."

When we sink into our hara inside of shikantaza and zazen-only, we somatically experience that the still essence of total reality is intimately arising from the visceral center-point of our lower abdomen. To embody the still essence of total reality from the visceral center-point of your hara is to be somatically listening to a timeless moment of vast Oneness that flashes everywhere right here and now. This is how we experience the timeless nature of this Only Moment Body while our core-Self is viscerally listening to the vast Oneness and boundless intimacy of total reality. All this is viscerally transmitted and somatically experienced far beneath the cerebral functioning of ego-self and thinking mind inside of zazen-only. All that is viscerally transmitted and somatically experienced inside of zazen-only is passionately embodied, gratefully acknowledged, and continuously verified in our daily practice of shikantaza.

Beyond Forced Sitting

When we wakefully embody the still center-point of our lower abdomen inside of zazen-only, we do not think about our hara, contemplate our body core, imagine our boundless intimacy with all beings and things, or ponder our vast Oneness with total reality. Nor do we grasp at the experience of core-Self arising in this Only Moment Body. Our Way of being core-Self in non-thinking while viscerally listening to the vast Oneness and boundless intimacy of total reality cannot be mentally created, emotionally fabricated, or physically forced to arise in the fixed stillness of zazen-only.

When we sit in the behavioral form of zazen-only, we do not practice patiently sitting still. We do not use the power of our mental discipline to endure the physical stillness of zazen-only. Nor do we forcefully exert the power of our will to sit fixedly even through pain. In our Way, we compassionately embody the refuge of zazen-only by not ignoring the arising of physical pain. All of us know that physical pain is associated with actual or potential tissue injury and bodily damage. Ignoring pain in zazen-only is the cultivation of ignorance in the field of delusion. This is why we do not forcefully hold our body in the fixed stillness of zazen-only while experiencing tingling, numbness, or increasing physical distress. In our Way, we express a conscientious caring, an attentive compassion, and a genuine tenderness toward our whole body in zazen-only. We slowly and gently make necessary somatic adjustments to any area that is experiencing numbness, tingling, or physical pain while totally honoring the ancient seal of zazen-only. We do this by continuing to be viscerally alive through our hara while abiding in the still vibrancy of our gut-core intelligence during each somatic adjustment.

Our Way is to somatically linger with ease and joy in the physical stillness of zazen-only while waiting forever for nothing to happen. We just sit inside of zazen-only with nowhere to go, nothing to be, and not one thing to achieve. This is the Way we surprisingly bloom into a radical human being with not one thing lacking. Our Way is entirely organic and beyond any mental, emotional, and behavioral exertion of ego-self. As we sit down in zazen-only, we do not grasp at being listening in non-thinking. We do not patiently wait for the intimate arrival of timelessness or expect the somatic realization of boundless intimacy. Nor do we anticipate the core-Self transmission of vast Oneness. We just cherish the profound ordinariness of each breath, delight in the sensual Ki of our hara, abide in the vibrant Ki of our core-Self, and wholeheartedly enjoy being alive as an ordinary human being far beneath thinking. When you practice zazen-only just like this, you will forget about the passage of linear time and viscerally blossom into the precious flower of timelessness, boundless intimacy, vast Oneness, and ungraspable enlightenment itself. All that viscerally blossoms in the embodiment of zazen-only is somatically practiced as the Way of shikantaza. To wholeheartedly live the somatic practice of shikantaza is to openly love and receive love beyond fear while passionately expressing tender caring and compassion toward all beings and things within the ordinariness of everyday life.

Thank you.

"The zazen-only I speak of is not just learning
meditation. It is simply the Dharma gate of repose
and bliss, the practice-realization of totally culminated
enlightenment. It is the manifestation of ultimate reality.
Traps and snares can never reach it. Once its heart is
grasped, you are like the dragon when he gains the
water, like the tiger when she enters the mountain.
For you must know that just there (in zazen-only)
the right Dharma is manifesting itself, and
that, from the first, dullness and
distraction are struck aside."

Eihei Dogen
Fukan-Zazengi
(1200-1253)

I have often talked to you about a frog,
and each time everyone laughs. But a frog is
very interesting. He sits like us, too, you know.
But he does not think that he is doing anything so
special. When you go to the zendo (meditation dojo)
and sit (in zazen), you may think that you are doing some
special thing....That may be your understanding of zazen.
But look at the frog. A frog also sits like us, but he has no
idea of zazen. Watch him. If something annoys him,
he will make a face. If something comes along to
eat, he will snap it up and eat it, and he eats
just sitting. Actually, that is our zazen.
We are not doing any special
thing by just sitting].

Shunryu Suzuki-roshi
(Zen Mind, Beginner's Mind)

CHAPTER 2

Core-Self Alignments

Faith, Wonder, and Compassion are the Real Treasures of our Life.

"To see form and clarify the mind, to hear sound and
come to realization is attainment of the Way with the body.
Thus, when you practice just sitting and continuously give up
all thoughts and views, the Way becomes more and more
intimate. So attaining the Way means attaining
it completely with the whole body."

Eihei Koroku
(Dogen's Extensive Record)

Introduction

In our Way of traditional Zen practice, we live according to seven core-Self alignments that uphold our daily experience of well-being, joy, ease, and sensual vitality in this Only Moment Body. Here, I will describe how we practice these seven alignments to nourish clarity, harmony, integrity, and authenticity in our everyday life and relationships. The seven somatic alignments of core-Self include: (1) alignment to postural ease and physical balance; (2) alignment to abdominal breathing and peak body metabolism; (3) alignment to biochemical integrity and felt cerebral harmony; (4) alignment to a viscerally anchored mental functioning; (5) alignment to synergy and causal interdependency; (6) alignment to transpersonal unity and interpersonal practice; and (7) alignment to living beyond grasping and pushing away.

The order in which I present these seven daily alignments does not reflect a valuing of one over another. Nor does the order presented here mean that you have to practice each one before you go on to the others. You will find yourself practicing several alignments simultaneously or practicing only one or two according to the ever shifting circumstances and challenges of your everyday life. Just remember that each one of the seven daily alignments works interdependently with all the others to nourish your vital wellness, your felt wholeness, your ever fresh clarity, your visceral integrity, and your continuous Way of being core-Self in this Only Moment Body. As I describe the seven daily alignments of core-Self, you will begin to realize how they compliment each other to sustain your behavioral wisdom, your beginner's heartmind, and your compassionate Way of practicing shikantaza and zazen-only.

Postural Ease And Physical Balance

Our first alignment as core-Self is to the daily practice of postural ease and physical balance. Alignment to postural ease and physical balance is based on our deep visceral intimacy with the still center-point of gravity located in the middle of our lower abdomen. As you will remember, the still center-point of gravity is where we intimately experience the arising of core-Self in shikantaza and zazen-only. Our abdominal center-point of gravity is an ever dependable reference point for establishing the postural ease and physical balance of this Only Moment body.

As we abide in the abdominal center-point of gravity and the still arising of core-Self in shikantaza and zazen-only, we cultivate the daily experience of postural ease by embodying an effortless spinal uprightness. By effortless spinal uprightness, I mean the Way that the still center-point of gravity naturally aligns all of our spinal vertebrae into an erect S-shaped curve without creating muscular tension or tightness. Our effortless spinal uprightness establishes the body of postural ease while allowing our vertebral column to remain pliable and always ready to withstand varying degrees of stress as we physically move and act in everyday life.

Our Way is to prevent needless muscular tension or excessive stress on our spinal column and its intervertebral discs as we embody shikantaza and zazen-only. We are constantly aligning to an easeful and effortless postural uprightness from the still center-point of our visceral core-Self. Our core-Self alignment to an effortless spinal uprightness during the activities and behaviors of our everyday life sustains our experience of postural ease while keeping our vertebral column healthy, strong, and flexible.

As we embody shikantaza and zazen-only, we viscerally abide in the still center-point of our core-Self, compassionately practice the easeful and effortless uprightness of our posture, and continuously nourish our physical balance during the activities and affairs of our everyday life. Our alignment to physical balance includes an ever deepening core-Self intimacy with gravitational forces that are always interacting with our body. These shifting gravitational forces have an impact on our total muscular-skeletal system whether our body is in a behavioral state of stillness or movement. When we practice an effortless postural uprightness in shikantaza and zazen-only, we experience how the still center-point of our visceral core-Self somatically unifies and balances all the gravitational forces that impinge upon our body as we abide in seated stillness or arise to engage in motion.

When we embody the still center-point of core-Self, we are able to viscerally discern and instantly integrate all the gravitational forces that immediately influence the degree and quality of our postural ease and physical balance while sitting, walking, pushing, stretching, bending, pulling, rotating, lifting, running, and jumping. As core-Self, we remain inwardly attentive to the Way that gravitational forces immediately impinge on our total muscular-skeletal system while continuously making corrective adjustments to our spinal uprightness, our shifting physical balance, and the intensity or angle of our physical exertion. Our compassionate adjustments in each moment decreases muscular tension and tightness, diminishes mental and emotional stress, supports the healthy functioning of our vertebrae, bones, joints, and ligaments, and enhances our daily experience of being core-Self in reposed vitality, gentle uprightness, easeful balance, and grounded tenderness.

As the still center-point of core-Self naturally functions in dynamic interdependency with gravitational forces far beneath ego-self and thinking mind, all earth dwellers are able to experience the effortless embodiment of physical balance, the surprising wholeness and gentle efficiency of all their movements, and the easeful and joyful Way of being still or active in everyday life. To practice core-Self alignment to postural ease and physical balance is to wholeheartedly perform your daily activities with compassionate attentiveness to ergonomic safety, graceful movement, easeful productivity, and behavioral wisdom. As you continue to practice in this Way, your simple and ordinary muscular-skeletal adaptations to ever shifting gravitational forces will become more synergistic, amazing, spontaneous, delightful, and intriguing.

Abdominal Breathing And Peak Body Metabolism

Our second alignment as core-Self is to the continuous practice of abdominal breathing and the cultivation of peak cellular metabolism during stillness, rest, movement, and vigorous activity. When we embody shikantaza and zazen-only, we always nourish an intimate relationship with the depth, rhythm, and fullness of our abdominal breathing. As we do just this, we also sustain a meticulous core-Self attentiveness to our body's immediate need for oxygen during cellular metabolism. Cellular metabolism includes the tens of thousands of chemical reactions that take place within all our cells to maintain the healthy functioning of our body. The bright wisdoming process of metabolism transforms oxygen and digested nutrients into cellular matter and bioenergy. Cellular metabolism uses oxygen just like food to create body heat and all the fuel necessary for thinking, emoting, sensing, feeling, and moving in everyday life. Each time we inhale, oxygen is captured by tiny blood vessels within our lungs and immediately taken to all the cells of our body by way of our circulatory system. After all our cells metabolize oxygen and nutrients, they release carbon dioxide. Carbon dioxide is essentially a toxin generated after we inhale. All the cells of our body release carbon dioxide into the blood stream as part of the metabolic process. Our blood stream then delivers carbon dioxide to our lungs where it is expelled from our body with each exhalation.

We practice core-Self alignment to continuous abdominal breathing and peak metabolic functioning whether we are easefully at rest, mentally and emotionally active, or engaged in behavioral movement. During periods of embodied stillness or inactivity, we gently inhale using our diaphragm muscle and allow our lower abdomen to tenderly extend itself. By doing just this, we provide our body with an abundant level of cellular oxygenation to easily sustain our resting metabolic threshold while enhancing our immediate oxygen reserves. When we engage in any play, work, or movement that increases our body's oxygen needs beyond our resting metabolic threshold, we consciously maximize our cellular oxygenation by deeply and rhythmically breathing into our lower abdomen. We oxygenate our body through abdominal breathing because it is far more efficient than chest breathing. As we relax our lower abdomen and engage the diaphragm muscle in the act of breathing, our lungs expand to twice the volume they usually do when we breathe only by engaging our chest and shoulder muscles.

Most people do not understand how important abdominal breathing is to our health and well being. Our physical body is designed to discharge at least seventy percent of all its biotoxins through the breathing process. The other thirty percent of our biotoxins are discharged through our sweat, defecation, and urination. If we are not breathing deeply by engaging our diaphragm and relaxing our lower abdomen, our cells do not receive the maximum oxygen needed to establish and sustain a peak level of metabolic functioning. This diminishing of peak metabolic functioning happens during periods of rest as well as periods of vigorous activity and athletic performance where the need for more oxygen increases rapidly. When our peak metabolic functioning is constantly diminished and challenged by the ineffectiveness of our shallow chest breathing, our body also becomes less efficient in ridding itself of its biotoxins. As oxygenation for peak cellular metabolism remains diminished and biotoxins continuously buildup, the healthy and harmonious functioning of our body becomes adversely affected. This is why our constant practice of diaphragmatic breathing is extremely important in sustaining our peak metabolic functioning and our continuous embodiment of vitality, immunity, health, healing, wellness, and longevity during the passage of our everyday life.

As we embody shikantaza and zazen-only, we sustain our maximum oxygenation, strengthen our immunity to illness, and optimize our metabolic functioning through our devoted and continuous practice of diaphragmatic breathing. At the same time, we practice a devoted core-Self attentiveness to our oxygen saturation threshold, to our immediately felt oxygen expenditures, to the fullest release of biotoxins through each exhalation, and to the enhancement of our oxygen reserves in each passing moment. When we practice our second core-Self alignment in this Way, we intimately discern how our deep abdominal breathing, our maximum level of oxygenation, and our peak metabolic functioning continually enhance our mental clarity, our emotional buoyancy, our behavioral stamina, and the ever fresh Way that we experience this Only Moment Body of ease and joy.

Biochemical Integrity And Felt Cerebral Harmony

Our third alignment as core-Self is to the compassionate cultivation of biochemical integrity and felt cerebral harmony during the embodiment of shikantaza and zazen-only. By "biochemical integrity," I mean the Way that we experience the natural and balanced chemical functioning of our whole body. Many of us reveal our somatic intimacy with the biochemical integrity of our body when we speak about our chemistry being off or imbalanced. By "felt cerebral harmony," I mean the way in which we physically experience the clear, easeful, and crisp functioning of our brain generated consciousness. We practice our third alignment by maintaining a compassionate core-Self intimacy with our body's total biochemistry and our felt cerebral functioning in everyday life. We notice how our ever shifting biochemistry and our cerebral experience of consciousness are constantly being affected by the shallowness and depth of our breathing, the foods, liquids, supplements, and drugs that we ingest into our body, and the efficiency or inefficiency of our cellular metabolism. This is why we practice being somatically and viscerally mindful of the substances we take into our body, how they affect our dynamic biochemical integrity, and how they influence our heady experience of cerebral consciousness. When we practice just like this, we become intimately aware of subtle changes in our biochemistry that enhance or diminish our felt experience of being fully alive, sharply alert, and crisply aware as this Only Moment Body. We begin to see how these subtle changes in our biochemistry directly influence the felt texture and quality of our embodied experience while determining the dimness, clearness, murkiness, freshness, or dullness of our cerebrally generated consciousness. We begin to notice that their is a direct causal relationship that exists between what we ingest and metabolize and our emergent physical and emotional experience of vigor, lethargy, anxiety, edginess, anger, depression, fatigue, and exuberance.

When we are somatically aware of our ever shifting biochemistry, we begin to develop an intuitive visceral understanding of how our whole body seeks to maintain a true biochemical integrity and an easeful and harmonious cerebral functioning.

Our body seeks biochemical integrity and an easeful cerebral harmony so that it can nourish and sustain its ever fresh sensory experience of total reality, its visceral joy and delight in being fully alive right here and now, and its peak physical vigor, mental clarity, and emotional buoyancy during the passage of everyday life.

There are two principles that guide our alignment to biochemical integrity and felt cerebral harmony during our practiced embodiment of shikantaza and zazen-only. The first principle is the avoidance of all manufactured and organic psychotropic drugs. These drugs affect the central nervous system, alter the natural embodiment of cerebral consciousness, and cause significant changes in perception, experience, and behavior. Rather than establish visceral intimacy with the still vibrancy of our core-Self, psychotropic drugs overpower our developed ego-self functioning, disrupt our logical and rational way of thinking, reinforce depersonalization, inundate our senses with overwhelming stimulation, create an illusory and transient emotional euphoria, amplify the diffuse and ambiguous nature of physical reality, and chemically disconnect a fabricated cerebral consciousness from the felt experience of being this Only Moment Body. Some people go on to assume that their psychotropic state of disembodied consciousness has liberated them from the physical world and the lawful functioning of cause and effect. Others view their fabricated cerebral consciousness as the realization of a higher state of transcendental being and the harbinger of humanity's spiritual evolution. However, they do not viscerally comprehend that any psychotropic alteration of cerebral consciousness is far removed from the pristine sensual embodiment of their hara, the still brilliance of their core-Self, the undefiled exuberance of their beginner's heartmind, and the profound simplicity and ordinariness of their everyday life. This is why we do not rationalize the ingestion of psychotropic drugs as a justifiable means to experience a religious, shamanic, or mystical state of fabricated cerebral consciousness.

The second principle that guides our alignment to biochemical integrity and felt cerebral harmony is the principle of accountability to the bright wisdoming of vast Oneness in this Only Moment Body. We practice the principle of embodied accountability by honestly and compassionately appraising all our somatic experiences and daily behaviors that are associated with our eating and drinking. We ingest foods, drinks, supplements, and necessary medicines as long as the kind, quality, or quantity does not adversely affect our somatic well-being, our felt biochemical integrity, our cerebral clarity, our visceral groundedness, and our loving, caring, and empathic availability to others. As we appraise the kind, quality, and quantity of the substances that we ingest, we value the effortless embodiment of moderation and renunciation. Our Way of embodying moderation and renunciation is without forced discipline. What others see as willpower or self-discipline is really our Way of cherishing and honoring moderation and renunciation as two important pillars that support our health, wellness, clarity, and longevity.

We hold true to the principle of embodied accountability by honestly witnessing the times we ingest unhealthy substances or take in more food, drinks, supplements, and prescribed medicines than we really need. Most of us are driven toward overconsumption and the ingestion of unhealthy substances because we want to distract ourselves from social anxiety and emotional discomfort, to diminish the arising of stress and tension throughout our body, or to avoid facing and consciously processing our grief, anguish, anger, fear, boredom, resentment and other difficult feelings. To be somatically mindful of how overconsumption and the ingestion of unhealthy substances has diminished visceral intimacy with our core-Self is to instantly comprehend how we have upset the dynamic biochemical integrity of our body, how we have disrupted our cerebral clarity and harmony, how we have depressed our ever fresh, easeful and wakeful alertness, and how we have been keeping ourselves from being wholeheartedly present with others. To remain true to the principle of embodied accountability is to continuously discern whether we are honestly, courageously, and creatively meeting the challenges of everyday life without diminishing our physical health and well-being, perpetuating unhealthy karma, generating mental drama, or attaching to the dysfunctional emotional states of denial, avoidance, and resistance.

Viscerally Anchoring Our Mental Funtioning

We practice our fourth core-Self alignment by viscerally anchoring our mental functions within the still center-point of our lower abdomen. When we viscerally anchor the mental functions of ego-self and thinking mind within the still center-point of our lower abdomen, we somatically discern that core-Self can sensibly and skillfully employ them without needing to identify with them. This Way of viscerally anchoring in the still center-point of our core-Self while skillfully employing our ego-self and thinking mind is somatically transmitted inside the seated stillness of zazen-only. It is in zazen-only that we somatically learn how to meticulously refine and spiritually develop our ego-self and thinking mind, how to compassionately molt off our karmic attachment to dysfunctional behaviors, how to live in boundless intimacy with all beings and things, how to blend with the bright wisdoming of vast Oneness, how to conscientiously and tenderly take care of our everyday life, and how to viscerally abide in the stillness of total reality during the passage of linear time.

As we arise from zazen-only to viscerally embody our core-Self inside of shikantaza, we continue to somatically discern the insubstantiality of our ego-self and thinking mind while experiencing the fleeting impermanence of all our thoughts, feelings, and sensations. It is in shikantaza and zazen-only that core-Self silently illuminates the illusory nature of our personal beliefs and opinions, the emptiness of our perceptual biases and blind prejudices, and the futile mental posturing and emotional armoring of our egoself-centricity. When all this is fully illuminated within shikantaza and zazen only, we viscerally comprehend that the armoring and posturing of our egoself-centricity fosters cognitive inflexibility, diminishes empathy, advances physical rigidity, reinforces behavioral reactivity, and increases our susceptibility to stress and tension. We become aware that seemingly stressful situations are not inherently stressful in and of themselves. We come to realize that the experience of stress and tension usually arises when we meet the challenges of everyday life from our guarded and vulnerable egoself-centricity. This is why we viscerally anchor all our cerebral mental processes within the still vibrancy of our core-Self that is far beyond the unhealthy, defensive, aggressive, and narcissistic posturing of egoself-centricity.

When we practice our core-Self alignment to a viscerally anchored mental functioning, we entrust our whole life to the intelligent non-thinking stillness of our core-Self. By "non-thinking," I do not mean to imply that thinking is not an important mental process or that the still intelligence of core-Self cannot function in the midst of cerebral thinking. Rather, I am referring to the Way that we passionately live from the visceral center-point of non-thinking that silently illuminates the surface and depth of our everyday life. This visceral center-point of non-thinking is exactly the still intelligence of our core-Self that somatically exists underneath the cerebral functioning of ego-self and thinking mind. To viscerally embody our core-Self in shikantaza and zazen-only is to somatically realize that living from the still discernment of non-thinking is a healthy and pragmatic Way to live everyday life while being in boundless intimacy with all beings and things.

As we embody the still brilliance of core-Self in non-thinking, we silently illuminate how the futile posturing and armoring of egoself-centricity can keep us from living a deeply fulfilling, compassionate, loving, peaceful, and lasting life. We begin to recognize that our singular and exclusive identification with the cerebral functioning of egoself-centricity creates a false sense of mental and emotional stability. We begin to see how the myopic nature of egoself-centricity is perpetuated by endless narcissistic thoughts about I, me, and mine. We begin to recognize that egoself-centricity keeps us from seeing what we are looking at, diminishes our sensory freshness and our exuberant aliveness, distracts us from empathizing with the feelings and emotions of others, hinders the clarity of our logical and rational thinking, and obstructs the embodied expression of behavioral wisdom, boundless intimacy, and compassionate action in our everyday life. To silently illuminate the dysfunctional nature of egoself-centricity from the still discernment of non-thinking is to viscerally liberate the wondrous exuberance, profound humility, and magnanimous authenticity of beginner's heartmind. To experience the liberation of beginner's heartmind is to somatically comprehend our precious Way of living from the still brilliance of nonthinking. This is our beginner's Way of clearly seeing all beings and things just as they are, of always enjoying the pristine simplicity and ordinariness of everyday life, and viscerally honoring our boundless intimacy from the still center-point of non-thinking.

Causal Interactivity And Relational Synergy

So far I have described how embodiment of core-Self in shikantaza and zazen-only includes our alignment to postural ease and physical balance, our alignment to abdominal breathing and peak cellular metabolism, our alignment to biochemical integrity and felt cerebral harmony, and our alignment to a viscerally anchored mental functioning. Although these four alignments are each distinct and unique in their somatic practice focus, we do not view them as being totally separate and independent from one another. Our fifth core-Self alignment involves a wakeful and compassionate attentiveness to the causal interactivity and relational synergy that exists between our first four somatic alignments. By "causal interactivity and relational synergy," I mean the Way that our first four alignments causally interact and relationally influence each other to synergistically nourish and sustain the peak functioning of this Only Moment Body.

While practicing one core-Self alignment, we remain viscerally mindful of how it causally interacts in dynamic relationship with the other three. In this Way, we begin to learn that our practice of one core-Self alignment is important to the synergistic and harmonious functioning of all four somatic alignments. For example, when we practice our alignment to postural ease and physical balance, we notice how it also enhances our intimacy with abdominal breathing, improves our metabolic efficiency, advances our biochemical integrity, augments our felt cerebral harmony, and promotes the visceral grounding of all our mental functions. Likewise, as we practice our alignment to abdominal breathing, our heady mental functions begin to sense their visceral grounding, our body experiences less tension, stress, and tightness, our center-point of gravity is intimately felt, our postural ease and spinal uprightness are somatically encouraged, our cerebral harmony is nourished and enhanced, our attentiveness to ergonomic safety and physical balance is facilitated, and our metabolic functioning and chemical balance immediately begin to improve.

We practice core-Self alignment to causal interactivity and relational synergy from the moment we awaken in the morning to the moment we go to sleep at night. As we practice being compassionately attentive to the causal interactivity between our first four somatic alignments, we viscerally comprehend that the still brilliance of our core-Self advances their relational synergy and harmonious functioning beyond thinking. To advance the relational synergy and harmonious functioning of our first four somatic alignments from the still brilliance of our core-Self is to remain deeply rooted in our physiological processes while simultaneously living in boundless intimacy and vast Oneness from the quantum depth of this Only Moment Body.

Transpersonal Unity And Interpersonal Practice

Our sixth alignment as core-Self is to cultivate transpersonal unity with the still essence of total reality while practicing clarity, authenticity, empathy, and loving kindness in all our interpersonal relationships. By "transpersonal unity," I mean a viscerally based unity with the vast Oneness that upholds our boundless intimacy and limitless interdependency with all beings and things. To be in transpersonal unity through our core-Self in shikantaza and zazen-only is to somatically comprehend the ungraspable nature of transpersonal unity Itself. This means that transpersonal unity cannot be cerebrally grasped by our ego-self nor caught by the traps and cages of our thinking mind. To confidently be transpersonal unity in shikantaza and zazen-only is to have no desire to mentally grasp or personalize the ungraspable nature of Unity itself. As we have no desire to mentally grasp or objectively personalize the ungraspable nature of transpersonal unity, we do not use our cerebrally generated intelligence to project our own humanity, our moral reason, our ethical vision, our willful nature, or our personal realization of "I am" onto the still essence and vast Oneness of total reality.

To live in transpersonal unity is to viscerally comprehend that the still essence of total reality flashes as our core-Self in this Only Moment Body while upholding our boundless intimacy with all beings and things. In our Way, we do not grasp at transpersonal unity or the boundless intimacy of total reality. Nor do we push away or negate the great functioning of duality that allows us to relate to others as separate human beings and unique individuals. We treasure the great functioning of duality that is the genuine bases for enjoying and sharing our personality within the dynamic interpersonal fabric of everyday life. We treasure the individuality of all human beings while recognizing, honoring, and respecting their inherent dignity, their wholesome emotional boundaries, and their healthy ego-self functioning that sustains their separate and accountable identity within society.

When we embody our core-Self inside of shikantaza and zazen-only, we experience transpersonal unity far beneath the daily functioning of our ego-self and thinking mind. To be anchored in our visceral core-Self is to somatically realize transpersonal unity no matter where we are, no matter how we feel, no matter what we are thinking, no matter what we are doing. To be core-Self in transpersonal unity is to gratefully embody the tranquility of heart not-wanting and the clarity of mind not-knowing. We call this precious embodiment of heart not-wanting and mind not-knowing the liberation of our beginner's heartmind. To embody transpersonal unity and experience the liberation of our beginner's heartmind is to passionately enjoy the pristine simplicity and profundity of each moment far beyond our cerebral thinking. Our Way is to always be a wondrous beginner who remains somatically attentive to the vast Oneness of total reality that continues to intimately arrive in the ordinariness and impermanence of everyday life. We gratefully embody a beginner's somatic attentiveness by anchoring all our mental functions within the still vibrancy of our core-Self where transpersonal unity is viscerally realized and silently illuminated at the surface and depth of total reality.

In our Way, we place an absolute priority on embodying transpersonal unity with vast Oneness whether we are sitting alone in the silence of zazen-only or living our everyday life and relationships in the practice body of shikantaza. We take refuge in transpersonal unity because core-Self in transpersonal unity guides us through the difficulties, joys, challenges, and blessings that arise in our interpersonal practice of relationships. Interpersonal practice includes all relationships associated with family life, marriage, intimate couples, close friendships, religious fellowships, work associates, and daily social acquaintances. We reach-out from our core-Self in transpersonal unity to practice the duality of interpersonal relationships with empathy, clarity, openness, caring, authenticity, and integrity.

Although the practice of interpersonal relationships is predominately heart-based, it is viscerally anchored in the still integrity of our core-Self that cherishes transpersonal unity and accountability to the vast Oneness of total reality. As we viscerally anchor in the still integrity of our core-Self, we wholeheartedly listen to the thoughts of others while empathically being with their feelings and emotions just as they are. In our Way, we employ the cerebral functions of ego-self and thinking mind to truthfully communicate from the still integrity of our core-Self. When we anchor within the still integrity of core-Self during interpersonal dialogue, we faithfully honor the uniqueness of our individuality and the individuality of the other, clarify and inspire the healthy functioning of our ego-self and thinking mind, and remain true to the vast Oneness and boundless intimacy of total reality.

As we listen and dialogue with others from the still integrity of our core-Self, we naturally extend a healthy boundary of Ki awareness around our whole body. As we do just this, we honestly share our thoughts, feelings, needs, and desires. We speak our truth while courageously meeting and exposing the full range of our humanness from the still integrity of our core-Self. To courageously expose the full range of our humanness from the still integrity of core-Self is to instantly drop off the mental, somatic, and emotional armoring of our ego-self and thinking mind. This is the Way we open ourselves to the power of truth, forgiveness, healing, compassion, wisdom, and love. To be in interpersonal dialogue from the still integrity of core-Self is to practice tenderness and deep caring toward self and others while embodying the authenticity, humility, flexibility, and magnanimous openness of beginner's heartmind.

Living Beyond Grasping And Pushing Away

We practice our seventh core-Self alignment by passionately living beyond grasping and pushing away. To passionately live beyond grasping and pushing away is to throw our whole life force into somatically being the truth while viscerally embodying total reality just as IT is. To viscerally embody total reality and somatically be the truth is to live everyday life from the still essence of core-Self and the noble wholeness of our beginner's heartmind. We practice somatically being the truth and viscerally embodying total reality whether we feel pleasant or unpleasant, delighted or disturbed, energized or exhausted, fearful or at ease, distressed or composed.

Somatically being the truth and viscerally embodying total reality are both dependent on our daily practice of accepting things just as they are and taking care of things just as they come. In our Way, we do not clutch or grasp at situations, activities, and experiences that our ego-self preferentially desires and wishes to prolong. Nor do we ignore or push away situations, activities, and experiences that our ego-self preferentially dislikes and wants to avoid. If something needs to be done, we practice doing it with wholehearted attentiveness and an upright conscientiousness. If uncomfortable feelings or difficult emotions arise that we do not want to face, we courageously and honorably illuminate them from the still integrity of our core-Self while compassionately embracing them with the unintrusive curiosity and gracious wonder of our beginner's heartmind.

To sit as core-Self inside of zazen-only with the unintrusive curiosity of beginner's heartmind is to behaviorally express our deepest yearning to somatically be the truth just as IT is, see all beings and things just as they are, and viscerally embody total reality before thinking. Our somatic practice of shikantaza and zazen-only is not about avoiding the truth or mentally creating a fabricated or preferential experience of embodied reality. To somatically practice shikantaza and zazen-only is to unhesitatingly bow to the truth and viscerally embody the unfabricated nature of total reality moment by moment. To unhesitatingly bow to the truth while viscerally embodying total reality is to molt off our tenacious attachment to cerebral thinking and our ego-self's persistent addiction to grasping and pushing away. This is how we naturally live the body of truth in our everyday life, see all beings and things just as they are, and viscerally be total reality just as IT is. To see beings and things just as they are is to see them beyond our mental chatter, our emotional prejudices, and our perceptual biases. To viscerally be total reality just as IT is means to courageously embody the ungraspable nature of core-Self, to compassionately embrace the vast impermanence of all beings and things, and to joyfully live in the vast Oneness and flashing stillness of everyday life that is happening far beneath our cerebral thinking.

As we unconditionally live from the ungraspable nature of core-Self, our daily embodiment of total reality is brilliantly clear and far beyond doubt. To be brilliantly clear and far beyond doubt is to see that our addiction to grasping and pushing away keeps us from joyfully embodying our vast Oneness and boundless intimacy with total reality. When we somatically live the truth, compassionately accept beings and things just as they are, realize our visceral clarity and integrity far beyond doubt, and express deep caring and tenderness toward all beings and things, we unfold boundless intimacy and ungraspable enlightenment within the ordinariness of our everyday life. Anyone who viscerally practices shikantaza and zazen-only in this Way is a genuine and trustworthy human being who lives beyond grasping and pushing away.

Thank you.

"The entire body is illumination;
the entire body is the entire mind.
When the entire body is the entire
body, there is no hinderance."

Eihei Dogen
Ikka Myōju
"One Bright Pearl"

"The phrase, 'learning the
Way through the body,' means
that we learn the Way by means
of the body, that we learn the Way
by means of our living flesh."

Eihei Dogen
Shinjin Gakudō
Studying The Way Through Bodymind

• CHAPTER 3 •
Marks Of Core-Self

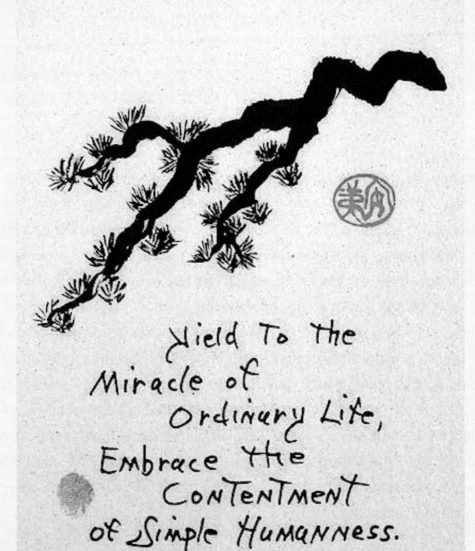

Yield To The
Miracle of
     Ordinary Life,
Embrace the
     Contentment
of Simple Humanness.

"Behind the head [beyond sight and knowing],
the path of genuine intimacy opens wide;
in front of the face [seeing total reality],
not-knowing is a good friend."

Eihei Koroku
(Dogen's Extensive Record)

The Taproot of Humanness

We embody the radical taproot of humanness by just sitting as core-Self inside of zazen-only. When I speak of the "radical taproot of humanness," I am referring to the pristine and inclusive Way of living as a somatically grounded and viscerally rooted human being. One way to understand the radical taproot of humanness is to imagine a huge tree with a large trunk, gnarled branches with leaves, and a broad root system emerging from a very deep central taproot. The central taproot keeps the whole tree firmly anchored to the earth while reaching deeply for water and minerals. The growth, development, and longevity of the tree is nourished and sustained by the central taproot. Now imagine that the tree I am referring to is the ancient tree of our radical or original humanness. The branches of this ancient tree represent the cultural, racial, spiritual, religious, scientific, and philosophical views of humanness that have emerged throughout mankind's history. The deep taproot of our radical humanness is exactly the embodiment of our visceral core-Self in shikantaza and zazen-only.

When we somatically realize the visceral taproot of our radical or original humanness in shikantaza and zazen-only, we experience the sensual innocence, exuberant vitality, and still brilliance of core-Self in this Only Moment Body. To live everyday life from the radical taproot of humanness is to live as core-Self before the dawning of history and linear time, before the emergence of cultures, languages, and racial identities, and before the development of ego-self and thinking mind. As the deep visceral taproot of our radical humanness, core-Self sustains the peaceful and harmonious Way of living in boundless intimacy and ungraspable enlightenment with all beings and things.

When I say that the practice of shikantaza and zazen-only somatically awakens the visceral Way of passionately living as a radical human being, I am not talking about a transcendental or disembodied state of cerebral consciousness. Our Way of living everyday life through the radical taproot of humanness is the somatic Way of being viscerally grounded in the sensuality of our hara and the still vibrancy of our core-Self. When we fully embody everyday life through the still vibrancy of our core-Self, we liberate the clarity and exuberance of our beginner's heartmind and recover the radical taproot of all human beings. To passionately live through the radical taproot of all human beings is to viscerally comprehend the basic goodness, profound humility, and brilliant spontaneity of beginner's heartmind. To behaviorally express our basic goodness, our beginner's heartmind, and the vast inclusiveness of our radical humanity is to somatically realize the ever intimate arrival of an enlightened human being in everyday life. As we embody core-Self in shikantaza and zazen-only, we continuously verify the radical taproot of all human beings, openly enjoy our boundless intimacy with all beings and things, and unfold ungraspable enlightenment beyond efforting, gaining, owning, or attaining.

A Trustworthy Criteria

The embodied taproot of core-Self exhibits six illuminating marks that together reflect the true nature of radical humanness. We viscerally grasp and somatically verify the illuminating marks of core-Self through our daily practice of shikantaza and zazen-only. To viscerally embody the six illuminating marks of core-Self in shikantaza and zazen-only is to somatically comprehend the completion and total fulfillment of our radical humanness far beneath cerebral thinking. When we somatically realize the completion of our radical humanness inside of zazen-only, we confidently arise in shikantaza to behaviorally express our boundless intimacy with all beings and things, our passionate alignment with the vast Oneness of total reality, and our endless gratitude for being core-Self in this Only Moment Body.

When we embody the six illuminating marks of core-Self, we can sensibly discern how social norms, political views, religious doctrines, and cultural traditions either encourage or obstruct the somatic realization of our radical humanness, the visceral recognition of our vast Oneness with all beings and things, and the innocent sensual brilliance of our beginner's heartmind that passionately enjoys the ever fresh impermanence of everyday life. We can genuinely appraise the value and integrity of any personal or collective view by asking whether it inspires or distracts human beings from the embodiment of core-Self and its six illuminating marks. To the degree that a personal or collective view inspires and advances the embodiment of core-Self and its six illuminating marks, then to that degree we can be certain that the view is in accord with our radical humanness, our basic goodness, our boundless intimacy, and our vast inclusiveness. On the other hand, to the degree that any personal or collective view obstructs or discourages the embodiment of core-Self and its six illuminating marks, then to that degree we can be certain that it will hinder the visceral discernment of our boundless intimacy, the fulfillment and completion of our radical humanness, and the somatic liberation of our beginners heartmind that passionately enjoys the vast Oneness of total reality.

Impermanence

The first illuminating mark of core-Self is deep visceral intimacy with vast impermanence. To be core-Self in deep visceral intimacy with vast impermanence is to somatically comprehend that vast impermanence is happening at the surface and depth of total reality. As we embody core-Self in shikantaza and zazen-only, we somatically discern that the surface of vast impermanence is the fleeting existence of all beings and things and the transitory nature of our birthing, living, and dying. Likewise, in shikantaza and zazen-only, we somatically experience that the depth of vast impermanence is exactly the still flashing of this only moment that continuously integrates the total dynamic functioning of the whole universe. This is the Way we viscerally comprehend the surface and depth of vast impermanence in shikantaza and zazen-only

At the surface of vast impermanence, we all experience death, dying, old age, grief, and loss. These unavoidable human experiences empathically bind us together far beyond our social, racial, cultural, and individual differences. This is why we reach out with compassion, caring, loving kindness, and understanding when we meet any human being who is facing these difficult experiences. This is the Way that core-Self empathizes with all human beings while viscerally sharing the depth of vast impermanence that is humanity's eternal refuge far beyond separation, duality, and extinction.

Most of us are constantly grasping at permanence while living in rapid change and endless impermanence at the surface of everyday life. To grasp at permanence at the surface of reality is to push away the crossroads of life and death that are always arriving to somatically meet us right here and now. To push away the crossroads of life and death at the surface of reality is to push away the depth of vast impermanence that is exactly the stillness of an eternal moment flashing far beyond the passage of linear time. In our Way of living as core-Self in this Only Moment Body, we do not grasp at permanence nor push away the unavoidable reality of death and dying. When we practice just sitting as core-Self inside of zazen-only, we inhale each breath as the passionate expression of our momentary aliveness without grasping at permanence. We joyfully embody endless gratitude and treasure the revitalization of our life force that is the inhalation itself. At the end of each inhalation, we just let go with ease and trust into the outward flow of our exhalation. To be each exhalation in zazen-only is to totally release our life force beyond grasping. To release our life force beyond grasping is to viscerally meet the crossroads of life and death right here and now. To viscerally meet the crossroads of life and death right here and now is to somatically realize that the still flashing depth of vast impermanence is eternally upholding this only moment of total reality. This is why we take refuge in vast impermanence as we continue to compassionately meet the crossroads of life and death through our core-Self far beneath cerebral thinking.

As we continue to compassionately meet the crossroads of life and death through our core-Self, we viscerally experience that the stillness of core-Self is the eternal flashing depth of vast impermanence itself. This is why our ego-self and thinking mind cannot objectify, analyze, or measure core-Self in this Only Moment Body. Our Way is to faithfully embody core-Self as the mark of vast impermanence while viscerally enjoying our everyday life as the still flashing freshness of total reality. As core-Self just sitting as core-Self inside of zazen-only is far beyond the traps and cages of ego-self and thinking mind, we call it the visceral Way of embodying this only moment of vast impermanence that eternally refreshes the boundless intimacy and limitless interdependency of total reality.

Interdependency

The second illuminating mark of core-Self is daily living within a limitless web of interdependent and interconnected causes and conditions that function harmoniously together to manifest the whole universe. We call this our Way of living in interconnected harmony with all beings and things. By viscerally living in interconnected harmony, we somatically realize that no being or thing exists independent or separate from all other beings and things throughout space and time. All beings and things throughout space and time exist in interdependency with no exception. No being or thing, no matter how microscopically small or immensely large, exists by itself or only through itself. All beings and things coexist in limitless interdependency until they meet specific causes and conditions that propel them toward extinction. We call this the Way of living and dying through the law of interdependent arising and passing away. We come to somatically verify the law of interdependent arising and passing away through the still vibrancy of our core-Self inside of zazen-only. Just as core-Self viscerally discerns the vast Oneness of total reality in zazen-only, so too core-Self somatically comprehends that all beings and things interdependently arise, temporally exist, and finally pass away within a vast interconnected network of causes and conditions.

Our existence as human beings becomes truly meaningful and deeply fulfilling when we viscerally realize our vast Oneness with total reality while somatically verifying our limitless interdependency and interconnectedness with all beings and things. When human beings experience just "This," they express their overflowing gratitude by embodying the tenderness of love, by living with compassion and love in everyday life, and by wholeheartedly receiving love and compassion from others.

This is the unfabricated Way of living and loving as a radical human being who embodies core-Self far beyond figuring and thinking. Just like the mark of vast impermanence is a mark that we compassionately share together, the mark of interdependency reveals our precious interconnectedness with each other and our boundless intimacy with total reality. This limitless web of interconnectedness and vast interdependency that operates harmoniously at the surface and depth of total reality upholds and sustains the life of our bodies, the existence of our natural world, the social, cultural, and technological interactions of everyday life, and the total dynamic functioning of the universe as a whole.

When we viscerally experience the core-Self mark of interdependency and the law of interdependent arising and passing away, we reach out to all beings and things equally with deep caring, attentiveness, intimacy, and gratitude. This means that the mark of interdependency is the compassionate mark of core-Self that values all beings and things equally in the vast interconnectedness of total reality. As core-Self reaches out in everyday life through its cherished interconnectedness with all beings and things, it honors each being and thing as the great functioning of vast Oneness arising in relational interdependency with this Only Moment Body right here and now. In our Way, we somatically bow in interdependency with the vast Oneness of total reality that continuously arrives through each being and thing that meets us in everyday life. To somatically bow to each being and thing in our everyday life is to viscerally confirm that each being and thing is not more or less than any other being or thing that exists in the whole universe. As the great functioning of each being and thing is an expression of the great functioning of vast Oneness, we honor and respect all beings and things that constantly arrive to engage core-Self in the dance of boundless intimacy and ungraspable enlightenment within the profound ordinariness of everyday life.

Transparency

The third illuminating mark of core-Self is the mark of transparency. This mark of transparency has two principles that we practice and embody in our everyday life. The first principle of transparency reflects the Way core-Self openly and honestly engages in daily interpersonal relationships. This means that our core-Self relates to others transparently without hiddenness, slyness, pretense, or deceit. The transparency of core-Self is the mark of living as a radical human being with visceral integrity, childlike authenticity, intellectual honesty, and empathic clarity in the relationships of everyday life. It is the core-Self mark of being totally genuine and trustworthy to others. This mark of transparency is the mark of being passionately real within and beyond thinking. When we are being completely real and transparent from our core-Self, people wholeheartedly trust our visceral integrity in the same Way that they trust the felt heaviness of stones, the texture of tree bark, and the wetness of water. When we live transparently through our core-Self, we inspire and encourage everyone we meet to be totally real and transparent in their daily relationship to others.

The second principle of transparency reflects the Way that the still brilliance of our core-Self silently illuminates the insubstantial nature of our ego-self identity, our passing thoughts and thinking mind, our personality, our immersion in linear and historical time, and our cultural, racial, political, and religious views and beliefs. These cerebrally generated mental transparencies overlay one another to provide us with a cohesive and conscious view of our personality, our individuality, and our distinct behavioral and emotional way of being in relationship with nature, with people in everyday life, and with the infinite universe as a whole. Although they are transparent and insubstantial, our cerebral overlays function together to help us mentally grasp the meaning and purpose of our own existence while empowering us to objectify and manipulate physical reality to constantly fulfill our basic needs. The same cerebrally generated overlays help to establish and sustain our personal, social, and individual accountability to each other while mentally enabling us to communicate our unique feelings, beliefs, values, and thoughts in everyday life.

This transparent set of cerebral overlays that mentally help us to communicate in everyday life have a great pragmatic function within the world that we live in and share together. However, people forget that these transparent and insubstantial overlays are deeply rooted in our brain's evolution, have been developed through the cerebral power of our minds, currently exist within our own mind and the minds of others, and are socially and culturally reinforced during the passage of everyday life. Many of us disremember that these cerebral mental overlays are fundamentally transparent and insubstantial in nature. This means that they do not inherently exist in the same way that physical reality objectively exists. Our evolutionary attachment to these transparent cerebral overlays hinders our visceral realization of core-Self, our somatic verification of the vast Oneness of total reality, and our pristine embodiment of boundless intimacy and ungraspable enlightenment beyond I, me, and mine. This is why we constantly sink into the still essence of our core-Self, silently illuminate the transparent functioning of our heady ego-self and thinking mind, openly live from the inclusive nature of our radical humanness far beneath our personal beliefs, and freely express the wonder and exuberance of our beginner's heartmind that cherishes the ever fresh impermanence of total reality.

Not-Knowing

The fourth illuminating mark of core-Self is the mark of not-knowing. Our Way is to confidently embody the mark of not-knowing while passionately living as core-Self in the ordinariness of everyday life. When I speak of "the mark of not-knowing," I am referring to the still brilliance of core-Self that silently illuminates our boundless intimacy and limitless interdependency far beneath the functioning of our ego-self with its cerebral way of thinking and knowing. To confidently embody the mark of not-knowing in shikantaza and zazen-only is to enjoy the still brilliance of core-Self in non-thinking as it viscerally arises beyond all doubt. To enjoy the still brilliance of core-Self in non-thinking is to somatically discern the vast Oneness of total reality without experiencing the slightest need to grasp IT, name IT, or own IT.

When we embody the still brilliance of core-Self in non-thinking, we viscerally discern that our ego-self is constantly driven by ignorance and fear to mentally uphold its own substantiality even in the midst of vast impermanence. This is why our ego-self sustains an endless mental chatter about itself, tenaciously adheres to group views and beliefs to fortify its own existence, attaches to a delusive and false freedom by remaining in bondage to grasping and pushing away, validates its own supremacy by separating itself from Nature, and all the while advances its cerebral power of objective labeling, thinking, and knowing. This driven way of upholding our own existence had its innocent beginnings during our early ego-self development. It was then that we began to cerebrally identify with our given name, our use of verbal language, our inner mental chatter about I, me, and mine, and our growing ability to think about our thoughts, our feelings, and our maturing experience of everyday life and relationships.

Over time, our heady ego-self development overshadows the pristine nature of our beginner's heartmind while distancing us from the still brilliance of core-Self in non-thinking. To wholly identify with our developed ego-self and the cerebral power of our thinking is to diminish our visceral intimacy with vast Oneness that is the ever fresh flashing of core-Self in this Only Moment Body. To viscerally realize core-Self as the ever fresh flashing of vast Oneness far beneath our ego-self functioning is to somatically comprehend that the mark of "not knowing who we are" is always intimately arriving right here and now. In our Way, we treasure the ungraspable nature of our core-Self even as we confidently take care of our everyday life with our thinking mind, joyfully share our individuality with others, and conscientiously embody our ego-self identity with responsibility and accountability to society. When we embody core-Self in shikantaza and zazen-only, we confidently accept the mark of not knowing who we are with childlike humility, simplicity, and openness. We call this childlike Way of confidently embodying the mark of not-knowing, "The Way of beginner's heartmind." To openly accept the mark of not knowing who we are with beginner's heartmind is to honor the ungraspable nature of vast Oneness that continuously arises as the flashing stillness of core-Self far beneath I, me, and mine.

In our Soto Zen tradition, there is a legend about the first Chinese Patriarch named Bodhidharma (470 AD - 543 AD). The legend portrays Bodhidharma as a radical human being who confidently embodied his core-Self while openly expressing the mark of not-knowing with the directness and honesty of beginner's heartmind. According to legend, Bodhidharma visited Chinese Emperor Wu in 520 AD. At their meeting, the Emperor asked Bodhidharma, "What merit have I gained by building Buddhist temples and funding many monastic communities?" Bodhidharma replied, "No merit whatsoever." Bewildered and upset by Bodhidharma's answer, the Emperor said, "Who are you to talk to me like this?" Bodhidharma instantly responded, "Your Highness, I do not know." Bodhidharma's reply, "I do not know," is the still integrity of core-Self flashing as vast Oneness beyond the traps and cages of ego-self and thinking mind. This was Bodhidharma's upright Way of speaking from core-Self, faithfully being true to the mark of not-knowing, and teaching the profound humility and authenticity of beginner's heartmind. Just like Zen Master Bodhidharma, all of us can courageously embody the mark of not-knowing who we are as we passionately live our everyday life in shikantaza and zazen-only. This is the Way all radical human beings passionately live as core-Self, openly accept the truth of not-knowing, and confidently share personal views, political opinions, and religious beliefs with the profound humility and magnanimous openness of beginner's heartmind.

Completion And Wholeness

The fifth illuminating mark of core-Self is the mark of completion and wholeness. Wholeness refers to our core-Self that exists in an undivided state of vast Oneness with nothing wanting. Completion refers to our core-Self as it enjoys boundless intimacy and total fulfillment with not one thing lacking. When we just sit down as core-Self inside of zazen-only, we experience completion and wholeness far beneath our figuring, criticizing, judging, and thinking. As we embody the wholeness of our core-Self during the practice of shikantaza, we behaviorally express our completion as a radical human being by tenderly cultivating our loving relationships, by freely disclosing our boundless intimacy with all beings and things, by sharing the exuberance and wonder of our beginner's heartmind, and by taking refuge in the vast Oneness of total reality.

When we are cerebrally embodied as an ego-self, our experience of everyday life is limited to the surface of reality. To live solely from our cerebral ego-self embodiment at the surface of reality is to remain in bondage to linguistic labeling, perceptual duality, spacial locality, temporal duration, logical thinking, and reflective analysis. To be exclusively embodied as a cerebral ego-self is to be removed from our visceral experience of boundless intimacy and vast Oneness at the surface and depth of total reality. To be removed from our visceral experience of boundless intimacy and vast Oneness is to somatically discern a persistent lacking and wanting. This persistent lacking and wanting drives our cerebral ego-self to find happiness, fulfillment, completion, and wholeness at the surface of reality. We do not realize nor clearly discern that our persistent lacking and wanting is encouraging us to viscerally embody our boundless intimacy and vast Oneness with all beings and things. Not clearly discerning the inward direction toward deep fulfillment and completion beyond lacking and wanting, we search outward while ignoring our core-Self in this Only Moment Body. Some of us are driven to satisfy or extinguish our deep lacking and wanting by adhering to an exclusive and dogmatic religious tradition, by dabbling in the occult or multiple New Age paths, by idealizing and worshiping spiritual and religious leaders, and by proselytizing "holy texts" to advance our egoself-centricity, our species-centric superiority, and our ethnocentric biases. Others are driven to constantly increase their credit and income, to impulsively buy material goods and technological toys, to grasp at ever higher levels of consciousness, to embody a transcendent ecstasy through drugs, or to gain greater power, fame, knowledge, and wealth. Our ego-self falsely assumes that one or all of these behaviors will totally satisfy or extinguish our persistent lacking and wanting.

As our ego-self is driven outward to totally satisfy or extinguish its persistent sense of lacking and wanting, we experience a widening discrepancy between where we are and where we would like to be. When we emotionally comprehend this discrepancy between where we are and where we would like to be, we judge and criticize ourselves for falling short of a felt wholeness and total completion that would liberate us from our bondage to lacking and wanting. The greater the discrepancy between where we are and where we would like to be strengthens our inner critic while keeping us in bondage to drivenness, grasping, and attachment. This is why we continue to feel that we are never enough, never have enough, and never will be enough. To never be enough and never have enough is to cultivate a world of greed, hatred, anger, ignorance, frustration, and suffering. There isn't any exclusive religious belief, idolized spiritual leader, or New Age ideology that will ever extinguish the felt discrepancy that exists between where we are as an ego-self and where we would like to be. There is nothing outwardly that will ever heal our felt separation, estrangement, and isolation from the vast Oneness and boundless intimacy of total reality.

In our Way, we turn the light of our embodied awareness inward and do not search outward. We viscerally embody core-Self inside of shikantaza and zazen-only, enjoy the liberation of our beginner's heartmind, and somatically realize a vast Oneness that extinguishes all lacking and wanting. When we somatically experience vast Oneness and boundless intimacy far beyond lacking and wanting, we naturally dwell in the fulfillment of our radical humanness far beneath our figuring, judging, thinking, and comparing. When we live through our core-Self, we do not experience the discrepancy between where we are and where we would like to be. As core-Self, we are not driven to constantly gain something that we are missing or lacking. When we viscerally embody core-Self in shikantaza and zazen-only, we somatically verify that all radical human beings can live in total completion far beyond lacking, desiring, and wanting.

All of us can experience the completion and wholeness of our radical humanness by living through our core-Self in this Only Moment Body. When we viscerally embody core-Self in deep completion and wholeness with nothing wanting and not one thing lacking, we do not compare our radical Way of being human to an idealized image of humanness projected by any culture, religion, or science. To identify with our ego-self is to always seek completion and fulfillment by attaching to an idealized image of humanness that is far removed from where we are as human beings right here and now. On the other hand, to viscerally embody the still brilliance of core-Self while passionately enjoying the liberation of beginner's heartmind is to somatically realize the total completion and wholeness of our radical humanness right where we are. To experience the total fulfillment and completion of our radical humanness in shikantaza and zazen-only is to viscerally and somatically verify that we have always been infinitely more than enough just as we are. In our Way, to be infinitely more than enough is to viscerally comprehend that our core-Self is in boundless intimacy and vast Oneness far beyond our imaging, figuring, judging, comparing, and thinking.

When we viscerally realize the completion and wholeness of our core-Self, we are always ready to let go and meet the blooming of death and dying without regret. However, this does not mean that we do not passionately explore future goals, work diligently to accomplish our life purpose, arouse a determination to manifest a better world, tenderly take care of this Only Moment Body in everyday life, and entangle with the Way of loving and being loved as a radical human being. This means that our embodiment of core-Self in completion and wholeness does not negate the continuation of our personal growth, our planning and accomplishing of daily agendas, our devoted ambition to better our life and the life of our loved ones, and our fervent desire to realize, accomplish, and conscientiously express our true calling for the benefit of others. As we embody core-Self in total completion, fulfillment, and wholeness beyond lacking and wanting, we do not stop mentally, emotionally, or spiritually growing and evolving. However, we always somatically realize that the true horizon of completion and wholeness is exactly where we viscerally embody our core-Self in boundless intimacy and vast Oneness within shikantaza and zazen-only.

Our devoted embodiment of core-Self within shikantaza and zazen-only is the intimate arrival and total completion of ungraspable enlightenment itself. So when I say that there is no where to go, nobody to become, and nothing to do, I am pointing to your total completion and wholeness as core-Self with nothing wanting and not one thing lacking. When we do not intimately live through the completion and wholeness of our core-Self, we create more stress, frustration, tension, and suffering for ourselves and others. Our deep feeling of always being incomplete will continue to arise if we limit our human embodiment to just being a separate ego-self at the surface of reality. If we only embody our ego-self with its persistent lacking and wanting, we will remain in bondage to our outward drivenness, our inner discrepancy, our felt inadequacy, and our deep sense of incompletion. Our Way is not like this. We do not chase outwardly or remain in the tension and frustration of inner discrepancy. We just rest as core-Self inside of shikantaza and zazen-only, totally enjoy our precious life beyond thinking, dwell in completion and wholeness with every step we take, and wholeheartedly practice the Way of loving and being loved with endless gratitude.

Inner Peace

The sixth illuminating mark of core-Self is the mark of inner peace. We come to somatically know the illuminating mark of inner peace when we viscerally linger in the felt completion and wholeness of our core-Self inside of zazen-only. Inner peace naturally arises as we wholeheartedly abide in our seated stillness, our wakeful uprightness, our vibrant readiness, our genuine tenderness, our visual inclusiveness, our somatic easefulness, our still composure, and our boundless intimacy with the vast Oneness of total reality. When we arise from zazen-only to live our everyday life as core-Self in the practice body of shikantaza, we continue to viscerally confirm the mark of inner peace by behaviorally expressing our boundless intimacy with all beings and things, by joyfully sharing the liberation and exuberance of our beginner's heartmind, and by passionately blending all our activities and relationships with the vast Oneness and limitless interdependency of total reality. This is how we somatically continue to abide in completion and inner peace as we viscerally embody core-Self inside of shikantaza and zazen-only.

As we viscerally embody and behaviorally express the Way of inner peace during the passage of everyday life, we passionately love and receive love beyond resistance and fear while romancing total reality with our beginner's heartmind. To romance total reality, openly love beyond resistance and fear, and behaviorally express inner peace in everyday life is to remain somatically mindful that vast impermanence is always touching us far beneath our ego-self and thinking mind. In our Way, we do not push away or suppress the visceral experience of vast impermanence that continues to intimately arrive in shikantaza and zazen-only. To viscerally meet vast impermanence as this Only Moment Body is to embrace the crossroads of life and death right where we are. As we continue to meet the crossroads of life and death in shikantaza and zazen-only, we do not grasp at the sensual embodiment of our core-Self or the romantic exuberance of our beginner's heartmind. Our Way is to courageously meet the blooming of vast impermanence with each breath while tenderly abiding in inner peace far beyond grasping and pushing away. To viscerally embody core-Self at the crossroads of life and death while romancing total reality with beginner's heartmind is to brilliantly enhance the inexhaustible value of each moment while meeting the immediacy of vast impermanence with inner peace. To somatically comprehend that we are viscerally being the mark of inner peace in the midst of vast impermanence is to molt off our karmic drama, our needless distress, anxiety, worry, and apprehension, our unhealthy agitation, aggravation, and fragmentation, and our harmful stress and tension.

Our Way softens and eases the endless striving and drivenness of ego-self in everyday life. We accomplish this by abiding in the visceral composure of our core-Self, by embodying the marks of completion, wholeness, and inner peace as our true nature, and by wholeheartedly enjoying this Only Moment Body at the ever fresh crossroads of life and death. We cherish the blessing of being born in each moment while accepting and embracing death as our intimate companion. This allows us to tenderly embody our core-Self, efficiently accomplish the goals, activities, and business of everyday life, completely delight in the pristine freshness of our beginner's heartmind, and passionately live the Way of loving and being loved. Intimacy with death and vast impermanence is a reference point for always living from the compassion, integrity, and bright wisdoming of our core-Self in this Only Moment Body. When death is held as imminent in each moment, all our arrogance, pride, righteousness, pretension, false humility, and worldly power, wealth, fame, and social status are seen as superficial, unimportant, and simply molt away.

We somatically realize inner peace and serenity in shikantaza and zazen-only when we devotedly nourish an ever deepening intimacy with our breath, gratefully embody the still brilliance of our gut-core intelligence, faithfully recover the basic goodness of our beginner's heartmind, and fearlessly entrust the passage of each moment to the vast Oneness and boundless intimacy of total reality. To viscerally embody core-Self in inner peace is to honestly engage all beings and things without burdening them with our biased perceptions, our fears and resistances, and our mental and emotional prejudices. This is the Way we preserve all beings and things just as they are. This is the Way we take care of them with clarity, compassion, and tenderness. When we compassionately attend to each being and thing without complaint, resistance, or avoidance, we honor the vast Oneness of total reality, behaviorally express the power of inner peace, and unfold ungraspable enlightenment and boundless intimacy in the ordinariness of everyday life.

The Map is Not the Territory

As you embody shikantaza and zazen-only, you do not have to keep the six illuminating marks of core-Self in your thinking mind. The marks of core-Self are not mental things that you have to think about or diligently remember either individually or collectively. Do not view them as Zen meditation skills or mindfulness techniques that you have to consciously apply in all the activities, situations, and relationships of everyday life. This is a very important point to understand because the six illuminating marks of core-Self are always being viscerally transmitted and somatically discerned within shikantaza and zazen-only.

Although I have linguistically mapped the marks of core-Self with meaningful words and ideas, please remember that the map I have created is not the actual embodiment of the territory itself. It would be a mistake to assume that mentally knowing the map is viscerally knowing your core-Self and its six illuminating marks that are both far beyond thoughts and thinking. Remember that the ideas you are trying to mentally comprehend are not the viscerally embodied experience itself. You cannot embody the six illuminating marks of core-Self by just reading and conceptually knowing through your thinking mind. You have to physically sit down in the behavioral stillness of zazen-only, sink into the sensuality and still vibrancy of your gut-core intelligence, keep your eyes gently open to reflect the surface and depth of total reality, and all the while remain passionately wakeful and somatically at ease in the midst of vast impermanence. Only then will you come to viscerally embody the central taproot of your radical humanness, somatically discern the six illuminating marks of core-Self, and experientially realize your boundless intimacy and vast Oneness with all beings and things.

Thank you.

"The true
human being is
not anyone in particular;
But, like the deep blue color
of the limitless sky, it is everyone,
everywhere in the world."

Dogen Zenji

"Practice without an idea of gaining
is called Buddha's practice. If we become
attached to enlightenment or to the profundity of
the teaching, we will lose the point. When we just
practice zazen as a human being without any idea
of gaining we have the universality of the teaching,
and also its individuality and validity.....So the
point is to practice our pure way as human
beings, with sincerity and without
an idea of gaining."

Suzuki-roshi

"Zen is not
some fancy, special art
of living. Our teaching is just
to live, always in total reality, in
its exact sense. To make our effort,
moment after moment, is our Way."

"For us, you know, even though
you attain enlightenment, you are
also a human being — "buddha" is
another name for human being.
buddha and human being is
the same nature, same
one quality...."

Suzuki-roshi

CHAPTER 4

Still Paradox Of Reality

Love is the Sword
of Wholeness—
It cuts off all
Separateness and
makes us One.

"Enlightenment is intimacy with all beings and things."

Eihei Dogen

Advancing The Timeless Way

There is a timeless Way of living within a precious and limitless network of interdependent relationships. This timeless Way of living is based on the practiced embodiment of three Zen principals. To embody these three Zen principles is to nourish and sustain a life of radical humanness, vast Oneness, boundless intimacy and ungraspable enlightenment. The first Zen principal is to abide in the still brilliance of core-Self while silently illuminating the total dynamic functioning of our ego-self, our thinking mind, and all our passing thoughts, feelings, sensations, and behaviors. The second Zen principal is to wholeheartedly care for all beings, things, and events that continuously come forth to advance the boundless intimacy of our core-Self while encouraging our precious accountability to the vast Oneness of total reality. The third Zen principle is to vigorously embody our core-Self while faithfully practicing a beginner's tender Way of loving and being loved, of peacefully abiding in vast impermanence, of sincerely and transparently being the body of endless gratitude, and of courageously living and dying in shikantaza and zazen-only. This is the timeless Way that we viscerally embody core-Self while passionately unfolding ungraspable enlightenment in the ordinariness of our everyday life.

The Way to embody ungraspable enlightenment and compassionately live within a vast network of interdependent relationships is to throw your whole life force into viscerally realizing the still essence of your core-Self inside of shikantaza and zazen-only. When I speak of viscerally realizing the still essence of core-Self inside of shikantaza and zazen-only, I am not asking you to throw your whole life force into cerebrally concentrating on your hara or mentally focusing on the visceral center-point of your lower abdomen. Rather, I am asking you to tenderly and courageously let go of your cerebral power that traps a dominant portion of your total body awareness within your head. By just letting go in this Way, you liberate the trapped body awareness that was cerebrally localized within your head and allow it to naturally sink into the visceral center-point of your hara with each inhalation. To naturally sink into the visceral center-point of your hara is to compassionately rest the drivenness of your localized cerebral power and enjoy the still and sensual arising of core-Self. To let go of your heady cerebral power and sink into the still and sensual vibrancy of your core-Self is to viscerally discern that you have arrived as a radical human being who is somatically confirming boundless intimacy and timeless interdependency far beyond the traps and cages of ego-self and thinking mind.

When we throw our whole life force into actualizing the three Zen principles of everyday life, we tenderly embody the Way of all radical human beings who live magnanimously, love passionately, and die courageously from the still essence of core-Self. To faithfully embody the still essence of core-Self is to viscerally comprehend that boundless intimacy, timeless interdependency, and ungraspable enlightenment are the three treasures that nourish and sustain our inner peace far beneath I, me, and mine. To peacefully live beneath I, me, and mine is to honor the vast Oneness of total reality. To honor the vast Oneness of total reality is to extend a tender attentiveness, a genuine acceptance, and a compassionate caring to all the beings, things, and events that come forth during the passage of everyday life to engage our core-Self in the timeless dance of boundless intimacy and ungraspable enlightenment itself. To somatically practice this timeless dance is to nourish our physical health and wellness, our cerebral clarity and easefulness, our emotional stability and buoyancy, our deep serenity and inner peace, and our core-Self composure in the midst of rapid change and vast impermanence. This is how we come to know beyond all doubt that this gentle and timeless Way is vital to the well-being and longevity of this Only Moment Body.

As we respectfully advance and honorably refine our everyday life in our timeless Way, we do not perpetuate unhealthy aggravation, tension, stress, anger, resentment, fear, and frustration in our body. This is because we do not burden beings, things, and events with any ego-self drama, any species-centric bias, any bigoted perceptions, any false expectations, any desire or need for perfection, any aggressive drivenness, any grasping or pushing away, or any obsession with control. Our Way is to honor the interconnectedness of total reality by practicing not dominating, not controlling, not interfering, not grasping, and not pushing away. This is how we practice respectfully seeing and meeting all beings, things, and events just as they are in the vast Oneness of total reality. This is how we live in limitless interdependency with all beings and things while passionately advancing and refining our everyday life through the healthy dance of boundless intimacy that is ungraspable enlightenment itself.

The Quantum Depth of Core-Self

In our Way, we live in boundless intimacy and limitless interdependency through the still essence of our core-Self. The still essence of our core-Self is exactly core-Self viscerally arising as the still center-point of total reality. To experience core-Self as the still center-point of total reality is to somatically discern that the still essence of core-Self is not stillness as we usually comprehend it. The still essence of core-Self is the flashing of a vast Oneness that refreshes each moment of total reality far beyond the passage of linear time. To viscerally realize that core-Self is the still flashing of vast Oneness in this Only Moment Body is to effortlessly refresh our boundless intimacy and limitless interdependency without owning, controlling, dominating, or interfering. In our Way, we passionately enjoy being the still paradox of core-Self that cannot be gained, grasped, or attained. This is the Way we embody core-Self as the still paradox of total reality while tenderly and brilliantly advancing our everyday life in boundless intimacy and ungraspable enlightenment far beneath the functioning of I, me, and mine.

Our Way of being the still essence and vast Oneness of total reality in this Only Moment Body cannot be fully comprehended unless we frame the paradox of core-Self within the scientific field of quantum physics. While examining the true nature of matter, physicists have discovered that all beings and things throughout the universe are composed of atoms. Investigating deeper within the structure of the atom, physicists have found that all atoms are made up of subatomic particles that are essentially vibratory bundles of quantum energy. At the depth of total reality, these vibratory bundles of quantum energy can exist simultaneously as a wave and a particle without hinderance, obstruction, or contradiction. In other words, a vibratory bundle of quantum energy can behave as a localized particle or a distributed wave within the continuum of space and time. When physicists think of a quantum of energy appearing as a particle, they imagine a string-like vibration located at a specific point in the space-time continuum. On the other hand, when physicists think of the same quantum of energy appearing as an undulating wave, they imagine a smooth wavy motion extending itself within the space-time continuum. Physicists are currently trying to understand how all these vibratory bundles of quantum wave energy can manifest the separateness of all beings and things while being entangled in boundless intimacy and vast Oneness at the surface and depth of total reality.

While performing their empirical research, quantum physicists have discovered that a very peculiar phenomenon occurs during their quantum-scale experiments. When a quantum-scale experiment is being conducted, the cerebral ego-self objectification and observation of the quantum-scale event changes the outcome of the experiment itself. This "observer effect" in quantum physics research is clearly showing us that the cerebral power to objectively observe quantum-scale events through ego-self functioning is paradoxically entangled with the boundless intimacy and vast Oneness of total reality. Thus, anyone observing and objectifying a quantum-scale event through their cerebral ego-self functioning will profoundly affect the research experiment itself, the quantum-scale event being investigated, the emerging data within the experiment, the theoretical and mathematical analysis of the data, and the way in which one integrates the theoretical and mathematical findings within any given scientific paradigm.

When investigating the quantum depth of total reality, twenty-first century physicists are not attached to the classical view that a value free and totally unbiased ego-self observer can objectively, logically, and mathematically discern the true nature of matter and energy in the whole universe. Although the classical view has helped us to develop knowledge of separate atoms and discrete subatomic particles, its limitations are becoming increasingly apparent as physicists probe deeper into the quantum depth functioning of total reality. This does not mean that the classical view is wrong or that we should no longer use it. The classical view is still highly respected as a method of inquiry that uses careful observation and controlled experiments to gather facts and evidence about the beings, things, and events in our universe. While still honoring and respecting the classical view with its methodology of objective observation, exact experimental procedures, mathematical reasoning, and analytical inquiry, quantum physicists are always seeking a more fruitful and non-interfering Way to intimately explore, thoroughly investigate, and simply comprehend the profound functioning of quantum depth reality.

Our modern empirical and theoretical research in quantum physics is beginning to reveal a quantum depth entanglement or interconnectedness that extends indefinitely throughout the space-time continuum. Quantum physicists are showing that all beings and things are not just composed of separate atoms and discrete subatomic particles. Underneath the atomic and subatomic composition of all beings and things is a vast relational web of interconnected quantum wave vibrations that together uphold the total dynamic functioning of all matter, energy, and vast impermanence at the surface and depth of total reality. We now know that this vast relational web of interconnected quantum wave vibrations is inadvertently affected by the observing and objectifying functions of ego-self and the cerebral generation of our thinking. This is a very important point to understand. It reveals why our Way viscerally softens attachment to ego-self, somatically yields to the vast Oneness and boundless intimacy of total reality, and effortlessly transmits the still brilliance of core-Self far beyond observing and thinking in shikantaza and zazen-only.

Not Observing Or Concentrating

When we embody shikantaza and zazen-only, we do not mentally concentrate on the center-point of our hara. Nor do we engage our cerebral power of observation. We do not count each breath, label passing thoughts and sensations, or mentally and emotionally anticipate the still arising of core-Self in this Only Moment Body. To engage the cerebral power of our ego-self by mentally observing, anticipating, expecting, or intending to experience the still essence of total reality is to cultivate a field of boredom, impatience, doubt, sleepiness, fidgeting and agitation. The more we cerebrally grasp at the still center-point of our lower abdomen, the more that core-Self remains hidden within the magnanimous openness of total reality. The more we mentally force ourselves to sit through physical pain in zazen-only, the more we express our deep lack of confidence that the still essence of core-Self naturally arises from the visceral center-point of our lower abdomen. When we arrogantly assume that we can establish the still essence of total reality by cerebrally subjugating our body in the physical stillness of zazen-only, we only confirm the nonexistence of our core-Self, verify the separateness of all beings and things, perpetuate the isolation of our ego-self functioning, mentally realize the meaninglessness of change and impermanence, and remain in bondage to our deep lacking and wanting. This is how the observing, objectifying, grasping, and controlling functions of ego-self and thinking mind inadvertently push away the still essence of total reality, the visceral arising of core-Self, the unfolding of ungraspable enlightenment in our everyday life, and the somatic confirmation that boundless intimacy and vast Oneness constitute the true nature of all radical human beings just as they are.

When we temporarily rest our ego-self functioning, set aside the cerebral power of our thinking, soften our attachment to objective observation, and embody the genuine humility and openness of our beginner's heartmind, we tenderly invite the still essence of total reality to emerge as core-Self inside of shikantaza and zazen-only. This is how the still essence of core-Self is viscerally realized in this Only Moment Body beyond ego-self grasping, owning, controlling, or gaining. To viscerally realize core-Self as the still essence of total reality is to somatically confirm that core-Self and vast Oneness are the still flashing of vast impermanence far beyond the objectifying and observing functions of ego-self and thinking mind. This means that underneath the impermanence of everyday life is a deeper layer of vast impermanence that flashes everywhere beyond motion to brilliantly refresh the still essence and quantum interconnectedness of total reality. To viscerally embody core-Self as the still flashing of vast impermanence is to somatically comprehend that the quantum depth entanglement of total reality is constantly being refreshed in boundless intimacy and vast Oneness without hinderance, contradiction, or obstruction. In our Way, we viscerally accept vast impermanence as the still non-locality of our core-Self and the still flashing of vast Oneness that has no coming or going. As we viscerally accept and faithfully embody this paradox of total reality, we tenderly and conscientiously take care of the activities and affairs of our everyday life, passionately share the freshness, wonder, and humility of our beginner's heartmind, and joyfully practice the Way of loving and being loved while living in boundless intimacy and vast Oneness with all beings and things.

Still Entanglement

While enjoying our deep visceral composure in shikantaza and zazen-only, we somatically discern that the boundless intimacy of our core-Self is being upheld by the entangled interconnectedness of quantum depth reality. This limitless web of entangled interconnectedness exists far beneath the cerebral functioning of our ego-self and thinking mind. To viscerally entangle with all beings and things through the still flashing interconnectedness of quantum depth reality is to somatically realize that core-Self is silently illuminating the vast Oneness of total reality. We call this silent illumination of vast Oneness, "The ungraspable enlightenment and boundless intimacy of all beings and things." To silently illuminate vast Oneness from our core-Self is to instantly awaken from our cerebral sleeping and dreaming in ego-self and thinking mind. When we somatically awaken from our cerebrally generated sleeping and dreaming, we also awaken to the still power of our core-Self in lucid dreaming and the Way that all beings and things are being dreamed within the still essence of total reality. To viscerally awaken to the power of core-Self in lucid dreaming is to passionately advance our personal dreams while remaining in respectful entanglement with all beings and things. To remain in respectful entanglement with all beings and things is to blend our endless awakening, our lucid dreaming, and the accomplishment of all our dreams with the vast Oneness of being dreamed in boundless intimacy and limitless interdependency far beneath our thinking.

In our Way, to embody core-Self in boundless intimacy with all beings and things does not hinder or obstruct our cerebral power to distinctly observe, objectively examine, logically comprehend, and efficiently take care of the activities, challenges, and responsibilities of everyday life. However, the first priority of our traditional Zen practice is to embody core-Self in still entanglement with the vast Oneness of total reality before we conscientiously take care of our daily activities, affairs, and relationships. This is how we continuously prioritize our still entanglement with vast Oneness while practicing shikantaza and zazen-only. In our Way, we live ungraspable enlightenment by tenderly practicing the Way of loving and being loved, by passionately enjoying, honoring, and respecting the great functioning of duality, by constantly refining the wholesome application of our ego-self and thinking mind, and by always cherishing our still entanglement with the vast Oneness and boundless intimacy of total reality.

When we embody core-Self in shikantaza and zazen-only, we somatically discern that our still entanglement with vast Oneness originates at the center-point of gravity within our lower abdomen. To be in still entanglement with vast Oneness from our body's center-point of gravity is to somatically realize that core-Self is the still flashing interconnectedness of total reality. To viscerally realize core-Self as the still flashing interconnectedness of total reality is to somatically comprehend that peace has no coming or going, no birthing or dying. This is the Way we experience our body's center-point of gravity that intersects with the still flashing of total reality to continuously refresh the boundless intimacy and vast Oneness of our core-Self.

When we experience our body's center-point of gravity intersecting with the limitless quantum entanglement of all beings and things, we viscerally discern that the still flashing essence of vast Oneness is the illuminating lamp of core-Self. To embody the lamp of core-Self is to enlighten the total dynamic functioning of our body, our ego-self, and our thinking mind. To viscerally realize the still illuminating lamp of core-Self in shikantaza and zazen-only is to somatically meet the still brilliance of non-thinking. To viscerally meet the still brilliance of non-thinking is to somatically comprehend that the lamp of core-Self silently illuminates our boundless intimacy and vast Oneness at the heart of duality. This is how the lamp of core-Self viscerally transmits a New World where all radical human beings prioritize their still entanglement with the vast Oneness of total reality, continuously refresh their boundless intimacy in the midst of vast impermanence, lucidly and compassionately express the still brilliance of non-thinking, and respectfully advance the healthy functioning of their ego-selves and their thinking minds.

Being Total Equality

When we live in the timeless and wondrous Way of shikantaza and zazen-only, we viscerally discern that the still flashing of vast Oneness is arising as the still essence of our core-Self while simultaneously upholding the total dynamic functioning of this Only Moment Body, the boundless intimacy of all beings and things, and the infinite entanglement of quantum depth reality. To embody the still essence of core-Self as the still flashing of vast Oneness is experientially accepted beyond doubt when we viscerally realize that the depth of total reality is continuously transmitting the still nature of quantum interconnectedness through the center-point of gravity within our lower abdomen. In our Way, to be the still quantum paradox of core-Self arising as vast Oneness in this Only Moment Body is not ego-self aggrandizement or the inflation of our individual personality. We embody core-Self as interdependently equal to all beings and things because all beings and things are exactly the great functioning of vast Oneness at the heart of duality.

Our Way is to passionately embody core-Self as the still flashing wholeness of total reality while respectfully honoring our boundless intimacy and interdependent equality with all beings and things. This is why we wholeheartedly bow to all beings and things that co-arise with our core-Self to unfold our daily life in ungraspable enlightenment itself. When we behaviorally express our interdependent equality in this Way, we viscerally confirm that the vast Oneness of total reality is infinitely greater than the fleeting and precious life of core-Self in this Only Moment Body. To somatically and viscerally realize all of this in shikantaza and zazen-only is to fully accept and embrace this world of vast impermanence as heaven itself. When we simply embrace vast impermanence as heaven itself, we naturally throw our whole life force into the practice of loving and being loved beyond hesitation, resistance, and fear. As we faithfully practice the Way of loving and being loved just like this, we embody the peaceful completion of a radical human being who wholeheartedly bows in endless gratitude for living an authentic life of boundless intimacy, vast Oneness, and interdependent equality with all beings and things.

Devoted Accountability

We behaviorally express the still integrity and moral uprightness of our core-Self by continuously living in devoted accountability to the vast Oneness and limitless interconnectedness of total reality. In our Way, we viscerally confirm our life of boundless intimacy and ungraspable enlightenment by embodying the still integrity of our core-Self far beneath the grasping and possessing nature of I, me, and mine. When we wholeheartedly embody core-Self in devoted accountability far beneath the functioning of I, me, and mine, the boundless intimacy of total reality viscerally transmits the respectful Way to meet all beings and things with equality, appreciation, and deep caring. Our practice of living in devoted accountability to the vast Oneness of total reality is the authentic basis for embodying a beginner's Way of freshly seeing things just as they are while always being ready to begin again with humility, clarity, compassion, and endless gratitude.

When we honorably practice devoted accountability to vast Oneness while deeply treasuring a beginner's Way of freshly seeing things just as they are, the still integrity of core-Self silently illuminates our ingrained patterns of grasping and pushing away, our somatic and emotional armoring, our defensive projections and rationalizations, our hidden motivations and agendas, and the unhealthy traits and characteristics of our unique personality. This is how our core-Self silently illuminates the biases and prejudices of our ego-self, the delusive, deceitful, and deceptive patterns of our thinking, and our individual maladaptive ways of relating, perceiving, knowing, emoting, and behaving. To silently illuminate all of this from the still integrity of our core-Self is to compassionately comprehend how we can lose our Way. As we compassionately comprehend how we can lose our Way, we viscerally authenticate the embodiment of devoted accountability, the wholehearted buoyancy of a true beginner who is ready to begin again, and the brilliant arrival of a radical human being who is unfolding in ungraspable enlightenment with all beings and things.

When we embody core-Self in shikantaza and zazen-only, we also see how we can be misguided and relentlessly driven to grasp at power, fame, money, material goods, mind altering substances, higher states of consciousness, dogmatic beliefs, intolerant political views, and radicalized religious doctrines. We come to viscerally realize that grasping at any of these behavioral options tends to distance us from our boundless intimacy with total reality while perpetuating a world filled with conflict, anger, greed, dissatisfaction, suffering, and endless drivenness. As core-Self silently illuminates all of this in shikantaza and zazen-only, we clearly see our bondage to the emotional armoring and defensiveness of our ego-self, our enslavement to the maladaptive traits of our personality, and the true Way to liberate a radical human being who values boundless intimacy far beyond the relentless drivenness of I, me, and mine.

When we practice living in devoted accountability, we continuously refine the healthy functioning of our ego-self while encouraging the surprising and brilliant transformation of our personality. To promote the healthy and transparent functioning of our ego-self while remaining open to personal healing, growth, and transformation is to live beyond rigidness, inflexibility, and stagnation. This is how we viscerally embody a beginner's true Way of unfolding in ungraspable enlightenment while passionately loving and being loved in the boundless intimacy of total reality.

Transpersonal Empathy

As we embody shikantaza in our everyday life, we extend transpersonal empathy and deep visceral caring to all beings, things, activities, and events that co-arise with our core-Self to interdependently unfold the vast Oneness, boundless intimacy, and ungraspable enlightenment of total reality. This means that our Way of Zen life extends transpersonal empathy and deep visceral caring to all beings, things, activities, and events from the still center-point of our lower abdomen. Extending transpersonal empathy and deep visceral caring from our core-Self is not the same as extending an exclusive heartfelt empathy only to people. We all know that empathizing with our heart involves the act of emotionally reaching out to understand the feeling life of another human being. All of us deeply appreciate a person's willingness to wholeheartedly empathize with our feelings without trying to fix them, figure them out, or own them. When we extend heartfelt empathy to others in this way, they feel completely understood rather than being objectified, judged, and labeled.

We are able to extend interpersonal empathy to each other because we share the same experiential range and depth of human feelings and emotions. This allows us to empathically mirror, intimately share, and wholeheartedly feel into other people's emotions of joy, sadness, fear, loneliness, grief, pain, and suffering. When we fully empathize with another person, we effortlessly direct a loving acceptance and a tender caring toward their whole being. When we emotionally experience empathy from another human being, we totally comprehend its deep value in nourishing authenticity, intimacy, and felt understanding within the interpersonal relationships of everyday life. To emotionally experience the deep value of interpersonal empathy is to practice, encourage, and exemplify it at home, work, and play. Likewise, to viscerally extend transpersonal empathy from the still quantum interconnectedness of our core-Self is to somatically comprehend its deep value in nourishing health, peace, composure, creativity, wisdom, and compassion during the activities, affairs, and relationships of everyday life.

Just like our shared human feelings and emotions empower us to extend interpersonal empathy and loving tenderness to each other, the still interconnectedness of quantum depth reality empowers our core-Self to extend transpersonal empathy and deep visceral caring to all sentient and insentient beings far beneath the isolated cerebral functions of ego-self and thinking mind. To extend transpersonal empathy and deep visceral caring from the still integrity of our core-Self is to somatically know beyond doubt that we are in boundless intimacy and limitless interdependency with any being, thing, activity, or event that exists in the vast Oneness of total reality. Our Way is to joyfully extend interpersonal empathy, loving kindness, and heartfelt caring to all the people in our life while simultaneously extending transpersonal empathy and deep visceral caring to all the creatures we meet, all the things and objects that we use, all the activities we engage in, and all the challenges, events, and circumstances that arise in our everyday life.

Noninterference

When we wholeheartedly live with interpersonal empathy while embodying core-Self in transpersonal empathy with all beings, things, and events, we viscerally confirm that the vast Oneness of total reality is unfolding our everyday life in boundless intimacy and ungraspable enlightenment itself. To viscerally confirm the richness of living in boundless intimacy and the limitless value of embodying everyday life as ungraspable enlightenment itself is to somatically verify that our core-Self is faithfully heeding the Way of noninterference. To faithfully heed the Way of noninterference is not the embodiment of detachment, aloofness, or noninvolvement. Noninterference is not turning our life force away from beings, things, and events, but rather respectfully, earnestly, and honorably engaging in their blooming and their completion. Our Way of noninterference is not distancing ourselves from our feelings and emotions or being indifferent to the feelings and emotions of others. Noninterference is the Way of blending with the vast Oneness of total reality by anchoring our ego-self identity and all our thinking, speaking, feeling, and behaving in the still discernment of our core-Self. This is the Way we compassionately embody noninterference whether we are engaging in loving relationships or diligently and conscientiously taking care of the social activities, affairs, and responsibilities of everyday life.

When we live as core-Self while faithfully heeding the Way of noninterference, we do not entangle with beings, things, and events from the mentalization of reality, from personal biases and emotional prejudices, from dreamy projections and rationalizations, from behavioral urgency and drivenness, or from a greedy, aggressive, and assertive egoself-centricity. We honor our core-Self and respectfully embody the Way of noninterference by not engaging in activities, affairs, and relationships to gain personal advantage at the expense of others. We do not exploit or manipulate beings and things to confirm the cerebral power of our ego-self, to enhance the prestige and influence of our individual personality, or to validate the narcissistic embodiment of everyday life and relationships. Because we wholeheartedly trust the Way of noninterference, we do not fear the extinguishing of our physical body, our ego-self, our personality, and our thinking mind.

When we embody the Way of noninterference, we do not reinforce the inner cerebral chatter that perpetuates the seeming substantiality and illusory separateness of our ego-self functioning. We live the true Way of noninterference when we do not control, use, or grasp at outward beings, things, and events to satiate an unknown inner longing and a deep inner lacking that can only be inwardly fulfilled far beneath the functioning of ego-self and thinking mind. In our Way, we viscerally realize human completion and wholly satiate our deep inner longing by faithfully embodying the still paradox of core-Self, by continuously living the Way of noninterference, and by respectfully honoring the limitless value and interdependent equality of all beings and things that exist within the vast Oneness and boundless intimacy of total reality.

When we are living the Way of noninterference, our core-Self is always ready to instantly respond in the moment, to momentarily wait before compassionately engaging with beings and things, or to just let beings and things unfold in ungraspable enlightenment without the interference of our ego-self or thinking mind. To let beings and things unfold in ungraspable enlightenment is to viscerally entrust their interdependent arrival, their ingenious blooming, and their surprising completion to the still flashing of vast Oneness that is exactly the boundless intimacy of total reality. Our Way is to always honor the timeless presence of vast Oneness and the limitless interconnectedness of total reality as we diligently take care of our daily activities, affairs, and responsibilities within the great functioning of linear time. This is how we somatically live the Way of noninterference by thinking clearly, speaking honestly, and acting spontaneously from our core-Self, by blending all our doing, loving, and being with the vast Oneness of total reality, and by faithfully embodying the humility of a respectful beginner who honors the boundless intimacy, limitless value, and interdependent equality of all beings and things.

Our Mirrored Way

We live the Way of noninterference whether we are settled as core-Self in the formal and motionless body of zazen-only or settled as core-Self in the informal and spontaneous body of shikantaza. This means that we practice being fully alive and alert from the still vibrancy of our core-Self whether we are just sitting inside of sitting or just sitting inside of living. We call this ancient Way of continuously embodying the still essence of core-Self, "Our mirrored Way of living in boundless intimacy and ungraspable enlightenment with all beings and things."

Whether we are just sitting as core-Self inside of just sitting or just sitting as core-Self inside of just living, we are passionately alive while enjoying the total completion and fulfillment of our radical humanness. To somatically confirm our radical humanness is to viscerally embody core-Self beyond all doubt, to wholeheartedly entrust our living and dying to the vast Oneness of total reality, to brilliantly clarify timelessness and noninterference during the passage of everyday life, and to compassionately meet all beings, things, and events with the pristine openness and respectful curiosity of beginner's heartmind.

Although we mentally comprehend shikantaza as shikantaza and zazen-only as zazen-only, we viscerally discern that zazen-only is exactly shikantaza and shikantaza is exactly zazen-only. Although they are not linguistically the same, they are viscerally not different. Although they are somatically one, they can still be behaviorally clarified as two. This is the paradox of a mirrored Way that silently illuminates core-Self in this Only Moment Body far beneath ego-self and thinking mind. Our Way of shikantaza and zazen-only gives birth to all radical human beings who cultivate the fruit of ungraspable enlightenment by faithfully living, loving, and dying in the boundless intimacy and vast Oneness of total reality.

When we throw our whole life force into living our mirrored Way, we experientially verify that core-Self is continuously settled as core-Self in this Only Moment Body. To be core-Self continuously settled as core-Self in this Only Moment Body is to viscerally clarify the great matter of life and death through the still brilliance of non-thinking. To be core-Self in the still brilliance of non-thinking is not someone doing shikantaza or zazen-only, not someone attaining radical humanness, not someone owning ungraspable enlightenment, and not someone gaining boundless intimacy. Although all this is true, core-Self in shikantaza and zazen-only is passionately being the still brilliance of total reality, the completion and fulfillment of our radical humanness, the luminous clarity of ungraspable enlightenment itself, and the vast Oneness and limitless interconnectedness of all beings and things.

Effort And Discipline

Our Way of throwing our whole life force into shikantaza and zazen-only involves some effort and discipline. However, this is a gentle effort and tender discipline that does not attempt to attain or gain, that does not willfully subjugate the body, that does not exert cerebral power to break through delusion, and that does not seek ungraspable enlightenment apart from shikantaza and zazen-only. When people hear of effort and discipline in our Way, they think that they have to exercise great will power and mental concentration to embody shikantaza and zazen-only. However, our gentle effort and tender discipline does not involve the exertion of our will power or the cerebral focusing of our mind. When we practice shikantaza and zazen-only in our tender and gentle Way, we do not mentally arouse a strict discipline and forceful effort in the wholehearted discipline and passionate effort that we make. From the very first time we embody shikantaza and zazen-only, we are naturally drawn into the sensuality of our hara, the still vibrancy of our core-Self, and the pristine vitality of our beginner's heartmind. Although it may be necessary to be compassionately mindful of effort and discipline at first, as you continue to practice shikantaza and zazen-only, your mindfulness of effort and discipline will disappear from the very mind that originally resisted effort and discipline itself. When you come to somatically know all of this far beyond your willful exertion of effort and discipline, you will viscerally comprehend how all radical human beings easefully throw their whole life force into living the Way of shikantaza and zazen-only.

The True Spirit Of Our Way

We embody the radical root nature of humanness and the true spirit of our Way by passionately living and gracefully dying from the still composure of our core-Self, by sharing the simplicity, curiosity, and exuberance of our beginner's heartmind, by continuously extending transpersonal empathy and interpersonal caring in our everyday life, and by spontaneously bowing in endless gratitude to the vast Oneness and boundless intimacy of total reality. This is the Way we compassionately live and die as a radical human being who simply embodies the still composure of core-Self far beneath the cerebral functioning of ego-self, personality, and thinking mind. To viscerally embody the still composure of core-Self is to continuously meet the crossroads of life and death with no regrets and with not one thing lacking. This is how we practice living and dying in the true spirit of our mirrored Way.

When we practice in the true spirit of our Way, we confidently navigate our everyday life and relationships with clarity, compassion, and wisdom. We live in the true spirit of our mirrored Way for its own sake. We do not practice our Way to grasp enlightenment, gather wisdom, gain wealth or fame, attain social or political power, transcend our karmic past, obtain a good reincarnation, confirm our moral salvation, or assure our place in a heavenly afterlife. If we allow worldly or spiritual desires, ambitions, and expectations to steer our mirrored Way, the still brilliance of total reality will not be viscerally realized, our boundless intimacy will not be somatically verified, and this life of ungraspable enlightenment will continue to recede into confusion and doubt. This is why we do not seek to gain or attain anything by practicing shikantaza and zazen-only. Even so, when we practice in the true spirit of our Way, we effortlessly clarify and heal our karmic past, live the present moment in boundless intimacy with the vast Oneness of total reality, and embody our surprising future in the timelessness of ungraspable enlightenment right here and now.

We live everyday life in the true spirit of our Way by acknowledging and honoring the vast Oneness of total reality, by respectfully living in boundless intimacy and limitless interdependency, and by always heeding the Way of noninterference. All this is very different from living through an ego-self that wields cerebral power, that mentally ignores the vast Oneness of total reality, and that arrogantly dismisses the boundless intimacy and limitless interdependency of all beings and things. To live through such egoself-centricity is to advance our deep sense of lacking, our endless wanting, our habitual drivenness, our inflexible beliefs, our intolerant views, and our cerebral isolation. As we continue to advance all of this, we leave ourselves vulnerable to stress and tension, to muscular armoring and emotional defensiveness, to mental fragmentation and behavioral fatigue, and to a growing aggravation, worry, pessimism, and frustration. In our mirrored Way, we heed the bright wisdoming of our vulnerability, take refuge in the humility and honesty of our beginner's heartmind, extend unconditional compassion to the totality of our lived experience, soften our attachment to egoself-centricity, tenderly sink into the visceral center-point of our whole body, and faithfully recover the still composure of core-Self inside of shikantaza and zazen-only.

Our Way Is Total Completion

When we practice in the true spirit of shikantaza and zazen-only, our core-Self clearly discerns that the great functioning of each being and thing is the great functioning of vast Oneness meeting us in the ordinariness of ungraspable enlightenment itself. This is why we unhesitatingly bow to all beings and things that call forth our core-Self to dance in boundless intimacy with the vast Oneness of total reality. To spontaneously dance in boundless intimacy with the vast Oneness of total reality is to somatically verify the limitless value of respectfully yielding to the Way of noninterference. When we respectfully yield to the Way of noninterference, the Way of noninterference liberates us to instantly respond beyond thinking and empowers us to easily wait in a still timelessness far beyond the discipline of patience. Whether we instantly respond or easily wait in the still timelessness of total reality, our responding and our waiting are spontaneous, unfabricated, and free from deceit, duplicity, or hidden agenda.

When we live from the still brilliance of our core-Self, we compassionately dance in boundless intimacy, gracefully bow in limitless interdependency, and wholeheartedly yield to the Way of noninterference. This holds true whether core-Self is silently illuminating our ego-self, our thinking mind, our personality, our needs, sensations, feelings, and desires, or any being, thing, activity, or event that enters the immediate field of our lived experience. To embody core-Self while behaviorally yielding to the Way of noninterference is to somatically verify that this life of ungraspable enlightenment is exactly our joyful readiness to instantly respond or easily wait in the still timelessness of forever.

Our Way of living as core-Self in ungraspable enlightenment is all-pervading, complete in itself, and fully accessible to all human beings who cherish limitless interdependency, who honor the vast Oneness of total reality, and who unhesitatingly bow to the Way of noninterference. When we embody core-Self as the still paradox of total reality, we do not seek fulfillment and completion by traveling here or there, by searching after this or that, by taking psychotropic drugs, by ingesting shamanic substances, by tightly clinging to an exclusive religious dogma, by attaching to an ego-self serving and divisive political view, by idealizing spiritual leaders, by grasping at occult teachings, by idolizing ancient scriptures, or by going from one New Age spirituality to another. This is not our Way.

Our Way does not look outward for completion. Nor do we look beyond the present moment for total fulfillment. We do not seek to gain a "perfect enlightenment" in some distant future. We do not grasp at the still brilliance of core-Self by cerebrally focusing the mind, by intensifying our mental concentration, by willfully subjugating our body in the stillness of zazen-only, or by extinguishing our ego-self and thinking mind. In our Way of shikantaza and zazen-only, we viscerally confirm that our core-Self is originally still and silent, free from craving, desiring, and wanting, and entirely undefiled by purity, sinfulness, ignorance, enlightenment, and holiness. This is why we confidently abide in the still essence of our core-Self that transmits the inherent sacredness, boundless intimacy, and limitless interconnectedness of total reality. This is why we faithfully embody ungraspable enlightenment as the profound ordinariness of everyday life, respectfully honor equality and interdependency in the Way of loving and being loved, openly share the exuberance and wonder of our beginner's heartmind, and simply enjoy the total fulfillment and completion of our radical humanness far beyond lacking or regret.

Thank you.

"[People] say, great enlightenment or perfect
enlightenment, but Dogen Zenji says, "Intimate
Enlightenment." Most intimate One is enlightenment.
Most intimate One to you is enlightenment....Of course,
if it is something beyond you, that is not intimate. Even
if it is something to attain, it is not the intimate One.
[Dogen] says, "Intimate Enlightenment." This
intimacy to [ungraspable] enlightenment
is our practice....It is so intimate,
that we do not realize [or grasp]
enlightenment. That is
what {Dogen}
means."

Shunryu Suzuki-roshi
Soko-ji Temple-San Francisco

"One is led to a new
notion of unbroken wholeness
which denies the classical idea of analyzability
of the world into separately and independently existing
parts . . . We have reversed the usual classical notion
that the independent 'elementary parts' of the world are
the fundamental reality. . . Rather, we say that inseparable
quantum interconnectedness of the whole universe is the
fundamental reality, and that relatively independently
behaving parts are merely particular and
contingent forms within this Whole."

David Bohm
American Physicist
(1917-1992)

"A human being is part of the whole
called by us universe, a part limited in time
and space. We experience ourselves, our thoughts
and feelings as something separate from the rest.
A kind of optical delusion of consciousness. This
delusion is a kind of prison for us, restricting us
to our personal desires and to affection for a
few persons nearest to us. Our task must
be to free ourselves from the prison by
widening our circle of compassion
to embrace all living creatures
and the whole of nature
in its beauty."

Albert Einstein
1879-1955

• PART II •

ILLUMINATION

"When we thoroughly explore
what the great Way of the buddhas
is, we find that It is liberation from delusion
and letting our true Self manifest to the full. For
some, this liberation from delusion means that life
liberates us from life, and death liberates us from
death. Both our getting out of birth-and-death and
our entering into birth-and-death are the great
Way. Laying birth-and-death aside and going
beyond birth-and-death to the other
shore are both the great Way."

Dogen Zenji
(1200 AD to 1253 AD)

CHAPTER 5

Sitting Inside Of Sitting

Being Faith
Before Beliefs,
Yielding To the Wisdom
of a Whole Universe.

"At the very moment of just sitting [in zazen-only],
investigate what sitting [in zazen-only] really is. Is it
unimpeded freedom? Is it a state of vigorous energy? Is
it thinking or not thinking? Is it doing or not doing? Is
there sitting inside of 'just sitting'? Is it 'just sitting'
inside of bodymind? Is it sitting letting go of
'just sitting' in sitting? Or is it total freedom
from 'just sitting' inside of body and
mind? Investigate all of this in
every possible way!

Dogen Zenji
Zanmai-O-Zanmai
(Monarch of Still Illumination)

The Needle of Zazen-Only

In our Way, we deeply honor and respect two ancient Zen poems. The first poem was written by the great Chinese Zen master Hongzhi (1091-1157). Old Hongzhi is the patriarch of the Cáo-dòng Zen lineage that viewed zazen-only as the Way of "silent Illumination." Our Japanese Soto Zen lineage is deeply rooted in the Cáo-dòng Zen lineage of Master Hongzhi. Old Hongzhi entitled his poem "Zuochan Zhen" which means "The Acupuncture Needle of Zazen-Only."

The second poem was written by Dogen Zenji in 1242. Dogen's poem intimately reflected and spoke to Hongzhi's original version. This shows just how much Dogen Zenji admired and respected Hongzhi. Dogen entitled his poem "Zazen-Shin," which in Japanese also means "The Acupuncture Needle of Zazen-Only." By using the metaphor of Chinese acupuncture to describe zazen-only, Hongzhi and Dogen illuminate our Zen practice as the true Way of being vitally alive and fully embodied as a healthy human being.

In Chinese acupuncture, the insertion of medicinal needles in various parts of the human body stimulates, generates, and regulates the flow of our vital life energy. In China this vital life energy is called "Qi" or "Chi," while in Japan it is called Ki. Chi flows and circulates along bio-energy pathways or meridians that extend throughout the body. When the natural circulation of Chi becomes blocked or hindered, illness and disease can result if the flow is not restored.

Chinese acupuncture has used the insertion of medicinal needles for thousands of years to promote the health, healing, and longevity of human beings. I believe that Hongzhi and Dogen intentionally placed the embodiment of zazen-only within the ancient model of Chinese acupuncture to reveal its significance in promoting our physical, mental, emotional, and spiritual health and wellness.

When we view the traditional practice of Zen from the perspective of Chinese acupuncture, our embodiment of zazen-only is like a universal acupuncture needle that we freely and openly insert into all the activities, affairs, and relationships of everyday life. The pinpoint of this universal needle is exactly our core-Self in this Only Moment Body. In our Way, we somatically verify the pinpoint of zazen-only by sinking into the still composure and settled discernment of our core-Self. When we apply the needle of zazen-only by viscerally dwelling in the still pinpoint of our core-Self, we effortlessly generate and conserve our Ki energy, sustain our vital health and longevity, realize our boundless intimacy with total reality, and viscerally recover a compassionate and pristine Way of being that transforms each moment into ungraspable enlightenment itself.

The Poems of Hongzhi and Dogen

In this section, I will share with you the two poems by Master Hongzhi and Master Dogen. Before you read the poems, please take a moment to settle into your core-

Self and arouse the curiosity and openness of your beginner's heartmind. After you finish reading each poem, take three slow breaths into your hara and reread them again. Do not try to mentally investigate them; do not think about their subtle meaning. Just read the poems while grounding into the visceral center of your lower abdomen. Know that Hongzhi and Dogen are both freely and openly transmitting the embodiment of core-Self that they viscerally realized by just sitting inside of zazen-only. After reading both poems, you will be prepared to intimately understand my visceral entanglement with Hongzhi and Dogen. This visceral entanglement will become more apparent when you start reading "The Ancient Seal of Zazen-Only."

Now take a breath, sink into your gut-core Self,
and attend to the Zazen of Hongzhi.

The Zazen Needle of Hongzhi

Essential function of buddha after buddha,
Functioning essence of ancestor after ancestor.
It knows without touching things;
It illumines without facing objects.
Knowing without touching things,
Its knowing is inherently subtle;
Illuminating without facing objects,
Its illumination is inherently mysterious.
Its knowing inherently subtle,
It is ever without discriminatory thought;
Its illumining inherently mysterious,
It is ever without a hair's breadth of sign.
Ever without discriminatory thought,
Its knowing is rare and without peer;
Ever without a hair's breadth of sign,
Its illumining comprehends without grasping.
The water is clear right through to the bottom;
A fish swims lazily along.
The sky is vast without horizon;
A bird flies far, far away.

I really appreciate and respect this poem by Master Hongzhi. It is the authentic expression of core-Self in this Only Moment Body of zazen-only. As Dogen Zenji himself stated, "This one [Hongzhi's poem] says it right. It alone radiates throughout the surface and depth of universal truth. It is the statement of a [real] buddha and ancestor among all buddhas and ancestors past and present."

Before you go on, take another deep breath, sink into
core-Self, and consider the Zazen of Eihei Dogen.

The Zazen Needle of Dogen Zenji

Essential function of all the buddhas,
Functioning essence of all the ancestors;
It is present without thinking;
It is completed without interacting.
Present without thinking,
Its presence is inherently intimate;
Completed without interacting,
Its completion is inherently verified.
Its presence inherently intimate,
It is ever without stain or defilement;
Its completion inherently verified,
It is ever without the upright or inclined.
Intimacy ever without stain or defilement,
Its intimacy sloughs off without discarding;
Verification ever without upright or inclined,
Its verification makes effort without figuring.
The water is clear right through the earth;
A fish goes along like a fish.
The sky is vast straight into the heavens,
A bird flies just like a bird.

After writing his mirrored version of Hongzhi's poem, Dogen Zenji states, "It is not that Master Hongzhi has not said it right, but that it can also be said just like this. Above all, descendants of buddhas and ancestors should study zazen-only as the one great concern." When Dogen says that we should study zazen-only as the one great concern, he does not mean to read books and hear lectures about Zen meditation. By study, he means the daily embodiment of zazen-only. To embody zazen-only as the one great concern is to intimately study and resolve the great matter of life and death. To resolve the great matter of life and death is to fully embody the still paradox of core-Self inside this Only Moment Body of zazen-only.

The Ancient Seal of Zazen-Only

Now, I will share with you my Zen poem entitled "The Ancient Seal of Zazen-Only." I wrote this poem to encourage the daily practice of core-Self inside of zazen-only, to inspire the radical embodiment of humanness, and to revitalize the somatic investigation of life and death far beyond beliefs and thinking mind. "The Ancient Seal of Zazen-Only" is written in the poetic style of Master Hongzhi and Master Dogen who fully embodied the Way of core-Self inside of zazen-only.

As you read the poem, you will see how I entangle with Hongzhi and Dogen to viscerally transmit the non-thinking intelligence of core-Self that silently illuminates our boundless intimacy and vast Oneness with all beings and things. Although my poem is deeply entangled with the Zen poems of Hongzhi and Dogen, I have chosen to name it differently. Although the name is different, I am still speaking of the somatic needle of zazen-only and its visceral pinpoint of core-Self. Just like Hongzhi and Dogen both taught the embodiment of zazen-only according to their time, I teach the somatic needle of zazen-only and its visceral pinpoint of core-Self according to my own time.

In writing my poem, I am not saying that Master Hongzhi and Master Dogen did not hit the mark. Nor am I saying that they did not clearly illuminate core-Self as the visceral pinpoint of zazen-only. Rather, I am saying that the visceral pinpoint of core-Self and the somatic acupuncture needle of zazen-only can also be fully expressed, further studied, and intimately clarified just like this.

Stop! take a deep breath, sink into your your core-Self,
and become intimate with the Zazen of Shugyo Daijo.

The Ancient Seal of Zazen-Only

A fearless tiger settles with ease in the moonlit forest.
An awakened dragon spreads its wings in the fertile valley.
Just like this, all beings and things have a great functioning.
Here or there, inert or active, great functioning is only One.
The still functioning of core-Self is the essence of total reality.
Silently illuminating linear time and our five pristine senses,
Yet It is the timelessness of ungraspable enlightenment Itself.
Even as Its brilliance is before seeing, hearing, and touching,
Its still discernment and lucid composure are intimately felt.
Compassionately exposing the limitations of our thinking,
It clarifies everyday life through Its boundless empathy.
Although It is openly present in the midst of thinking,
It investigates matters independent of reasoning.
Revealing the surface and depth of total reality,
Its intimacy penetrates both life and death.
As It wholly fathoms both life and death,
Its still knowing is vast and without peer.
Honoring the useful function of ego-self,
It creates no enemy to be vanquished.
Ever beyond thinking and knowing,
It cannot be defined nor compared.
Far beneath naming and figuring,
Its discerning stillness apprehends
without grasping or pushing away.
Whether rippled or turbulent, the muddy
stream remains lucidly clear and undefiled.
A whale swims with ease in a waterless ocean.
Gliding across the vast Oneness of a blue sky,
the hawk remains completely nested in its flight.

The "Ancient Seal of Zazen-Only" depicts the original root Way of living as a radical human being through the silent illumination and still discernment of our core-Self. This radical root Way of being human in everyday life was fully embodied by the ancient Chinese sages (5000-4500 B.C.). Two Chinese texts reveal how these ancient Chinese sages embodied their visceral core-Self in everyday life. The first is called the "I Ching," or "The Book of Changes." It was written around 2953 B.C.. The I Ching encourages the harmonious human embodiment of change, impermanence, and duality while teaching people how to blend their everyday behavior with the dynamic functioning of a vast Oneness that unfolds the bright wisdoming of total reality itself. The second Chinese text is called the "Tao Te Ching," or "The Book of the Way and Its Virtue," which was written about 550 B.C.. The "Tao Te Ching" instructs people to return to their natural, original, or radical Way of being fully human. It encourages all of us to embody the virtuous root of humanity (core-Self) while yielding to the Way (vast Oneness) that upholds the integrity and interdependency of total reality.

Although these two texts indicate that the Chinese sages lived everyday life in the vast Oneness and boundless intimacy of total reality, no dominant figure in China transmitted the visceral integrity of core-Self within a traceable human lineage. However, in the sixth century B.C., near the eastern part of India, Shakyamuni Buddha embodied ungraspable enlightenment, somatically realized the boundless intimacy of our radical humanness, viscerally transmitted the still flashing of core-Self within a traceable human lineage, and established the Way of living and dying in shikantaza and zazen-only. This is why I respectfully practice the Buddha Way and gratefully embody the Way of Chinese sages.

TURNING THE LIGHT INWARD
Inside of Just Sitting

Introduction

The "Ancient Seal Of Zazen-Only" blends the embodied wisdom of Shakyamuni Buddha with the embodied wisdom of the Chinese sages. Just like the whole of this book, I used intimate language in a symbolic and metaphorical Way to create the poem from my visceral gut-core intelligence. I call this gut-core Way of using intimate language *the language of visceral intimacy.* In the *language of visceral intimacy*, there is no felt gap between the language describing experience and the felt experience itself. This Way of using language from our gut-core intelligence is the intimate language of core-Self. This *intimate visceral language* of core-Self is exactly the language that Hongzhi and Dogen used to write their own poems. Dogen referred to *intimate language* as "*mitsugo.*" *Mitsugo* is core-Self using intimate language to viscerally speak from core-Self. The *language of visceral intimacy* is not meant to be intellectually or mentally figured out. To speak and write from our core-Self is to use *intimate visceral language* that can be somatically grasped, intuitively discerned, and empathically comprehended.

In this section entitled "Turning The Light Inward," I will use *intimate visceral language* to unpack the teachings that exist within each line of my poem. I unpack these teachings to further clarify the total dynamic functioning of your core-Self, to advance the inclusive nature of your radical humanness, and to promote the brilliant embodiment of your beginner's heartmind.

GUIDING COMMENTARY

The Fearless Tiger

"A fearless tiger settles with ease in the moonlit forest."

The fearless tiger represents a still discernment, a settled composure, a wakeful readiness, and a flashing quickness of response. Whether we are just sitting as core-Self inside of zazen-only or just living as core-Self in our everyday life of shikantaza, we effortlessly embody a courageous readiness and a bright wakefulness to immediately respond like a fearless tiger in a moonlit forest.

The moonlit forest is a wild and intimate place that surrounds the fearless tiger. The dense forest is full of vital aliveness, deep tranquility, vast impermanence, vibrant freshness, and continuous growth and change. When we dwell in the intelligent visceral center of our lower abdomen, we are the fearless tiger resting in the unobstructed wildness and spontaneous freshness of our true nature. We are the fearless tiger of core-Self that confidently meets the dense forest of everyday life with wakeful readiness, settled compassion, and still discernment.

As core-Self is viscerally settled as core-Self in this Only Moment Body, we somatically experience our wild alertness and throbbing vitality, our easefulness and deep tranquility, our ever fresh impermanence, our felt completion in the midst of endless growth and change, and our brilliant and wondrous nature as an endless beginner. To become intimate with the tiger, the wildness, the forest, and the moonlight is to become intimate with our core-Self as it unfolds ungraspable enlightenment in limitless interdependency with all beings and things.

Whether we are just sitting as core-Self inside of just sitting or embodying core-Self inside of just living, we confidently meet the total reality of everyday life like the fearless tiger meets the surface and depth of the moonlit forest. The fearless tiger senses that she belongs in the wildness of the forest. She knows in her flesh, blood, bone, and marrow that the forest is a reflection of her true nature. She knows that anything can happen in the wildness of the forest. However, she is able to easefully dwell in the moonlit forest with alertness, wakefulness, and an instant readiness to respond to anything that arises. Her fearlessness comes from the deep settledness of her visceral intelligence. It is there that she realizes her vast Oneness with total reality. It is there that she knows her boundless intimacy with the wildness of the forest. It is from there that she expresses her visceral power to confidently recline with ease and alertness, or to quickly stride with an inner stillness and a flashing readiness to respond anywhere right here and now.

The Awakened Dragon

"An awakened dragon spreads its wings in the fertile valley."

The dragon in this poem is not the kind of dragon that destroys villages with its fiery breath, and is then hunted and killed by a brave warrior. That is more the Western understanding of a dragon. In China and other Eastern countries, dragons are regarded as mythical creatures that symbolize divine power, deep integrity, endless vitality, and profound wisdom. In our Way, we view the dragon as the protector of all radical human beings who fully embody their core-Self, who passionately enjoy the brilliance and humility of their beginner's heartmind, and who behaviorally express their endless gratitude for living in boundless intimacy with all beings and things.

The awakened dragon is a metaphor for letting go of our heady slumber in ego-self and awakening to the vast Oneness and boundless intimacy of core-Self. The fertile valley is the center of our lower abdomen where we experience the sensual vitality, pristine innocence, and visceral integrity of our core-Self. We awaken the real dragon by allowing our localized heady awareness to sink into the visceral center-point of our hara where core-Self intimately arises.

When you live through the visceral center-point of your lower abdomen, you become the real dragon of core-Self that silently illuminates the vast Oneness of total reality. This means that you are no longer fooled by the separate, transparent, and insubstantial nature of your ego-self, your passing thoughts, your personal beliefs, and the functioning of your thinking mind. When you just sit as core-Self inside of zazen-only and live through core-Self in everyday life, you are the real dragon that openly lives in boundless intimacy with all beings and things. You are the real dragon that freely unfolds ungraspable enlightenment through all the activities and affairs of everyday life.

Dogen said, "We wholeheartedly care for the real dragon instead of a carved one." The real dragon is core-Self just sitting as core-Self inside of zazen-only. Although zazen-only is not the real dragon, you will viscerally meet the real dragon inside of zazen-only. However, if you carve the behavioral stillness of zazen-only into the image of a dragon, you will never meet the real dragon inside of zazen-only. If you carve your teacher into a dragon, still he or she is not the real dragon that dwells in the center of your lower abdomen far beneath thinking. If you carve beliefs and scriptures into the caricature of a dragon, they will never be the real dragon of core-Self that viscerally awakens to the power of lucid dreaming and the still flashing of total reality inside of zazen-only. If you are skilled at carving replicas of dragons and attach to them in everyday life, you will never meet the vigorous dragon that spreads its wings in the fertile valley of boundless intimacy and ungraspable enlightenment itself.

As the fearless tiger represents the discerning stillness, settled composure, and instant responsiveness of core-Self, the awakened dragon represents the visceral integrity, insightful brilliance, noble presence, and silent illumination of our core-Self. When we live through our core-Self in intimate accountability to vast Oneness, we are the real dragon that lives in boundless intimacy and ungraspable enlightenment at the surface and depth of everyday life.

Great Functioning
"Just like this, all beings and things have a great functioning."

The great functioning of the dragon and the great functioning of the tiger represent the great functioning of all beings and things. When I speak of all beings and things, I mean all people, creatures, pets, plants, rocks, trees and all the objects that support our daily life no matter how simple, mundane, or utilitarian. This includes things like our working tools, smartphones, computers, purses, toys, shavers, clothes, backpacks, pillows, bedspreads, and toothbrushes.

In the morning and evening, when I squeeze toothpaste onto my toothbrush, I honor the great functioning of the tube of toothpaste and the great functioning of the toothbrush that receives it. I show my deep appreciation for their great functioning by meeting them with the ever fresh wakefulness of my core-Self. Likewise, when I brush my teeth, I honor the toothpaste and the toothbrush that function together to clean my teeth. The tube of toothpaste, the toothpaste, and the toothbrush, all come forth to verify and confirm the boundless intimacy of my core-Self far beneath thinking. This great functioning of all beings and things is exactly the great functioning of their true nature. To be intimate with the great functioning of their true nature is to be intimate with the vast Oneness of total reality.

When we acknowledge, honor, and appreciate the great functioning of all beings and things that support our everyday life, we are really acknowledging, honoring, and appreciating the great functioning of vast Oneness that upholds the boundless intimacy and interdependency of total reality. Both the wooden striker and the bell that I use to begin and close my daily meditation have a great functioning at the surface and depth of total reality. When the striker meets the bell with core-Self to proclaim that this only moment is happening everywhere right here and now, it completes its great functioning. As the bell deeply vibrates with core-Self to proclaim the ever freshness and vast impermanence of total reality, it fulfills its great functioning. Just like this, all beings and things come forth to fulfill their great functioning in boundless intimacy with core-Self while unfolding ungraspable enlightenment as the ordinariness and total reality of our everyday life.

IT is Only One

"Here or there, inert or active, great functioning is only One".

No matter whether it is a being, thing, activity, or event; no matter whether it is here or there, inert or active, incomprehensibly large or small, everything has a great functioning and a unique wholeness that is upheld in boundless intimacy and interdependency with total reality. We call this boundless intimacy and interdependency with total reality the great functioning of vast Oneness. As vast Oneness upholds the great functioning integrity and boundless intimacy of all beings and things, each being and thing that arises in the immediate field of our lived experience is absolutely equal to all beings and things that pervade the entire universe. In the great functioning of vast Oneness, there is not one being or thing that is higher or lower than any other being or thing. This means that the individual functioning of limitless beings and things is exactly the great functioning of only One.

In our Way, we experience our core-Self as exactly One with the great functioning of all beings, things, activities, and events that arise in our everyday life, just as they are, just as IT is. Just as they are means that core-Self sees each being, thing, activity, or event as entirely unique and beyond comparison. Just as IT is means that core-Self meets each being, thing, activity, or event through a boundless intimacy and a vast Oneness that is beyond all separation. We dwell in boundless intimacy with the great functioning Oneness of all beings, things, and events by meeting them through the transpersonal empathy of our core-Self.

No matter how seemingly great or insignificant according to social or cultural standards, we embrace each being, thing, activity, or event as the bright wisdoming of vast Oneness meeting us in boundless intimacy right here and now. In our Way, all beings, things, activities, and events come forth to illuminate vast Oneness and verify that our core-Self is living in boundless intimacy far beneath thinking. When we practice honoring the great functioning of all beings and things, all beings, things, activities, and events intimately engage our core-Self to illuminate the vast Oneness of total reality and unfold this life of ungraspable enlightenment without a trace of attainment or owning by I, me, or mine.

Absolute Stillness

"The still functioning of core-Self is the essence of total reality."

As vast Oneness is an absolute stillness that penetrates the great functioning of our core-Self while sustaining the individual and interdependent functioning of all beings and things throughout the whole universe, we call IT the still essence of total reality. This still essence of total reality is fully experienced in this Only Moment Body as the still illumination, discerning composure, and boundless intimacy of our core-Self.

It is from the still essence of total reality that core-Self confidently engages with the total dynamic functioning of everyday life.

We embody core-Self in everyday life to fully express the vast Oneness of total reality, to freely extend compassion, transpersonal empathy, and deep caring to all beings and things, to confidently respond to life's challenges from the still discernment of our lower abdomen, to practice the Way of loving and being loved as the fruit of ungraspable enlightenment itself, to somatically verify the completion of our radical humanness, and to openly share the exuberance of our beginner's heartmind.

We cannot embody the still essence of total reality if we are always preoccupied with our heady ego-self and thinking mind. We cannot experience the joy and fulfillment of living in boundless intimacy if we separate ourselves from all beings and things while ignoring our limitless interdependency with their great functioning. We cannot realize nor verify ungraspable enlightenment in the ordinariness of our everyday life if we continue to use people, objects, situations, and circumstances to fulfill our endless egoself-centric needs and desires.

When we attach to our mental chatter while meeting all beings and things with the cerebral power of our thinking mind, we constantly uphold the illusion of a permanent, controlling, and substantial ego-self. To see how our ego-self is driven to uphold its own existence is to realize our deeply seated fear of uncertainty, emptiness, and vast impermanence. To embrace the fear of vast impermanence is to intimately realize that our need to control and unfold reality beyond uncertainty and impermanence is delusion. On the other hand, to respectfully meet all beings, things, and events from the deep composure, flashing impermanence, and compassionate caring of our core-Self is to realize that the still essence of total reality is unfolding everyday life in boundless intimacy and ungraspable enlightenment far beneath the functioning of ego-self and thinking mind.

The Time Of Intimacy

"Silently illuminating linear time and our five pristine senses,
Yet It is the timelessness of ungraspable enlightenment Itself."

Normally, we experience all beings, things, and events happening within a linear time that moves at the same unchangeable speed for everyone. We view time as independent and separate from us. Most people accept that all beings, things, and events are embedded in a linear time that moves from past, present, to future.

Our ego-self thinks that it is necessary to view all beings and things objectively while investigating how they interact according to the law of cause and effect within linear time. When we experience everyday life through our ego-self functioning, this is the way we come to objectively know and think about all beings and things in the passage of linear time. Our ego-self thinks about its own time as moving in a trajectory from its birth, to its present life, to its future death. However, the way that our ego-self experiences linear time is only the surface of time that is embedded in the still wholeness of quantum timelessness itself.

When we fully embody our core-Self, we experience a quantum depth of timelessness that has no passage of linear time. This quantum depth of timelessness is absolutely still while flashing everywhere to brilliantly refresh the surface and depth of total reality. Although the passage of linear time and the still quantum depth of timelessness may seem contradictory and mutually exclusive, they naturally interact in a complimentary way during the practice of core-Self in everyday life. What I am saying here is that we are free to live as radical human beings who function efficiently and effectively within linear time while somatically being the still flashing of a timeless moment that continuously sustains our core-Self in boundless intimacy and ungraspable enlightenment itself.

When core-Self is being the still quantum depth of timelessness, we are not separate from being this only moment of timelessness that is flashing everywhere as vast impermanence itself. We are being this only moment of timelessness even as we embody the still vibrancy of core-Self within the passage of linear time. We call this our Way of being the wholeness of time in the vast Oneness of total reality. Although timelessness exists far beneath the functioning of ego-self and thinking mind, our core-Self viscerally realizes beyond all doubt that the still quantum depth of timelessness is the boundless intimacy of total reality that unfolds everyday life in ungraspable enlightenment itself. Even as core-Self is living in boundless intimacy with all beings and things through the still quantum depth of timelessness, it is not obstructed by the daily use of linear time that allows all human beings to live a productive, efficient, timely, honorable, and respectful life.

Non-Thinking Intelligence

*"Even as Its brilliance is before seeing, hearing, and touching,
Its still discernment and lucid composure are intimately felt."*

These two lines emphasize the Way we experience the still discernment and lucid composure of our core-Self as it is being the timelessness of boundless intimacy and vast Oneness in this Only Moment Body. When I speak of lucid composure and still discernment, I am referring to the non-thinking intelligence of our core-Self that continuously provides us with preverbal information about our everyday life activities, affairs, and relationships. As this preverbal information is viscerally experienced through the still non-thinking intelligence of our core-Self, it cannot be cerebrally comprehended by our ego-self and thinking mind. When I speak about the limitations of our ego-self and thinking mind. I do not want you to mistake this as the negation of our ego-self functioning or our ability to think, reason, and develop knowledge about ourselves and the total dynamic functioning of nature and the universe as a whole. Our insubstantial ego-self identity and our mental ability to rationally think, write, and orally communicate with words and ideas are all expressions of a wondrous human functioning that also promotes our personal, social, cultural, and scientific evolution across linear time.

In our Way, we honor the development of our ego-self, our personality, and our cerebral ability to use analysis, reason, and logic to take care of practical matters as they arise in the immediate field of our lived experience. This means that we employ our insubstantial ego-self identity and our thinking mind to help us conscientiously navigate and responsibly take care of the activities, affairs, and relationships of everyday life. However, we ground our insubstantial ego-self identity, our daily social interactions, and the functioning of our thinking mind in the boundless intimacy, timeless stillness, vast Oneness, and transpersonal empathy of our core-Self. To ground our insubstantial ego-self identity and thinking mind in our core-Self is to realize a more intimate Way of empathically meeting all beings, things, and events while viscerally discerning their uniqueness and limitless interdependency within the total dynamic functioning of our everyday life.

Clarifying Everyday Life

"Compassionately exposing the limitations of our thinking,
It clarifies everyday life through Its boundless empathy."

In our everyday life, we all meet challenging and difficult people. We all experience perplexing and bewildering situations, events, and circumstances that expose the limitations of our ego-self with its separate way of relating, knowing, controlling, and thinking. Dogen Zenji called these difficult and perplexing challenges the "genjo koans of everyday life." "Gen," the first part of "genjo," means to show up completely, to be wholly true and real, and to fully embody this only moment that is total reality itself. "Gen" is to realize and verify that this only moment is the moment of everywhere stillness and that everywhere stillness is this only moment right here and now. This only moment is the time where all beings, things, and events interdependently arise in boundless intimacy with core-Self to manifest the total dynamic functioning of vast Oneness in everyday life. When we embody the true meaning of "gen," we meet each being and thing in linear time while sharing a timeless moment of vast Oneness with all of them right here and now. This timeless moment is a flashing stillness where beings, things, and events show up to engage our core-Self in the dance of ungraspable enlightenment far beneath the functioning of our ego-self and thinking mind.

"Jo," the second part of "genjo," means to somatically realize ongoing completion and be viscerally present right here and now. To somatically realize ongoing completion and be viscerally present is to embody core-Self as the fundamental pinpoint of shikantaza and zazen-only. To embody the visceral pinpoint of shikantaza and zazen-only is to be a radical human being who lives in respectful interdependency with all beings and things. "Jo" is to embody core-Self as the radical root of all human beings that is far beyond lacking. As there is not one thing lacking in the radical root of all human beings, we gratefully live from our core-Self for its own sake. "Jo" means to continuously heal ourselves with all beings and things by realizing, actualizing, and verifying the pinpoint embodiment of core-Self that completes and fulfills our everyday life. Thus, Dogen Zenji's "genjo" means to be the true completion and fulfillment of core-Self in each flashing moment of total reality. We live the true meaning of "genjo" when we fully embody the visceral pinpoint of core-Self, extend transpersonal empathy to all beings and things, engage them with respect, equality, and composure, and wholeheartedly blend with the still essence of total reality that unfolds our everyday life as ungraspable enlightenment itself.

The word "koan," in Dogen's phrase "genjo koan," can best be understood as a perplexing or challenging situation, event, or circumstance that exposes the limitations of our ego-self and thinking mind. When we come across a perplexing event, situation, or circumstance, we view this as an opportunity to practice the "koan" of our everyday life. We do this by first acknowledging the exposed limitations of our ego-self and thinking mind. Then, we faithfully entrust our "daily life koan" to the still discernment and silent illumination of our core-Self. This way of entrusting our daily life koans to the still discernment and silent illumination of our core-Self is very straightforward. We come back to the vital flow of our breath, soften our attachment to ego-self and thinking mind, allow our embodied awareness to sink into the lucid composure of our core-Self, silently illuminate the vast Oneness of total reality, see things just as they are from a broader, clearer, and more inclusive perspective, and confidently respond with caring, compassion, and tenderness toward ourselves and others. When we continue to do just this, we viscerally confirm that "embodying genjo" and "clarifying the koans of everyday life" is the ancient Way of living in boundless intimacy and vast Oneness with all beings and things.

Independent of Reasoning

"Although It is openly present in the midst of thinking,
It investigates matters independent of reasoning."

When I say, "it is openly present in the midst of thinking," I mean that we do not have to stop our passing thoughts, still our thinking mind, or keep ourselves from talking to each other to fully experience the still discernment and illuminating composure of our core-Self that naturally arises from the visceral center of our lower abdomen. However, it is our daily practice of just sitting inside of zazen-only that provides us with the experiential basis for embodying our core-Self while in the midst of living, thinking, talking, writing, and doing. When I say, "it investigates matters independent of reasoning," I mean that our core-Self clarifies and resolves the genjo koans of everyday life independent of our logical and rational way of thinking and knowing.

When genjo koans arise in my everyday life, including those that are associated with serious illness, loss, injury, death, dying, or seeing loved ones in pain and suffering, I remain eternally grateful that I am able to meet them from the discerning stillness and illuminating silence of my core-Self inside this Only Moment Body. I have had many difficult genjo koans in my life that have been openly met, intimately clarified, and fully resolved independent of reasoning. Here, when I say, "independent of reasoning," I mean through the still discernment of my core-Self inside of shikantaza and zazen-only.

When you see someone sitting with half opened eyes in the upright posture of zazen-only, you are not seeing someone who is meditating on a koan or a perplexing life issue in the sense of mentally, logically, or rationally thinking about it. Rather, you are seeing someone who is embodying the discerning stillness of their core-Self that is far beneath the functioning of their ego-self identity, the ideation and knowing of their thinking mind, and the impermanent passage of their thoughts and feelings.

In our Zen tradition, the statue of Buddha sitting upright in zazen-only intimately transmits the still discernment and illuminating composure of core-Self just sitting inside of just sitting. When we look at the statue of Buddha seated in Zen meditation, we see our core-Self silently illuminating the completion and fulfillment of our radical humanness inside of just sitting. The statue of Buddha seated in the tranquility of zazen-only depicts a radical human being who is courageously investigating total reality beyond the knowing of ego-self while openly enjoying core-Self in boundless intimacy with vast Oneness beyond thinking.

In contrast to the statue of Buddha seated in the tranquility of zazen-only is the statue of "The Poet" created by the great European artist Auguste Rodin. I am sure many of you have seen this statue of Rodin that depicts a muscular man seated hunched over while mentally struggling with an aspect of lived reality. The seated Poet is obviously exerting his thinking mind to the utmost. He embodies the state of mental tension and inner stress. Rodin's "Poet" is a perfect example of an embodied ego-self mentally preoccupied with resolving a perplexing genjo koan in everyday life. Because the statue of "The Poet" depicts a man struggling to understand something deeply through the thinking function of his ego-self, people began to call the statue "The Thinker." This is why "The Thinker" has become a recognizable icon of a tensely embodied ego-self facing the limitations of thought, logic, reason, and mental introspection.

When you see a statue of "The Thinker," you can almost feel the overwhelming stress of ego-self entanglement emanating from his muscular body. You sense the emotional frustration he is having while trying to resolve a difficult genjo koan within the exposed limitations of his rational analysis, logical thought, and ego-self way of knowing. You can see the mental and emotional tension that permeates the physical posture and musculature of the Thinker. On the other hand, when you see a statue of Buddha seated in the upright posture of zazen-only, you immediately feel the compassion, ease, joy, and peace emanating from it. This is why people who know nothing about Zen experience a deep feeling of embodied tranquility when they place a seated Buddha in their home or garden. When you see a statue of Buddha in seated meditation, you can almost taste his life of boundless intimacy and ungraspable enlightenment with your whole body. You sense that you are looking at a human being who is embodying peace while extending unobstructed empathy and compassion to all beings and things.

If you place a statue of the Thinker and a statue of the Buddha side by side, you can see and feel the obvious differences in meeting genjo koans through the exposed limitations of ego-self and thinking mind or through the brilliant stillness and discerning composure of core-Self inside of zazen-only. When you freely and openly meet the genjo koans of everyday life through your core-Self, you are like the historical Buddha who lived the peaceful Way of boundless intimacy and ungraspable enlightenment itself. On the other hand, if you continue to meet the genjo koans of everyday life from the exposed limitations of your ego-self and thinking mind, you will be like Rodin's "Thinker" who is eventually hunched over by mental drivenness, inner judgement, chronic stress, emotional frustration, and muscular tension.

Vast And Without Peer

"Revealing the surface and depth of total reality,
Its intimacy penetrates both life and death.
As It wholly fathoms both life and death,
Its still knowing is vast and without peer."

In these four lines, I am speaking of our core-Self intimacy with vast impermanence. When we practice grounding into the visceral center of our lower abdomen, we experience the deep refuge of living through the still composure of our core-Self as we continue to intimately arrive at the crossroads of life and death right here and now. When I say that we experience core-Self as a profound refuge at the ever present crossroads of life and death, I am referring to the confidence, composure, and calmness that we experience while living in wholehearted companionship with the intimate reality of death in everyday life. Our felt calmness with the immediacy of death and our felt composure with having death as our intimate companion arise together while sitting as core-Self inside of just sitting.

When we are just sitting as core-Self inside of zazen-only, we viscerally realize that vast Oneness sustains the continuity, wholeness, and boundless intimacy of life and death within the timeless stillness of our everyday life. Our sciences are able to investigate how matter and energy lawfully function to uphold the dynamic integrity of life and the total reality of existence. However, our sciences have not been able to investigate the still essence of vast Oneness that upholds the unity of life and death and the total reality of nonexistence. Even so, the still composure of core-Self viscerally comprehends the timeless unity of existence and nonexistence at the depth of total reality. We call this, "Viscerally resolving the great matter of life and death far beyond scientific paradigms, religious beliefs, and atheistic perspectives."

Our core-Self viscerally realizes the continuity and wholeness of life and death by intimately penetrating the reality of death in this very life. This intimate visceral comprehension of death through core-Self is like intuitively sensing or feeling one of the four seasons before it really happens. I think we all have had this kind of experience. I have had it many times during my own lifetime. For example, you wake up one day in the middle of winter. You go outside, feel the morning sun on your face, and smell the crisp dawn air. Just then, you feel that you are viscerally experiencing all of spring right here and now. Your ego-self and thinking mind know that it is not spring. It is the middle of winter. However, right at that moment, in the middle of winter, your still visceral center intimately knows the total immediate presence of spring. You feel that you are being the totality of spring within the total reality of winter. Even so, you realize that spring is spring and winter is winter. It always amazes me to sense the totality of the next season right in the middle of the present season. So when I say that our core-Self intimately experiences the total reality of death in this very life, I am referring to this kind of visceral experience in this Only Moment Body of zazen-only.

When we are seated as core-Self inside of zazen-only, we viscerally comprehend the total reality of death within the total reality of life. However, we also come to intimately know that the season of life is just life and the season of death is just death. In life, there is nothing but the totality of life. In death, there is nothing but the totality of death. We intimately know that being alive is our place at this moment in linear time. Our life has a past, a present, and a future unfolding in the timeless stillness of total reality. Our death and dying are moments in linear time that also have a past, a present, and a future in the timeless stillness of total reality. In our Way, we face and actualize the reality of life moment by moment through the timeless stillness and felt composure of our visceral core-Self. As death continues to intimately arrive, we face and actualize the reality of death through the timeless stillness and felt composure of our visceral core-Self. This is our Way of freely living our life and openly dying our death within the timeless stillness of vast Oneness that is the essence of total reality. This is our Way of living and dying as core-Self in boundless intimacy with vast Oneness while sharing this Only Moment Body of ungraspable enlightenment with all beings and things.

As our core-Self comes to viscerally know the immediacy of death in the reality of life right here and now, it does not sense death as an abyss to fear. It senses that the reality and immediacy of death is like the curvature of a circle rather than a sharp and final edge on a flat plane. Just like we dropped-off dread and fear when we realized that our world was round and not flat, our body experiences deep ease and tranquility when core-Self viscerally comprehends the natural curvature, continuity, wholeness, and vast Oneness of life and death. This is how we live and die as core-Self in the timeless stillness and profound richness of total reality.

Establishing No Enemy

"Honoring the useful function of ego-self,
It creates no enemy to be vanquished."

It is core-Self that compassionately accepts and embraces the functioning of our ego-self. Even as core-Self compassionately embraces the early childhood development of ego-self and its healthy adult functioning in society, it silently illuminates the insubstantiality of ego-self, the virtual and illusory nature of its dualistic and limited way of thinking and knowing, and its urgent drivenness to protect and defend its personal, racial, cultural, political, and religious identity at any cost. This urgency of ego-self to reactively protect and defend its illusory identity at any cost is completely understandable when we realize that it is being driven by a deep fear of its nonexistence. We falsely assume that our real and substantial existence is based on the existence of our ego-self identity because we have been socially conditioned to only view ourselves and our human embodiment in that way. Most of us do not question how or why we exist as an ego-self within our own mind. We rarely ask why we identify with our thinking mind, our given name, our social roles, and our personal views and beliefs. We do not ask what is driving our constant mental chatter about who we are, what we believe in, what others think of us, what we think of ourselves, where we are going, and what we are doing moment by moment.

Below the level of conscious awareness, our ego-self assumes that as long as it thinks about itself, its personal views and beliefs, and the endless passage of its feelings and thoughts, it will continue to substantially exist and be alive as an embodied identity. This tightly held ego-self assumption was introspectively observed by the French philosopher Rene Descartes (1596-1650). Descartes brought to full awareness the unconscious assumption of his ego-self when he wrote the Latin phrase, "Cogito ergo sum," which means "I think, therefore I am." This sentence became the very foundation for acquiring our Western scientific knowledge of physical reality. The logic behind "cogito ergo sum" goes something like this: "I am an ego-self who is able to think; I am aware that thoughts are constantly arising in my thinking mind; as a thinking and knowing ego-self, I exist in my head separate from every being and thing out there; the logical thinking function of my ego-self is able to objectively know and manipulate physical reality; thus, I continue to realize and verify my ego-self existence by being aware of my endless mental chatter, by using my logical thinking mind, by constantly thinking about myself and who I am, and by using the language in my mind to talk to others about what I am thinking, how I am feeling, and what I am experiencing." This is clearly how many of us feel about existing as a substantial ego-self. However, we forget that our virtual ego-self identity is a cerebrally generated reality that we experience as a heady way of existing, thinking, knowing, and being.

In our Way, we do not view our ego-self as an enemy to be vanquished or annihilated. Our gradual mental development as a knowing and thinking ego-self helps to stabilize our embodied awareness in linear time, sharply defines the boundary of what is in here from what is out there, empowers us to safely and productively investigate the world of cause and effect, and provides us with a functional, responsible, and socially accountable way to relate to each other in everyday life. However, if we falsely assume that our illusory ego-self identity is the totality of who we are in this Only Moment Body, we get caught up in constantly upholding our own existence. When I say, "upholding our own existence," I mean that we become driven to constantly verify, defend, and protect our illusory ego-self identity while reinforcing our preoccupation with "I, me, and mine."

We become driven to uphold our own ego-self existence because we know at a very deep level that our ego-self cannot exist as a substantial reality like a rock, a boulder, or a mountain. Whether we think about a mountain or not does not make the mountain any more real or substantial than it already is. We are not in charge of upholding the mountain's substantial existence. We cannot say that the mountain substantially exists because we think about the mountain. The mountain exists as a substantial reality before we name it "mountain" or think about it as a "mountain." However, our ego-self does not substantially exist in the same way as rocks, mountains, or boulders. This is why Descartes's ego-self logically concluded, "Cogito ergo sum," I think, therefore I am. This is the only way that the ego-self can realize, uphold, and continuously verify its own illusory and virtual existence.

Having deeply accepted the logic behind "cogito ergo sum," we assume that if we stop our mental chatter and all our naming, comparing, judging, and thinking, we will not exist as a substantial ego-self identity in everyday life. Our bondage to "cogito ergo sum" is at the very root of our endless mental chatter, our deep attachment to personal views and beliefs, and all our drivenness to gain and sustain fortune, fame, and power. In the midst of all this mental, emotional, and behavioral urgency to uphold our illusory ego-self identity, we naturally experience the still illuminating power of core-Self as a threat to our very existence. This is why many of us exhibit physical, mental, and emotional resistances to embodying core-Self far beneath our separate ego-self identity and all our thinking about I, me, and mine.

Many of us expend a large portion of our life force in resisting intimacy with our core-Self while upholding, defending, and protecting our illusory ego-self identity. When we continuously expend our life force in resisting the silent illumination of our core-Self while defending, upholding, and protecting the heady existence of our ego-self identity, we diminish the vitality, wellness, and longevity of this Only Moment Body, the ever freshness of our everyday life and relationships, and the visceral richness of living in vast Oneness and boundless intimacy. To awaken to the driven ego-self expenditure of our vital life force is to realize the ultimate necessity of courageously going beyond our resistances to core-Self intimacy. When we freely and openly dwell in our visceral core-Self, we know beyond thinking that we do not have to uphold the existence of our ego-self. We realize that our developed ego-self function, our mental ability to think logically with words and ideas, and the silent illumination of our core-Self are all being equally and simultaneously upheld by the vast Oneness and boundless intimacy of total reality.

Being IT

"Ever beyond thinking and knowing,
It cannot be defined nor compared."

This "It," ever beyond our thinking and knowing, refers to our core-Self as core-Self is flashing as vast Oneness inside of zazen-only. This means that the still wholeness of our core-Self is the still essence of vast Oneness that pervades the surface and depth of total reality. To be core-Self as the still flashing of vast Oneness is to intimately "Be IT" without grasping, owning, or gaining. Being IT is viscerally confirming our boundless intimacy and interdependent equality with all beings and things far beneath the functioning of our ego-self and thinking mind. This means that core-Self is exactly the still flashing of vast Oneness even as vast Oneness is far beyond our core-Self in this Only Moment Body.

When we sit down in zazen-only and sink into the still center-point of our lower abdomen, we viscerally realize that IT (vast Oneness) is upholding the holistic functioning of our bodymind. To viscerally realize that vast Oneness is upholding the holistic functioning of our bodymind in each passing moment is to somatically verify that core-Self is exactly the felt functioning wholeness of our bodymind right here and now. On the other hand, when we viscerally clarify that vast Oneness is sustaining this bodymind in boundless intimacy and limitless interdependency with all beings and things, we somatically confirm that the vast Oneness of total reality is undefinable and incomparable. To viscerally realize that vast Oneness is beyond defining and comparing is to realize that being IT cannot be caught by the traps and cages of ego-self and thinking mind. Likewise, the vast Oneness of total reality cannot be mentally or emotionally understood simply by projecting human attributes onto IT's eternally still, ever flashing, and boundless nature. Although vast Oneness cannot be contained within any cultural, historical, or species-centric view of a supreme being, IT's still timelessness, IT's universal lawfulness, IT's holistic and interdependent functioning, and IT's eternal flashing as vast impermanence cannot be ignored if we want to fully comprehend the true nature of total reality.

As we are being vast Oneness through our core-Self in zazen-only, our boundless intimacy with all of IT is far beyond the "either-or" logic of ego-self and thinking mind. Our "either-or" logic seeks to mentally understand vast Oneness as either personal or impersonal, something or nothing, being or non-being, mind or no-mind, spirit or matter. However, when we dwell in the still discernment of our core-Self we viscerally realize that vast Oneness is both personal and impersonal, spiritual and material, finite and infinite, being and non-being, something and nothing, mind and no-mind, and a bright wisdoming that is far beyond our human understanding of knowledge, consciousness, intelligence, and awareness. This is how core-Self viscerally transmits the refuge of being IT while wholly accepting the finiteness of core-Self in this Only Moment Body.

When core-Self is viscerally being IT, we say that the deep refuge of vast Oneness is intimately felt as Nothing holy and everything sacred in our everyday life. This is the joyful Way of embodying the blessing of core-Self inside of zazen-only. "Za" is core-Self just sitting as core-Self inside this Only Moment Body while peacefully being IT. "Zen" is being core-Self in this Only Moment Body while viscerally enjoying our boundless intimacy and vast Oneness with all beings and things. Shikantaza is spreading the wings of "Za" and "Zen" while tenderly and conscientiously taking care of the activities, affairs, and relationships of our everyday life. Whether one is a beginner or a veteran practitioner of core-Self in shikantaza and zazen-only, each moment of "Za" and "Zen" is the unfolding of ungraspable enlightenment itself.

Far Beneath Naming

"Far beneath naming and figuring,"

What is far beneath the cerebral functioning of ego-self with its reactive labeling, naming, and figuring is the transpersonal empathy of our core-Self that viscerally meets all beings and things within the boundless intimacy of total reality. Our visceral Way of meeting and knowing beings and things from the transpersonal empathy of our core-Self is very different from the detached and objective thinking and knowing that we commonly use in everyday life. We extend transpersonal empathy from our body's center-point of gravity that entangles with the still interconnectedness of quantum depth reality. This transpersonal empathic Way of knowing does not separate the still composure of core-Self from the still quantum depth of any being, thing, or event that is intimately known and understood within the flashing Oneness and vast impermanence of total reality.

On the other hand, our ego-self's way of knowing is based on the linguistic mental processing of any being or thing that is named, thought about, and figured out within the passage of linear time. Our ego-self is automatically driven to objectify, name, and figure out all beings, things, and activities that arise in our everyday life. This kind of automaticity and drivenness is called bondage to upholding our ego-self existence. It is bondage because our naming and figuring are not freely and openly chosen. Our constant naming and figuring are more like habitual mental reactions propelled by the two most basic fears of ego-self, the fear of nonexistence and the fear of not-knowing.

On the surface, it may seem that we freely choose to name and figure out all beings and things as they arise; but when we witness these mental processes closely, we see that they are based on the drivenness of our ego-self and the automaticity of our thinking mind. Our endless ego-self drivenness to objectify, name, judge, and figure out beings, things, and events in our everyday life deeply influences the way we view them, how we begin to reactively feel and think about them, and how we automatically grasp or push away their existence when facing them.

It is through our cerebral bondage to naming, judging, comparing, and figuring that we try to discern and comprehend the experiences, challenges, and relationships of everyday life. When we see, know, and meet all beings and things only through the cerebral functioning of our ego-self, our experience of reality is clouded by the drivenness of our naming and figuring, the reactive prejudices and judgments that distort our knowing, our need to protect our rationalizations and denials at any cost, and our constant grasping and pushing away. All this ego-self drivenness, distortion, delusion, and reactivity diminishes the vital potency of our sensory awareness, narrows the field of our immediate perception, keeps us in bondage to mental, emotional, and behavioral defensiveness, obstructs the completion and fulfillment of our radical humanness, hinders the recovery of our beginner's heartmind, and keeps us from viscerally realizing our birthright of boundless intimacy and ungraspable enlightenment in everyday life. On the other hand, when we embody the still discernment and lucid composure of our core-Self, we naturally soften our mental drivenness, clarify our delusory thinking, liberate ourselves from perceptual distortions, ease our attachment to emotional prejudices, and effortlessly molt off our reactiveness and defensiveness. When we do just this, we abide peacefully in the body of ease and joy, somatically listen and behaviorally yield to the vast Oneness of total reality, and practice loving and being loved with the fearlessness and exuberance of beginner's heartmind.

Not Grasping Or Pushing Away

"Its discerning stillness apprehends without grasping or pushing away."

The automatic and driven ego-self functions of naming, judging, comparing, and figuring are not the only cerebral functions that obstruct the visceral realization of core-Self in this Only Moment Body. Our ego-self is also enmeshed in another form of mental automaticity and emotional drivenness called "grasping and pushing away." As we go about our daily life, we are constantly driven to grasp at all that feels gratifying, enjoyable, and pleasurable while pushing away all that feels ungratifying, unenjoyable, and unpleasurable. This egoself-centric grasping and pushing away keeps us from somatically verifying the still discernment of our core-Self that completely accepts and unconditionally lives each moment of total reality. When we live from our egoself-centricity, we cope with unpleasant experiences by ignoring them, distancing ourselves from them, or by attaching to pleasant distractions that keep us from facing and living the unconditional embodiment of each moment. At the same time that our egoself-centricity tries to keep unpleasant experiences and activities from consciously being embodied within the passage of linear time, it engages in thoughts, feelings, and behaviors that perpetuate its own bondage to desiring, grasping, and clinging to ever more exciting and distracting experiences.

When you find that your inner mental chatter is filled with seemingly rational thoughts and ideas that justify your deep attachment to pride and anger, that uphold all your resistances to extend love and openly receive love, that continue to excuse your avoidance of interpersonal authenticity and intimacy, or that encourage your distraction and escape from doing what needs to be wholeheartedly done, this is usually a red flag that your ego-self is embodying dishonesty while being in bondage to grasping and pushing away. The rationalizations that we tightly cling to obstruct our embodiment of truth, deprive us of clarity and honesty in our thinking, inhibit the awareness of our boundless intimacy, impede the fullest extension of our visceral empathy, hinder our daily practice of tenderness and unconditional care, and diminish our felt interconnectedness with the quantum depth of total reality.

When we confirm and reinforce the embodiment of our egoself-centricity by reactively pushing away and resisting what we don't like while reactively clinging, craving, and grasping at what we like, we are embodying an ultimately false, unsatisfactory, and dishonorable way of being alive. Many people think that this constant grasping and pushing away is natural to our human nature that seeks comfort, pleasure, and happiness while avoiding discomfort, pain, and suffering. This is sometimes called the pleasure principle of human nature. The pleasure principle states that all human beings naturally seek out pleasure and avoid suffering in the process of living their everyday lives.   Our egoself-centricity sometimes uses the pleasure principle as a way to rationalize the validity of its constant grasping, coveting, craving, and pushing away. Our ego-self's rationalization of the pleasure principle is a delusion that ignores our deep bondage to desires, our growing dissatisfaction with the endless round of gratification, and our ever deepening experience of lack and incompleteness. The price we pay when we begin to accept our ego-self's rationalization of the pleasure principle is a gradual erosion of our confidence to honestly and courageously face total reality as a radical human being who fully embodies core-Self in boundless intimacy and cherished accountability to vast Oneness in the ordinariness of everyday life.

Over time, our bondage to grasping and pushing away tends to detrimentally impact our physical health and the felt quality of our wellness in everyday life. To help you understand this through your body, I would like you to extend your left arm horizontally right in front of you. Now make a closed grasping fist, as if you were holding on to something. Next extend your right arm horizontally and open your palm with fingers upward, as if you were pushing something away. Now exert some muscular tension into your grasping hand while simultaneously exerting muscular tension into the hand that is pushing away. Once you put this muscular tension in both hands, hold that tension for about thirty-seconds. Become aware of the subtle physical, mental, and emotional tension that is gradually arising throughout your body. This increasing tension that you are experiencing is caused by the muscular, mental, energetic, and emotional posture of grasping and pushing away. This is a tangible example of how our constant ego-self grasping and pushing away tends to generate a subtle form of physical, mental, and emotional tension in our everyday life. Over time, this subtle tension builds-up into the more tangible experience of "dysfunctional stress." Once the tension of grasping and pushing away reaches the threshold of dysfunctional stress, we begin to experience a mental, emotional, and physical agitation that diminishes our felt bodily ease, our physical vitality, our mental clarity, and our sense of emotional balance and wellness. Whether we acknowledge it or not, our endless grasping and pushing away will eventually degrade our health, the quality of our lives, and the authenticity, caring, tenderness, and integrity of our human relationships.

Our Way is to live through our core-Self that opens the hand of grasping and softens the hand of pushing away. I would like to have you physically experience our Way by asking you to extend your arms out again. Hold the hands with tension in the form of grasping and pushing away. Do this for twenty-seconds. Then immediately relax both hands, open them completely with palms upward, and hold your arms as if you were going to tenderly and caringly embrace someone right in front of you. Notice how the tension in your body subsides and melts away. Notice how you begin to feel a growing sense of ease, openness, and wellness. This is how we practice embodying core-Self while embracing the passage of our everyday life. In our Way, we soften both hands, relax our arms, and freely, openly, and courageously embrace total reality, just as we are, just as IT is.

A Muddy Stream Is Undefiled

*"Whether rippled or turbulent, the muddy
stream remains lucidly clear and undefiled."*

When I speak of "muddy waters," I am referring to the way we usually experience heart and mind from the perspective of our ego-self during its reactive and driven life of grasping, naming, figuring, and pushing away. The dualistic thinking function of our ego-self labels and separates our experience of heart from our experience of mind. This helps our ego-self to logically and knowingly differentiate the currents of our feeling life from the endless passage of thoughts at the surface of our embodied reality. Our dualistic ego-self way of knowing heart from mind helps us to mentally distinguish between the arising of thoughts that we locate in our head from the arising of feelings that we locate in our heart. However, this dualistic ego-self discernment of heart and mind is also the basis for the tension and struggle that we sometimes experience between our thinking and our feeling. We have all experienced a time where we tried to choose between meaningful feelings arising in our heart and logical thoughts arising in our head. At those times we may say to ourselves, "Do I listen to my heart or do I listen to my logical thinking mind." When we state this to ourselves, we are trying to see clearly through the muddy waters of our everyday life. Muddy waters exist because our ego-self is constantly naming, judging, and trying to figure out our felt experiences while simultaneously grasping, dramatizing, suppressing, or pushing away feelings according to its biased, defensive, driven, and reactive way of upholding an illusory and insubstantial identity.

Our ego-self's experience of heart and mind at the surface of embodied reality is not the completely clear and unified heartmind that we experienced when we were younger. We embodied our "original heartmind" before we knew our name or learned to talk and think with words and language. When we viscerally embody core-Self inside of zazen-only, we recover the pristine clarity and innocent freshness of our original heartmind. The unified nature and pristine clarity of our original heartmind is viscerally realized and somatically verified when we faithfully embody our core-Self in boundless intimacy with the vast Oneness of total reality.

As we embody core-Self just sitting as core-Self inside of zazen-only, we enjoy the arising freshness, wondrous openness, and pristine clarity of our original heartmind. In our Way, we say that the openness, oneness, clarity, and ever freshness of our original heartmind is the bright wisdoming of our core-Self. When we recover our originally unified heartmind as core-Self in zazen-only, we are really recovering the originally enlightened heartmind that is the birthright of all radical human beings. We call this originally enlightened heartmind, "beginner's heartmind." Our beginner's heartmind sees clearly through the murkiness of muddy waters because it intimately knows the tranquility of heart not-wanting and the brilliance of mind not-knowing. We naturally experience the original wholeness, exuberant freshness, and wondrous curiosity of our beginner's heartmind when we are intimately anchored in the unfabricated stillness and silent illumination of our core-Self beneath grasping, naming, figuring, and pushing away.

Our ego-self's view of heart and mind at the surface of embodied reality is based on a dualistic way of knowing that separates us from the original unfabricated oneness of our beginner's heartmind. It is important to remember that the wondrous openness, pristine clarity, and unfabricated wholeness of our beginner's heartmind are all firmly grounded in the vast Oneness and boundless intimacy of our core-Self. When we experience the duality of heart and mind through our ego-self at the surface of embodied reality, we become aware that our heart is constantly being stirred by ripples of passing feelings while our mind is constantly agitated by endless waves of thought. We notice that these ripples and waves come and go as our ego-self engages with the activities and affairs of everyday life. We all know from daily experience that our heart and mind are rarely calm and serene like a mountain lake that has no waves or ripples on the surface.

When we live only through our embodied ego-self at the surface of everyday life, we take the constant ripples of feelings and the endless waves of thought as the ultimate verification that we exist as a substantial ego-self. We cling to arising feelings within our hearts and attach to passing thoughts within our mind to further validate and uphold our virtual existence as an individual personality and a functioning ego-self. This means that our identification with passing thoughts and our clinging to passing feelings is deeply rooted in our habitual drivenness to exist as an ego-self with a unique and familiar way of thinking and feeling.

As you begin to practice just sitting as core-Self inside of zazen-only, you will illuminate just how much your heart and mind are constantly being stirred and muddied by your ego-self's way of grasping, naming, figuring, and pushing away. When you begin to consciously realize that the muddy waters of your heart and mind are always being stirred by your driven ego-self functioning at the surface of embodied reality, you may begin to feel disheartened and overwhelmed. You may think that you will never be able to experience the clear and unfathomable nature of your beginner's heartmind. You may begin to think that it is impossible to still the endless waves of thoughts, or calm the ever arising ripples and currents of feelings. You may even begin to think that you do not have enough sincerity or determination to intimately recover the original wholeness, wondrous clarity, and vital freshness of your beginner's heartmind. If you become disheartened and overwhelmed in this way, remember that right in the midst of muddy waters your originally enlightened heartmind remains unconditionally clear and entirely accessible right where you are. Remember that beginner's heartmind can be instantly realized and completely verified when you courageously sink into the felt sensuality, innocent presencing, and still composure of your core-Self that silently illuminates your humility, your sincerity, your completion, and your simplicity in zazen-only.

The Waterless Ocean

"A whale swims with ease in a waterless ocean."

The whale symbolizes core-Self swimming in the waterless ocean of vast Oneness and boundless intimacy with all beings and things. A whale can swim endlessly throughout the vastness of the ocean. The surface and depth of the great ocean embrace the whole body of the whale wherever it swims; and the whale is never abandoned by the vast ocean. Whether the whale surfaces to float on top of undulating waves or dives deep into an unfathomable stillness, it is always upheld and embraced by the great ocean. Wherever the whale is in the ocean, it will never fail to be intimate with the true nature of the whole ocean. The whale is unconditionally supported by the totality of the vast ocean to manifest the integrity, power, vitality, and buoyancy of its life force. Just like a whale is always at home at the surface and depth of the great ocean, so too our core-Self is completely at ease and fully at home at the surface and depth of total reality.

When we just sit down as core-Self inside of zazen-only, we cannot help but be the still essence and timeless depth of vast Oneness. We will never fail to realize the unfolding of ungraspable enlightenment as long as we continue to dwell in the still discernment of our core-Self beyond all thought of I, me, and mine. We will never fail to verify our life of boundless intimacy as long as we continue to practice deep caring and tenderness for all the beings and things that support our everyday life.

A Hawk Nested In Flight

"Gliding across the vast Oneness of a blue sky,
the hawk remains completely nested in its flight"

The hawk symbolizes the silent illumination, sharp insight, and still discernment of your core-Self. A hawk can soar freely and glide endlessly across the vast emptiness of a blue sky. Just like the whale is never abandoned by the ocean, the hawk is never abandoned by the blue sky. The blue sky never stops embracing the hawk wherever it flies.   As the hawk soars and glides across the vast sky of ungraspable enlightenment, it will never fail to be intimate with the whole sky that is everywhere right here and now. The hawk is constantly being supported and embraced by the totality of the vast blue sky just like the whale is constantly being supported by the totality of the great ocean. When you just sit as core-Self inside this Only Moment Body of zazen-only, you are the hawk that remains fully nested in the vital freshness of its flight. When I speak of the "vital freshness" of the hawks flight, I am referring to the vital freshness of your beginner's heartmind. As you openly dwell in your core-Self and freely express the magnanimous openness, exuberant spontaneity, and vital freshness of your beginner's heartmind, you will come to viscerally know that the true hawk of everyday life soars in the limitless sky of boundless intimacy while remaining tenderly nested in the vast Oneness of its flight.

Final Encouragement

To study the great matter of life and death is to courageously sink into the still vibrancy of your core-Self while molting off your ego-self identity far beyond fear. To molt off your ego-self identity is to recover the vital freshness, pristine clarity, and exuberant openness of your beginner's heartmind. When you recover the original unity of your beginner's heartmind and viscerally confirm the vast Oneness of total reality, you will somatically resolve the great matter of life and death, appreciate your boundless intimacy in each passing moment, and unfold ungraspable enlightenment with all beings and things far beyond doubt.

After you have viscerally settled the great matter of life and death, somatically touched the waterless ocean of boundless intimacy, and gratefully embodied the wings of ungraspable enlightenment itself, you will never be confused or turned around by the erroneous views, beliefs, and opinions of others. As you remain open, accessible, and inwardly illuminating, continue to blend with vast Oneness and respond to all beings and things with humility, clarity, wisdom, compassion, and deep caring.

Remaining ever simple, real, open, and genuine in all your relationships, continue to embody core-Self that silently illuminates the very foundation of your radical humanness and your boundless intimacy with all beings and things. Entrusting your journey through life and death to the vast Oneness of total reality, enjoy the still composure, tranquility, and wakefulness of your core-Self while openly expressing the vital exuberance and playful spontaneity of your beginner's heartmind.

When your beginner's heartmind is liberated and the boundless intimacy of your core-Self is fully realized with not one thing lacking, a precious lotus will bloom in the fertile valley and a vigorous dragon will emerge from the depths of the still mountain. Only then will you viscerally know the power of lucid dreaming, creatively actualize dreams in everyday life, and joyfully blend those dreams with the vast Oneness of being dreamed in ungraspable enlightenment with all beings and things.

Thank you.

"Silent and serene,
forgetting words, bright clarity
appears before you. When you reflect it,
you become vast; where you embody it, your
spirit is uplifted. Spiritually solitary and shining,
silent illumination restores wonder. Dew in the
moonlight, a river of stars, snow-covered pines,
clouds enveloping the peaks. When wonder
exists in serenity, all achievement is forgotten
in [still] illumination....What is this wonder?
Alertly seeing through confusion is
the Way of silent illumination
and the origin of subtle
radiance."

Chinese Zen Master Hongzhi
(1091 AD–1157 AD)

"The ancient sages were subtle, mysterious, and
profound. Their wisdom eluded men's knowledge.
As they eluded men's knowledge, I can only describe
their appearance. They were aware and cautious like
men crossing a frozen stream in winter; alert and
watchful like a warrior facing death on all sides;
polite and courteous like a guest; ever yielding
to reality like a melting cube of ice; genuine,
simple, and sincere like an uncarved block
of wood; openhearted and receptive like a
wide valley; and clear like muddy
waters allowed to settle."

Tao Te Ching
(Verse 15)

"Sages have
no [ego-]self, but there
is nothing that is not their Self.
This is the path of Illumination."

I Ching
Chih-hsu Ou-i

CHAPTER 6

Sitting Inside Of Living

Wandering –
Not Knowing
Where we Go,
Yet Never Leaving
our True Home.

"When you are able to practice shikantaza—when you experience shikantaza, and when you understand shikantaza, the meaning of your everyday life will [be] completely different."

"By shikantaza you will not gain anything, but you will be you your Self. So by shikantaza you will settle your Self on your Self."

Shunryu Suzuki-roshi
(Lecture: August 15, 1966)

Silent Illumination

Our Way of just sitting as core-Self inside of zazen-only is the authentic Buddha seal of "silent illumination." The Buddha seal of "silent Illumination" was first articulated by the great Chinese Zen Master Hongzhi (1091 AD–1157 AD). Hongzhi was the tenth Chinese patriarch in the Cáo-dòng lineage. The original founder of the Cáo-dòng school was Zen Master Dongshan (807 AD–869 AD). The Cáo-dòng school of Zen was transmitted in China for almost four hundred years. In China the Way of Zen is called "Chan" while zazen-only is called "zuo-chan." The Cáo-dòng school is also known as *Mo Zhao Chan* which means the *Zen School of Silent Illumination.* Master Hongzhi emphasized that the still brilliance of silent illumination is wholly embodied inside of zazen-only.

In the year 1224, the young Japanese monk, Eihei Dogen, traveled to China to find an authentic Zen teacher who fully embodied the Way of ungraspable enlightenment. After three years in China, Dogen stopped at Tiantong Temple where he met Zen Master Rujing (1163-1228). Master Rujing was the thirteenth Chinese patriarch in the Cáo-dòng lineage. He taught at the same Zen Temple where Hongzhi had been Abbot before him. Master Rujing openly transmitted the Way of just sitting in zazen-only while silently illuminating total reality. Rujing taught that sitting in zazen-only was the most intimate Way of realizing, embodying, and verifying ungraspable enlightenment in everyday life.

Under the guidance of Zen Master Rujing, Dogen diligently practiced "just sitting in silent illumination." One day while sitting in zazen-only, Dogen heard Rujing scold a fellow monk who was dozing while sitting. Rujing said firmly. "What do you expect to accomplish by dozing? Zazen-only is the dropping-off of body and mind." Just then, Dogen realized the vast Oneness and boundless intimacy of total reality. Afterwards, Dogen went up to Master Rujing's room and burned incense at the Abbot's altar. Watching him, Master Rujing said, "Why are you burning incense?" Dogen said, "Body and mind have been dropped-off." It was then that Rujing immediately approved Dogen's enlightened realization within the ancient Cáo-dòng Zen lineage.

Dogen's statement to Master Rujing, "Body and mind have been dropped-off," does not refer to a disembodied state of transcendent consciousness. Rather, it is exactly the molting off of an ego-self that sharply distinguishes and separates body from mind, thinking from feeling. It is the dropping-off of a driven ego-self that constantly seeks to own the physical body, the thinking mind, and all the ongoing mental and emotional processes that perpetuate its seemingly substantial existence. In the Buddha seal of silent illumination, we clearly verify that mind and body are not a duality and that the total dynamic functioning of bodymind cannot be owned by the ego-self. When we molt off our ego-self with its dualistic view of body and mind, we viscerally realize that our core-Self is in boundless intimacy with the vast Oneness of total reality. Just like this, Dogen embodied the completion of his radical humanness, instantly ceased his naming, owning, and figuring, dropped-off his dualistic view of body and mind, and confidently spoke from the visceral integrity of his core-Self. It was Dogen's core-Self that was sealed and verified by Master Rujing as boundless intimacy and ungraspable enlightenment itself.

The Way Of Shikantaza

In the year 1227, Dogen Zenji returned to Japan and founded our Soto Zen lineage that is the visceral transmission and true embodiment of the Cáo-dòng Zen lineage. Dogen passionately embodied, taught, and transmitted zazen-only as the authentic

Buddha seal of silent illumination. When Dogen started teaching the ancient Way of silent illumination, he referred to it as "shikantaza." "Shikan" means "only or nothing but," "Ta" means hitting the mark, "Za" is just sitting. So shikantaza is "Nothing but hitting the mark of just sitting." This "hitting the mark of just sitting" is really "hitting the mark of core-Self inside of just sitting." Dogen gave us the term "shikantaza" so that we may understand that zazen-only is viscerally hitting the mark of core-Self inside of just sitting. Shikantaza is core-Self just sitting as core-Self in this Only Moment Body of zazen-only. Our hitting the mark of core-Self inside of just sitting is the Way of silently illuminating our boundless intimacy and vast Oneness with all beings and things.

By using the term, "Shikantaza," Dogen reveals the profound significance of sealing the mark of core-Self inside of zazen-only. To live the Way of shikantaza is to be the sealed mark of core-Self with not one thing lacking. We somatically come to know the true meaning of shikantaza when we viscerally embody the mark of core-Self while living everyday life in boundless intimacy with all beings and things. Shikantaza is not a means to gain or attain an idealized enlightenment beyond our shared and normal experience of being human. Shikantaza is the still brilliance of core-Self that silently illuminates ungraspable enlightenment as the simplicity and ordinariness of our everyday life embodiment. This is true whether we are hitting the visceral mark of core-Self inside of zazen-only or hitting the visceral mark of core-Self while conscientiously taking care of our day-to-day responsibilities.

Shikantaza, as transmitted to us by Hongzhi, Rujing, and Dogen Zenji, is exactly core-Self settled as core-Self inside this Only Moment Body. Shikantaza is daily living as core-Self far beyond the traps and cages of ego-self and thinking mind. Do not confuse shikantaza with the physical stillness and silence of zazen-only. In the moment that we embody shikantaza by just sitting in zazen-only, core-Self dwells in the unborn stillness and birthless silence of core-Self that is far beyond the fabricated silence and stillness of zazen-only. This means that in the body of shikantaza that we call zazen-only, the still and silent embodiment of core-Self can never be achieved through any mental discipline or willful exertion to remain perfectly still and quiet in zazen-only. This is a very important point to understand.

As the still paradox of core-Self can never be created by any physical or mental effort to sit perfectly still in the body of zazen-only, all of shikantaza is the visceral realization that core-Self is freely and continuously transmitting core-Self whether we are physically active, speaking with others, or simply not moving. This is why our practice of shikantaza is not limited to hitting the mark of core-Self while just sitting in zazen-only. Shikantaza is also hitting the visceral mark of core-Self while just living, just walking, just talking, just playing, just loving, or just doing. When we practice shikantaza in our everyday life, we take refuge in the unborn stillness and birthless silence of our core-Self, openly extend compassion and transpersonal empathy to all beings and things, freely express the tender caring and exuberance of our beginner's heartmind, and passionately unfold our life of boundless intimacy and vast Oneness for its own sake.

The Fundamental Point

When we embody core-Self inside of zazen-only, we viscerally seal the Way of shikantaza. To viscerally seal the Way of shikantaza is to effortlessly hit the mark of boundless intimacy and ungraspable enlightenment itself. Our Way of hitting the core-Self mark of boundless intimacy and ungraspable enlightenment is far beyond gaining, possessing, attaining, or grasping. As we seal the Way of shikantaza in zazen-only, we take no-action to still our thoughts; we arouse no mindfulness of the moment; we do not concentrate on objects or mental images; we do not sit absolutely still through increasing pain; we do not count our breaths; we do not label our passing feelings and sensations; and we do not practice for worldly success or monetary gain. This is the Way we embody the fundamental point of zazen-only and seal the Way of shikantaza for its own sake.

Today, people practice many styles of meditation for a variety of reasons. They use techniques like guided visualization, mindful introspection, withdrawal of the senses, contemplative thinking, simply noting what arises in consciousness, focusing on the heart, minding each moment, listening to meditative music, or concentrating on a sound, a phrase, a word, or a symbol. However, all these techniques, and various others that are commonly practiced today, are not the authentic Buddha seal of silent illumination. When I say that all other forms of meditation are not the authentic Buddha seal of silent illumination, I do not mean that they are not valid or do not have a place in the enhancement of longevity and personal growth, in the promotion of interpersonal and spiritual development, in the facilitation of peak sports performance, and in the improvement of team synergy and creativity in business. However, they do not actualize the fundamental point of Dogen Zenji who taught us to daily embody the lamp of core-Self inside of zazen-only, to always value and cherish our beginner's heartmind, and to seal the Way of shikantaza for its own sake. Dogen taught us just like this to honor Shakyamuni Buddha who sealed vast Oneness inside zazen-only, who silently illuminated boundless intimacy for its own sake, who freely and openly transmitted the fulfillment of our radical humanness, who resolved the great matter of life and death for all sentient beings, and who embodied the still brilliance of total reality far beneath the functioning of I, me, and mine.

Actualizing the fundamental point of core-Self inside of zazen-only while viscerally sealing the Way of shikantaza is a natural, pristine, and unfabricated state of human embodiment. When I say that actualizing the fundamental point of zazen-only and sealing the Way of shikantaza are both a natural and unfabricated state of human embodiment, I mean there is nothing contrived, pretentious, or supernatural about either one. Although there is nothing supernatural about sealing the Way of shikantaza and embodying the Way of shikantaza in everyday life, all of shikantaza is a wondrous, extraordinary, and profound Way of living, loving, and being. Shikantaza is to faithfully embody the still paradox of core-Self while confidently and conscientiously taking care of our daily affairs, activities, and relationships. Shikantaza is core-Self empathically entangling with all beings, things, and events while silently illuminating vast Oneness and limitless interdependency far beneath figuring, comparing, judging, and thinking. This is how we continuously revitalize the wonder of our beginner's heartmind and the boundless intimacy of our core-Self as we practice the natural and unfabricated Way of shikantaza.

The True Buddha Seal

As shikantaza and zazen-only are exactly the Buddha seal of silent illumination, there is not a hairs gap between just sitting as core-Self inside of just sitting and just sitting as core-Self inside of just living. The eye and treasury of the true Buddha seal is exactly core-Self silently illuminating total reality while completely resolving the great matter of life and death far beneath the functioning of ego-self and thinking mind. Our Way of shikantaza and zazen-only is awakening from our dream in ego-self, visceral realization of core-Self and the power of lucid dreaming, endless refreshment of beginner's heartmind, and somatic verification that we are peacefully dwelling in the wholeness and completeness of our radical humanness with not one thing lacking.

We somatically verify shikantaza as the true Buddha seal by living our everyday life from the still and silent illumination of our core-Self. This means that the authentic Buddha seal of shikantaza is continuously embodied through the still vibrancy of our core-Self one breath and heartbeat at a time. This one breath and heartbeat at a time means not counting even one. It is just being core-Self with uncompromising simplicity in this Only Moment Body of total reality. Shikantaza is core-Self enjoying the visceral embodiment of core-Self, core-Self practicing the Way of loving and being loved with beginner's heartmind, and core-Self extending compassion and deep caring to all beings and things. When we embody core-Self in shikantaza just like this, we do not embody an altered state of consciousness; we do not transcend the practical matters and affairs of our everyday life; and we do not detach from our human feelings and emotions.

Our Way of zazen-only is core-Self awakening to boundless intimacy and the power of lucid dreaming. Our Way of shikantaza is core-Self actualizing the dreams of everyday life while blending those dreams with the vast Oneness of being dreamed with all beings and things. This is the shikantaza and zazen-only of the historical Buddha who faithfully embodied the still discernment of core-Self far beneath the sound, the fury, and the frenzy of everyday life. Just like the historical Buddha, we take refuge in shikantaza and zazen-only. This means that we take refuge in just sitting as core-Self inside of just sitting and just sitting as core-Self inside of just living. In our Way, we embody the Buddha seal of silent illumination to freely transmit the visceral integrity of core-Self, to openly share the basic goodness and innocence of beginner's heartmind, and to exemplify the fulfillment and completion of a radical human being who actualizes a shared future of boundless intimacy and ungraspable enlightenment right here and now.

Ungraspable Enlightenment

Whether we are actualizing the fundamental point of core-Self inside of zazen-only or actively living through the still discernment of our core-Self in shikantaza, we are embodying the authentic Buddha seal that unfolds our everyday life as the Way of ungraspable enlightenment itself. When I speak of "ungraspable enlightenment," I am referring to the Way that we experience the still and silent illumination of our core-Self, the Way we spontaneously love and joyfully receive love as radical human beings, the Way we playfully express the clarity and exuberance of our beginner's heartmind, the Way we embody our limitless interdependency with all beings and things, and the Way we blend our daily goals, activities, and affairs with the vast Oneness and boundless intimacy of total reality.

When I say that enlightenment is "ungraspable," I mean that our ego-self and thinking mind cannot mentally grasp or comprehend the Way that our core-Self enjoys boundless intimacy and flashes with the still Oneness of total reality. As our core-Self enjoys boundless intimacy and flashes with the still Oneness of total reality, we somatically verify that ungraspable enlightenment is the vibrant simplicity, vast impermanence, and ordinary brilliance of our everyday life. Our Way is to daily unfold our life of ungraspable enlightenment with all beings and things without grasping, owning, or attaining.

When we live as core-Self in the Way of shikantaza, we embody ungraspable enlightenment with the openness, freshness, and humility of our beginner's heartmind. To viscerally live as core-Self in the body of shikantaza is to tenderly and lucidly take care of our everyday life while in boundless intimacy with the still flashing of total reality. This Way of living ungraspable enlightenment while in boundless intimacy with the still flashing of total reality leaves no-trace of enlightenment itself. As no trace of enlightenment remains that can be owned or grasped, the traceless and ungraspable nature of enlightenment continues to unfold beyond the traps and cages of ego-self and thinking mind.

We viscerally realize and somatically verify core-Self living in ungraspable enlightenment when we throw our whole life force into being shikantaza and nothing else. To simply be shikantaza and nothing else is to viscerally embody our core-Self, to continuously align our postural ease and physical balance, to deeply appreciate our respiration and oxygenation, to delight in the pristine freshness of our beginner's heartmind, to compassionately sustain our chemical, mental, and emotional balance, to wholeheartedly engage in behavioral wisdom, and to openly practice our boundless intimacy with all beings and things. When we throw our whole life force into being shikantaza just like this, we continuously arrive in our radical humanness, actualize the fundamental point of the Buddha seal, and unfold this precious life of ungraspable enlightenment right here and now.

As our Way of embodying the boundless intimacy of core-Self with the basic goodness of our beginner's heartmind is exactly the total completion of our radical humanness and our sealed birthright of ungraspable enlightenment itself, we have no need for any contrived standards or fabricated techniques that perpetuate a righteous moral superiority, that advance stages of spiritual purification, that promote the historical Buddha as a deity, or that idealize an illusory and supernatural enlightenment. Our Way is to wholeheartedly embody the fundamental point of zazen-only, seal the Way of shikantaza for its own sake, and somatically enjoy our vast Oneness and boundless intimacy with total reality. We continuously seal the Way of ungraspable enlightenment by faithfully resting in our core-Self, by honoring our boundless intimacy with vast Oneness, by treasuring the wonder and humility of our beginner's heartmind, by deeply caring for all beings and things like our brothers and sisters, by living a true life of loving and being loved, and by delighting in the ordinary and surprising paradise of everyday life that has never abandoned us.

A Method of No-Method

When we sit down as core-Self in the body of zazen-only, we are training in the body of shikantaza itself. This means that we viscerally establish the somatic template for shikantaza in our daily practice of zazen-only. As embodying core-Self inside of just sitting and embodying core-Self inside of just living are both the original and pristine Way of being completely alive and totally fulfilled as a radical human being, shikantaza and zazen-only are not fabricated methods or techniques of meditation that can be willfully used to acquire or gain something that we lack. This is why we call shikantaza and zazen-only the Way of no-meditation.

When I say that shikantaza and zazen-only are the pristine Way of no-meditation, I mean that they are not something exclusive from everything else that we do, or something that we do that is separate from who we are. Both shikantaza and zazen-only are the total embodiment of who we really are in everything that we do with no exception. We embody zazen-only as the Way of just sitting as core-Self that is originally who we are. We embody shikantaza as the Way of just living as core-Self that is exactly who we are with not one thing lacking. When we practice the Way of zazen-only and live the Way of shikantaza, we are not doing a method or technique of meditation. Rather, we are viscerally and somatically expressing our full aliveness as a radical human being who embodies core-Self at the surface and depth of total reality.

Our daily practice of embodying core-Self is the Way of no-meditation because it is the organic and wholesome expression of being viscerally alert, somatically relaxed, empathically open, and sensually grounded in our hara or lower abdomen. When I say that shikantaza and zazen-only are not a fabricated Way of being fully and completely alive, I mean that they are not an altered or contrived Way of experiencing our daily embodiment. Shikantaza and zazen-only are the natural Way of embodying the visceral integrity of our core-Self while enjoying the pristine freshness, spontaneous playfulness, and surprising brilliance of our beginner's heartmind.

Whether we are seated in zazen-only or living our everyday life in shikantaza, we embody our core-Self without pushing, grasping, or forcing. We do this by tenderly practicing somatic intimacy with our abdominal breathing, somatic intimacy with the warmth and sensuality of our hara, and somatic intimacy with the visceral center-point of gravity in our lower abdomen. When we do just this, we continuously experience the still integrity of core-Self arising in this Only Moment Body. Our Way is to faithfully yield to the organic nature of vibrant sensuality, visceral stillness, and vital aliveness that magnetically draw us to embody core-Self while practicing shikantaza and zazen-only. Remember that our Way is not a method to attain enlightenment or to achieve an altered, detached, or transcendental state of consciousness. Rather, it is the natural Way of being vitally alert, passionately alive, and completely fulfilled as a radical human being who lives in boundless intimacy with the vast Oneness of total reality.

Our mirrored Way of shikantaza and zazen-only is fundamentally an unfabricated method of no-method. When I say that shikantaza and zazen-only are the daily practice of an organic method of no-method, I mean that they are both beyond all methods of meditation that focus on disciplining the mind, subjugating the body, exercising concentration, stilling passing thoughts and thinking, minding the present moment, gathering wisdom, attaining a future enlightenment, or attracting worldly fame, success, and wealth. Our mirrored Way of just sitting as core-Self in zazen-only and just living as core-Self in shikantaza are not a means to any of these ends. We just seal the fundamental pinpoint of zazen-only for its own sake and gratefully embody shikantaza with no thought of training, disciplining, gaining, minding, or attaining. When we let go of all views that regard meditation as a means to get what we want or desire, we liberate ourselves to authentically live the completion and total fulfillment of our radical humanness in shikantaza and zazen-only.

Do Not Miss The Mark

When we sit in zazen-only and live our everyday life in shikantaza, we experience the non-thinking intelligence of our core-Self as a discerning stillness and a silent illumination that precedes the evolutionary development of our ego-self and thinking mind. As the non-thinking intelligence of core-Self precedes the evolutionary development of ego-self and thinking mind, we call it the pristine or original Way that all radical human beings can fully engage their still brilliance to silently illuminate the surface and depth of everyday life. Our Way is to have deep confidence in the discerning stillness and silent illumination of our core-Self that is fully and unconditionally functioning within this Only Moment Body from birth to death. This means that we do not have to intensify our mental concentration, cerebrally arouse mindfulness in each moment, exercise the power of our will to subjugate our body, or perform any rigid ascetic disciplines to somatically experience the still discernment and silent illumination of our core-Self that is the radical birthright of all human beings without exception.

Our core-Self viscerally settled as core-Self in this Only Moment Body is all of brilliant stillness, discerning silence, basic goodness, boundless intimacy, vast Oneness, and ungraspable enlightenment itself. This means that all these precious qualities represent the radical root nature of core-Self that can never be gained, grasped, owned, or attained. Any spiritual or religious methods that are directed toward the attainment of these inherent qualities of core-Self completely miss the mark. We cannot do anything to gain these precious qualities of our radical humanness that organically emerge through the great functioning of our core-Self beyond willing, intending, grasping, owning, and lacking. If we try to mentally, emotionally, or behaviorally acquire the intrinsic qualities of our radical humanness, we reveal a deep lack of confidence in the still brilliance of our core-Self that is continuously and unconditionally flashing to refresh the vast Oneness and boundless intimacy of total reality.

Beyond Patience

Our Way is to simply enjoy the embodiment of core-Self inside of shikantaza and zazen-only with not one thing lacking and without being taken away by anything extra. Not one thing lacking means that desires and regrets do not arise within the settled composure, silent illumination, and still discernment of our core-Self. This is true whether we are seated as core-Self inside of zazen-only or living our everyday life as core-Self in shikantaza. Not being taken away by anything extra means that we gratefully embody the still intelligence of core-Self while passionately entrusting our life and death to the vast Oneness of total reality. Not lacking one thing and not being taken away by anything extra is to viscerally embody core-Self beyond all drivenness, dissatisfaction, incompletion, aggravation, and regret.

To effortlessly embody the sensual vitality, vibrant stillness, and wakeful alertness of core-Self in shikantaza and zazen-only is to molt off any practice of patience that is waiting for something to happen. This includes patiently waiting for still discernment, silent illumination, vast Oneness, and boundless intimacy. When we consciously try to be patient in shikantaza and zazen-only, we reveal our deep lack of confidence in the profound simplicity of this only moment that is flashing everywhere far beyond our patience, our grasping, our expectations, and all our desires. Molting off all effort toward being patient, we viscerally enjoy the vibrant sensuality of our gut-core intelligence that liberates us to "faithfully wait forever" for nothing to happen.

In our Way, we allow each moment of shikantaza and zazen-only to be just as IT is without patiently waiting for something to happen. When we allow each moment to be just as IT is, we come to viscerally realize that silent illumination, still discernment, and boundless intimacy can never be gained or attained by the cerebral power of our will or any diligent practice of patience. Whether we are embodying shikantaza or zazen-only, we are not trying to make something happen or get somewhere beyond where we already are. In our Way, we drop off all patience in zazen-only, embrace the flashing of this only moment just as IT is, compassionately arise to meet all beings and things in shikantaza just as they are, and faithfully entrust our journey of life and death to the vast Oneness of total reality. When we do just this, we somatically verify that core-Self viscerally arises far beyond any effort to be patient, any aspiration to be a compassionate being, any determination to achieve perfect wisdom, any intention to gain perfect enlightenment, any desire to transcend the ordinariness of everyday life, and any perseverance to sit through physical pain in the fixed stillness of zazen-only.

Our True Compass

Our Way of embodying shikantaza in everyday life is exactingly simple and utterly profound. When we live the fundamental point of zazen-only through the Way of shikantaza, we are continuously being guided to express behavioral wisdom, compassionate action, and deep visceral caring from the still and silent illumination of our core-Self. We call this still and silent illumination of our core-Self the brilliant non-thinking intelligence of our radical humanness. Whether we are just sitting as core-Self inside of just sitting (zazen-only) or just sitting as core-Self inside of just living (shikantaza), we are diligently embodying the brilliant non-thinking intelligence of our radical humanness that is the true compass of our life. It is this true compass of our radical humanness that helps us to navigate the inner reefs of greed, aggression, anger, shame, pride, guilt, ignorance, and delusion. This true compass of our radical humanness is the bright wisdoming of our core-Self that constantly encourages us to authentically express caring, gentleness, and tenderness toward ourselves and others. As we daily embody this true compass of our radical humanness, we continuously refresh our beginner's innocent Way of living with basic goodness while wholeheartedly practicing the Way of loving and being loved within the boundless intimacy, vast Oneness, and limitless interdependency of total reality.

Honor Your Sincerity

While you are trying to practice shikantaza and zazen-only in your everyday life, you may come to experience difficult feelings of shame, doubt, guilt, and a deep sense of inadequacy. These feelings arise when you think that the depth, consistency, integrity, or quality of your practice is not enough and that you will never be enough. You may feel totally inundated by your inner critic and your endless self-judgements. You may think that you are far from the still composure of core-Self, the clarity and exuberance of beginner's heartmind, and the fulfillment and completion of your radical humanness. However, there is a very subtle and compassionate teaching that is silently being illuminated at the very heart of your despondency, frustration, dissatisfaction, discontent, and felt inadequacy.

When you begin to feel that the depth, consistency, quality, and integrity of your practice are not enough, notice that you are focusing on an idealistic bench mark of true practice while entirely ignoring the sincerity and honorableness of your inner struggle. During times like this, remember that your inner struggle with not being enough or not doing enough is really a reflection of your true practice even in the midst of your harsh self-judgements. If you were not really sincere, dedicated, and conscientious about living our mirrored Way of shikantaza and zazen-only, you would not be struggling and questioning your resolve, your uprightness, and your commitment. It is your honorable inner struggle that clearly reveals the sincerity of your intention, the depth of your commitment, and the innocence of your inner longing to embody the still composure of core-Self while freely expressing the wild exuberance and playful spontaneity of beginner's heartmind. If you were not sincerely and conscientiously struggling you would only be experiencing indifference. However, you are sincerely struggling with your inner judgements and the felt inadequacy of your practice. Therefore, you are not indifferent or unconcerned. Your inner struggle shows that you are experiencing a genuine accountability to your core-Self. As you viscerally awaken to your sincerity, honorableness, and genuine accountability, you will come to somatically realize that core-Self is compassionately embracing your inner struggle while tenderly liberating the buoyant nature of your beginner's heartmind. Then, you will gratefully molt off your inner struggle and passionately begin again to practice the mirrored Way of shikantaza and zazen-only. When you begin again just like this, you will somatically verify the empowered humility and vigorous buoyancy of your beginner's heartmind.

Kindergarten

In our Way, we treasure the empowered humility of beginner's heartmind and the wondrous kindergarten of shikantaza and zazen-only. All that we viscerally realize and somatically verify about boundless intimacy and ungraspable enlightenment takes place in the practiced kindergarten of our everyday life. It is in the kindergarten of everyday life that we express the humility, curiosity, and exuberance of our beginner's heartmind. Our Way is never beyond beginner's heartmind and the kindergarten of shikantaza and zazen-only. Kindergarten is where we joyfully embody the still brilliance of core-Self and the ever surprising nature of beginner's heartmind.

As you practice shikantaza and zazen-only in the kindergarten of your everyday life, there may be times that you attach to your growing compassion, wisdom, and understanding. You might even feel like you are beyond kindergarten and that you have achieved a deep understanding of shikantaza and zazen-only. You may begin to think that you have finally arrived at the graduate school of silent illumination. You may even think that you are very special and above others. Attaching to your specialness and what you think you have accomplished in shikantaza and zazen-only, you may begin to distance yourself from the openness, wonder, and humility of your beginner's heartmind.   Just then, to your surprise, small events and circumstances will arise to challenge the seemingly firm and substantial ground of your specialness. However, do not be disheartened. These events and circumstances arise to intervene for your benefit. When you are completely baffled by their intervention, know that you are meeting the liberating genjo koan of your everyday life. Simply remain open and alert. Wholeheartedly embrace the intervention of total reality with beginner's curiosity. When you do just this, you will see that the intervention of total reality is calling forth the vast impermanence of your core-Self and the unownable nature of ungraspable enlightenment itself. To reawaken to the vast impermanence of your core-Self and the unownable nature of ungraspable enlightenment itself, is to simply embody a beginner's humility that confidently lives the brilliant Way of not-knowing. To confidently live the brilliant Way of not-knowing is to somatically meet the arrival of your radical humanness far beyond your illusory accomplishment and insubstantial specialness. When you somatically arrive as the radical human being that you already are, you will know what it means to be completely fulfilled by being no one special. To be no one special is to embody the integrity of your core-Self, to recover the curiosity of beginner's heartmind, and to return to the wondrous kindergarten of shikantaza and zazen-only. Then, you will come to realize that embodying humility, confidently accepting not-knowing, joyfully abiding in wonder, and being no one special are the true marks of core-Self that endlessly refresh the Way of beginner's heartmind.

Thank You.

"In our beginner's mind there is no thought,
"I have attained something." All self-centered thoughts
limit our vast [original] mind. When we have no thought
of achievement, no thought of ego-self, we are true beginners.
Then we can really learn something. The beginner's mind is the
mind of compassion. When our mind is compassionate, it is
boundless. Dogen-zenji, the founder of our school, always
emphasized how important it is to resume our boundless
original mind. Then we are always true to ourselves, in sympathy with all beings, and
can actually practice."

Shunryu Suzuki-roshi
(1905 - 1971)

"Dogen Zenji held up his
teaching whisk and said, "All
of you tell me, how do you intimately
see this and definitely know what it is
without being separated from it? Do you
want to completely understand this through
your body? At dawn, we are informed by
the calls of mountain birds; at the
beginning of spring we get the
news from the fragrance
of plum blossoms."

Eihei Koroku
Dogen's Extensive Record

CHAPTER 7

Lamp Of Ancient Buddhas

Resting in Silence,
a flower blooms
without the
slightest effort.

"The Great Way that buddha after buddha has transmitted
has continued on without interruption, and the merits of training
that ancestor after ancestor has revealed have spread far and wide.
As a result, having fully manifested the great realization and having
attained the Way without necessarily realizing that they have done
so, they reflect on what they have realized and take delight in it.
Then, emerging from their realization, they let go of it
and act freely, for this is what the everyday
life of buddhas and ancestors is."

Dogen Zenji,
Daigo
(Great Realization)

Introduction

Here, I will introduce you to the three roots of Zen life, illuminate the lamp of core-Self, and clarify the original seed of Zen transmission that is exactly core-Self viscerally transmitting core-Self in boundless intimacy and ungraspable enlightenment with not one thing lacking. I encourage you to temporarily set aside all you know about Zen and the transmission of Zen enlightenment. Diligently study, openly question, and experientially verify the integrity of this teaching. I have deep confidence that if you practice and investigate this teaching in everyday life, you will come to somatically comprehend that the birthright of all radical human beings is boundless intimacy with total reality, still entanglement with all beings and things, and unconditional transmission that we are all being dreamed in ungraspable enlightenment far beyond grasping, lacking, or pushing away.

Section One:

<u>THE INTERTWINING WAY OF KATTO</u>

"Because this very moment of now is an occasion [of intimately expressing the Way], we are intimate with Self, with the Self of others, with the buddhas and ancestors, and with all the different species. As a result, it is an intimacy on top of intimacy, ever anew. Because such teaching, practice, and awakening are what a buddha or an ancestor is, they comprise what buddas and ancestors intimately pass on.

Dogen Zenji,
<u>Mitsugo</u>
(Intimate Language)

Three Roots of Zen Life

Our Way is to live in the endless unfolding of ungraspable enlightenment by daily embodying, realizing, and verifying three ancient roots of Zen life. We call these three roots of Zen life boundless intimacy, precious entanglement, and unconditional transmission. We cultivate, digest, and metabolize these three roots of Zen life within our core-Self. This is true whether we are practicing just sitting as core-Self inside of zazen-only or living shikantaza as core-Self settled as core-Self in the practice of everyday life. As we cultivate, digest, and metabolize these three roots of Zen life, we do not have any thoughts or thinking about living Zen, willfully doing zazen-only, intentionally practicing shikantaza, becoming a buddha, gaining enlightenment, or attaining perfect wisdom.

This Way of cultivating, digesting, and metabolizing the three roots of Zen life was also addressed by Zen Master Dogen. Dogen viscerally realized and somatically verified the daily Way of living in boundless intimacy and ungraspable enlightenment with all beings and things. Dogen explored the farther reaches of precious entanglement, boundless intimacy, and unconditional transmission by embodying the still paradox of core-Self in shikantaza and zazen-only.

Master Dogen shared the true Buddha Way of living ungraspable enlightenment within his four-volume Japanese work entitled, "Shobogenzo." Shobogenzo means "The True Eye and Treasury of the Dharma." The Sanskrit word "Dharma" refers to the lawful integration and total dynamic functioning of the whole universe. Dharma is the bright wisdoming of total reality that upholds the boundless intimacy and limitless interdependency of all beings and things. The "True Eye" refers to the truthful eye of core-Self that compassionately witnesses the dynamic functioning of ego-self and thinking mind. "Treasury" refers to the treasured Way that core-Self lives in boundless intimacy and ungraspable enlightenment with all beings and things in the vast Oneness of total reality.

The Meaning of Katto

I am deeply indebted to Zen Master Dogen whose writings have encouraged me for over thirty-five years to live in boundless intimacy and unfold ungraspable enlightenment in the ordinariness of my everyday life. What has always stood out for me in Dogen's writings is his devotion to passionately teach, wholeheartedly embody, and unconditionally transmit ungraspable enlightenment in shikantaza and zazen-only. Dogen inspires, instructs, and challenges all Zen practitioners to somatically study the true nature of total reality, navigate life and death from the still compass of their radical humanness, and realize the farther reaches of living in boundless intimacy and vast Oneness with all beings and things.

The teachings in the "Shobogenzo" clearly reveal Dogen as a masterful Zen teacher, a true supporter and advocate of beginner's heartmind, a profound investigator of this only moment, and a gifted and unconventional writer who shared the still brilliance of core-Self in the language of his time. In the forty-seventh chapter of the *Shobogenzo* entitled "Katto," Dogen addresses the first Zen transmission of ungraspable enlightenment between Shakyamuni Buddha and his devoted disciple, Mahakasyapa.

The Japanese word "Katto" means "twining vines." Dogen uses the word "Katto" to elicit the mental image of Japanese wisteria that intertwine and entangle as they grow. Dogen's use of the term "Katto" refers to all Zen teachers and their student heirs who have entangled and intertwined for over twenty-five hundred years to meticulously transmit the total fulfillment of our radical humanness in shikantaza and zazen-only. This intimacy, entanglement, and transmission between Zen teachers and their student heirs is the interpersonal Way of confirming and publicly acknowledging that the ancient vine of the Buddha Way is still being cultivated at the heart of everyday life. As the outward interpersonal expression of "Katto," formal Zen transmission is determined by a Zen teacher who evaluates a student's visceral readiness to teach and exemplify the true embodiment of shikantaza and zazen-only while passing on the Buddha Way of living in vast Oneness and boundless intimacy with all beings and things. When student heirs receive formal Zen transmission from their Zen teacher, they become successors in an ancient Zen lineage that can be traced back to the first interpersonal transmission between the historical Buddha and monk Mahakasyapa.

The First Interpersonal Transmission

The first Zen transmission between Shakyamuni Buddha and monk Mahakasyapa happened on Vulture Peak, located near Rijgir in the land of India. At that time, hundreds of monks, nuns, and lay disciples had gathered to hear the Buddha speak on the Dharma of ungraspable enlightenment. After a long period of silence seated in zazen-only, Old Shakyamuni reached down on the ground, picked up a single flower between his thumb and forefinger, and held it up at heart level. This spontaneous act, originating from the still brilliance of core-Self and the simplicity of beginner's heartmind, was far beyond ego-self intending, expecting, owning, giving, or receiving.

All who had gathered on Vulture Peak looked on with awe and bewilderment. None who were in attendance could comprehend the true meaning of Shakyamuni Buddha's upheld flower. Only the monk Mahakasyapa viscerally understood that the still paradox of core-Self, embodied by Shakyamuni Buddha, had raised up one flower far beyond the traps and cages of ego-self and thinking mind. As

Mahakasyapa viscerally realized just this, he looked directly into Old Shakyamuni's eyes and spontaneously smiled. Mahakasyapa's smiling response instantly came from his core-Self to somatically confirm that Shakyamuni Buddha was wholeheartedly transmitting the boundless intimacy, vast Oneness, and ungraspable enlightenment of core-Self in shikantaza and zazen-only.

At that historical moment of mutual visceral acknowledgment, mutual entanglement with total reality, and mutual embodiment of beginner's heartmind, Shakyamuni Buddha said: "I embody the awakened eye and treasury of the true Dharma, the original heartmind of ever fresh nirvana, the precious Way of the formless, the gateless gate of limitless interdependency, the boundless intimacy of everyday life, and the Way of ungraspable enlightenment itself. I now publicly acknowledge that the eye and treasury of the true Dharma and the Way of living ungraspable enlightenment are wholly embodied by monk Mahakasyapa. After I am gone, he will continue to pass all this down to posterity with a sincerity and wholeheartedness that is far beyond transmitting, withholding, giving, and receiving."

This first Zen transmission between Old Shakyamuni and monk Mahakasyapa was all of core-Self interpersonally mirroring core-Self as the still quantum paradox of total reality. This is how monk Mahakasyapa became the first heir to publicly receive the seal of Zen transmission from his respected teacher Shakyamuni Buddha. It was this original Zen transmission that became the time honored template for publicly transmitting the lamp of core-Self and the peaceful Way of living and dying in shikantaza and zazen-only.

The Original Seed Of Transmission

Shakyamuni Buddha's embodiment of ungraspable enlightenment was intimately transmitted to monk Mahakasyapa far beyond transmitting. It was not dependent upon a mental belief or an act of worship. It was simply the flower of vast Oneness and boundless intimacy being viscerally raised by Old Shakyamuni and viscerally recognized by monk Mahakasyapa. This means that total visceral confirmation between Shakyamuni Buddha and monk Mahakasyapa was all of core-Self brilliantly holding up one flower and all of core-Self instantly smiling in response.

This mirrored core-Self confirmation between Old Shakyamuni and monk Mahakasyapa is honored in traditional Zen lineages as the first interpersonal transmission of ungraspable enlightenment. However, core-Self viscerally transmitting core-Self in this Only Moment Body is the original seed of Zen transmission itself. This original seed of Zen transmission was wholly embodied by the Buddha while sitting alone underneath the Bodhi tree in zazen-only. Shakyamuni Buddha's visceral awakening to core-Self transmitting core-Self in boundless intimacy and ungraspable enlightenment happened without a transmitting teacher. This is why Old Shakyamuni is honored as the original example of Zen embodiment and deeply respected as the first teacher who viscerally awakened to core-Self transmitting core-Self in zazen-only.

When Shakyamuni Buddha sat beneath the Bodhi tree in zazen-only, his half open-eyes caught a glimpse of the morning star. At that instant, while just sitting as core-Self inside of just sitting, he viscerally realized vast Oneness and boundless intimacy at the surface and depth of total reality. Old Shakyamuni awakened to his core-Self in lucid dreaming, verified the lamp of core-Self in silent illumination, and somatically confirmed that core-Self is being dreamed within the vast Oneness of total reality. As Shakyamuni Buddha viscerally awakened to core-Self transmitting core-Self inside of zazen-only, he said, "How wondrous! At this very moment, I have awakened to the vast Oneness of total reality! I am completely fulfilled beyond grasping, owning, gaining, lacking, or attaining. How amazing that this life of boundless intimacy and ungraspable enlightenment is being freely and openly transmitted everywhere. How surprising! It is the same life as before; but just Now, how brilliantly and pristinely it is illuminated!"

When Old Shakyamuni viscerally awakened to the still essence of total reality inside of zazen-only, he somatically verified that all of core-Self is boundless intimacy, vast Oneness, and limitless interdependency with not one thing lacking. To follow Buddha's example by just sitting as core-Self inside of zazen-only is to be viscerally immersed in the original seed of Zen transmission. It is this original seed of Zen transmission that is always viscerally blooming as this only moment of vast impermanence and ungraspable enlightenment with all beings and things. This holds true whether you are a beginner or a veteran practitioner of zazen-only. Whether it is your very first time of just sitting in zazen-only or your millionth time of just sitting inside of just sitting, know that the original seed of Zen transmission is always viscerally blooming into the boundless intimacy, vast Oneness, and limitless interdependency of your core-Self. This is true regardless of your mental capacity, the strength of your willpower, the diligent practice of your mindfulness, and the focus of your cerebral concentration in zazen-only.

As the original seed of Zen transmission is Old Shakyamuni awakening to the core-Self of all human beings, we say that Shakyamuni Buddha is always arriving as our core-Self inside of shikantaza and zazen-only. There, he is always holding up the flower of our core-Self, mirroring the vast Oneness of total reality, freely extending the fragrance of ungraspable enlightenment, and viscerally confirming our vast Oneness and boundless intimacy just as we are. When we meet Old Shakyamuni in this Way, we viscerally realize that the original seed of Zen transmission is far beyond religious and atheistic views even as it is the ultimate foundation for spiritual values, embodied faith, universal moral precepts, and ethical human behaviors.

The Unifying Lamp Of Transmission

What I have described thus far are two historical Zen transmissions of core-Self that to this day continue to motivate all Zen lineages to meticulously embody and earnestly transmit the ancient Way of living in ungraspable enlightenment with all beings and things. The first is the original seed of Zen transmission that Shakyamuni Buddha viscerally realized underneath the Bodhi tree inside of zazen-only. Again, this original seed of Zen transmission happened naturally and organically without a transmitting teacher. Somatic realization of the seed of transmission is exactly core-Self viscerally transmitting core-Self with not one thing lacking. The second historical Zen transmission happened publicly between Shakyamuni Buddha and monk Mahakasyapa. This interpersonal Zen transmission established the Way of publicly transmitting and orally confirming the resonant embodiment of core-Self within and between two human beings. Again, this interpersonal Zen transmission happens far beyond gaining, owning, withholding, and transmitting. These two viscerally based Zen transmissions continue to advance the still embodiment of core-Self as the brilliant lamp of ancient buddhas that silently illuminates the surface and depth of total reality. This brilliant lamp of ancient buddhas has inspired Zen practitioners throughout the ages to wholeheartedly sit in zazen-only, to viscerally embody the still mark of non-thinking, and to seal the Way of shikantaza for its own sake. This is how all Zen practitioners spread their wings of shikantaza and zazen-only, take flight in the sky of boundless intimacy and limitless interdependency, and unfold the Way of ungraspable enlightenment within the ordinariness of everyday life.

Master Dogen himself was deeply committed to teaching and transmitting the lamp of ancient buddhas. For Dogen, anyone who embodies silent illumination inside of zazen-only somatically verifies the vast Oneness of total reality, becomes empathically entangled with ancient buddhas and ancestral teachers, and viscerally confirms boundless intimacy and ungraspable enlightenment with all beings and things. Throughout the various chapters of the Shobogenzo, Dogen constantly encourages us to investigate the farther reaches of our radical humanness by daily embodying the mirrored Way of shikantaza and zazen-only. The elegant wholeness and empirical soundness of Dogen's teachings in the Shobogenzo inspire and encourage all Zen practitioners to viscerally entangle in the stillness of boundless intimacy, to always remain accountable to the vast Oneness of total reality, and to somatically verify that ungraspable enlightenment is organically unfolding at the ever fresh crossroads of life and death.

Unfolding The Way Of Enlightenment

In the next section entitled "The Treasury of Katto," I will further clarify the original seed of Zen transmission, the awakening of core-Self, the power of lucid dreaming, and the refuge of being dreamed within the vast Oneness of total reality. While you are reading and seeking to understand "The Treasury of Katto," I encourage you to ground your reading and your seeking within the visceral discernment of your core-Self. Do not try to understand or study "The Treasury of Katto" only from your heady ego-self and thinking mind. Above all, remember Shakyamuni's final encouragement to his disciples; "Be a lamp unto your Self. Hold fast to your Self as the lamp of truth."

To honor Shakyamuni Buddha's last words, do not accept "The Treasury of Katto" without somatically studying and viscerally examining its validity. Question it with the sincerity, curiosity, and wonder of your beginner's heartmind. Test it by throwing your whole life force into practicing the mirrored Way of shikantaza and zazen-only. If you question, investigate, and test "The Treasury of Katto" just like this, I am confident that you will confirm your somatic transmission into boundless intimacy, your visceral entanglement with the still essence of total reality, and your vast Oneness and limitless interdependency with all beings and things. Then, you will come to organically know beyond a doubt that you are actualizing the fundamental point of zazen-only, embodying shikantaza for its own sake, and unfolding your everyday life of ungraspable enlightenment far beyond grasping, owning, gaining, or attaining.

"An ancient buddha
once said, 'Now, I express the dream
within a dream for you. All buddhas in the past,
present, and future express the dream within a dream.
The six early generations of Chinese ancestors express
the dream within a dream.' Study and clarify these words.
Shakyamuni Buddha holding up the flower is exactly
the expression of a dream within a dream."

Dogen Zenji,
Muchū Setsumu
(A Dream within a Dream)

Section Two:

THE TREASURY OF KATTO

"Every crystal-clear manifestation
of the entire world is a dream; this dream
is none other than all things that are absolutely lucid.
One's doubt of this itself is a dream; life's confusion is
a dream as well. At this very moment, all these are a
dream, are within a dream, and expound a dream".

"Simply expressing the dream within a dream
is itself buddhas and ancestors, the assembly
of unsurpassable enlightenment."

Dogen Zenji,
Muchū Setsumu
(A Dream within a Dream)

Introduction

The *Treasury of Katto* includes: (1) falling asleep in thinking mind while non-lucidly dreaming of ego-self, (2) viscerally awakening to core-Self and the power of lucid dreaming, (3) endless entanglement with the humility of beginner's heartmind, and (4) somatic transmission of being dreamed in vast Oneness with all beings and things. Katto's treasury is core-Self living in boundless intimacy, core-Self entangled with ancient buddhas and venerable ancestors, and core-Self living the Way of ungraspable enlightenment with compassion, playfulness, accountability, loving tenderness, and a surprising brilliance beneath the cerebral functioning of I, me, and mine. All of Katto's treasury is continuously and unconditionally transmitted in the mirrored Way of shikantaza and zazen-only.

Sleeping And Awakening

All of us can understand that we fall asleep and dream at night. Although we may acknowledge that we sleep and dream at night, the fact that we are living our life while sleeping in the language of thinking mind and dreaming the non-lucid dream of ego-self continues to elude us. When we fall asleep in the language of thinking mind and the chattering dream of ego-self, we diminish visceral intimacy with core-Self and its unconditional transmission of boundless intimacy, limitless interdependency, and ungraspable enlightenment itself. Even as this is so, core-Self is continuously transmitting visceral realization of our illusory ego-self dreaming, our sleeping in thinking mind, our instant awakening to the power of lucid dreaming, and our being dreamed in vast Oneness with all beings and things.

Katto is somatic awakening to the lamp of core-Self, silent illumination of our ego-self functioning, compassionate entanglement with the logic and language of thinking mind, and visceral transmission that all of this is being dreamed within the vast impermanence of total reality. When we awaken to core-Self in lucid dreaming and the refuge of being dreamed in boundless intimacy with all beings and things, we rest in the tranquility of heart-not-wanting and the wonder of mind-not-knowing. To fully embody core-Self in shikantaza and zazen-only is to somatically verify visceral compassion for everyday life, visceral entanglement with the power of lucid dreaming, visceral reverence and deep gratitude for being dreamed as a radical human being, and visceral transmission that the depth of total reality is absolutely still.

Katto is core-Self viscerally transmitting how we fall sleep in thinking mind, how we immerse ourselves in the daily dream of ego-self, how we embody awakening to lucid dreaming, how we liberate the wholeness of beginner's heartmind, and how we blend our everyday dreams with the still essence of total reality. When we come to know that all our falling asleep in thinking mind, all our non-lucid ego-self dreaming, all our visceral awakening to core-Self, and all our somatic verification of lucid dreaming exist together in the vast Oneness of being dreamed in ungraspable enlightenment itself, we realize the completion and total fulfillment of our radical humanness far beyond lacking, judgement, or regret. To realize our radical humanness far beyond lacking, judgement, or regret is to viscerally embody the still brilliance of core-Self while compassionately entangling with ego-self and thinking mind during our everyday activities, relationships, and affairs.

If core-Self did not unconditionally transmit the still paradox of core-Self in shikantaza and zazen-only, there would be no treasury of Katto, no awakening to the power of lucid dreaming, no visceral entanglement with ancient buddhas, no silent illumination of ego-self functioning, no brilliant discernment of limitless interdependency, no liberation of beginner's heartmind, and no somatic realization that we are all being dreamed in boundless intimacy within the ordinariness of everyday life.

Not Fanciful Dreaminess

Our Way is to endlessly awaken to the still brilliance of core-Self, to somatically express the power of lucid dreaming, and to viscerally embody the transmission of being dreamed within the still essence of total reality. This is in contrast to staying fast asleep in the functioning of our thinking mind and our non-lucid ego-self dreaming. To constantly slumber in our non-lucid ego-self dreaming is to remain in bondage to our mental drama, our constant inner chatter, our rigid and exclusive beliefs, and all our conditioned ways of figuring, judging, thinking, emoting, and behaving.

Although Katto is awakening to core-Self and the power of lucid dreaming, visceral entanglement with ancient buddhas and venerable sages, and somatic transmission that one is being dreamed in the vast Oneness of total reality, do not mistake the treasury of Katto with dreamy fantasies, dreaminess, or illusory dreams that help people escape the mundane and ordinary passage of everyday life. This is not our Way. We viscerally embody the integrity of our core-Self, gratefully express the power of lucid dreaming, and passionately live the transmission of being dreamed with all beings and things while tenderly and conscientiously taking care of the challenges and responsibilities of daily life that advance the Way of boundless intimacy and ungraspable enlightenment itself.

Our Way is to be viscerally alert and somatically wakeful in the practice of shikantaza and zazen-only as we compassionately embrace and wholeheartedly take care of our everyday life far beyond grasping and pushing away. This includes our falling asleep in ego-self and thinking mind, being turned under by the wheel of dysfunctional karma, gratefully recovering our abdominal breathing, sinking into the liberating sensuality of our hara, endlessly awakening to core-Self and the power of lucid dreaming, continuing to practice the Way of loving and being loved with beginner's heartmind, and all the while deeply appreciating the refuge of being dreamed in boundless intimacy with all beings and things.

Compassionate Entanglement

When we awaken to the lamp of core-Self and the still power of lucid dreaming, we refine the healthy functioning of our ego-self, intelligently employ its dualistic way of logical thinking and rational knowing, envision and actualize everyday dreams with the buoyancy and humility of our beginner's heartmind, and all the while yield to being dreamed as a radical human being who remains devotedly accountable to the limitless interdependency of total reality. This is how we embody the treasury of Katto as core-Self continuously transmits the still paradox of core-Self during the passage of everyday life.

As the still paradox of core-Self flashes everywhere at the surface and depth of total reality, all of core-Self remains forever unstained and undefiled even as it entangles with the passage of linear time, the social functioning of ego-self, the language of thinking mind, and the logical, dualistic, and rational way of knowing. Being unstained and undefiled even as it compassionately entangles with everyday language and the functioning of ego-self and thinking mind, core-Self silently illuminates the still power of lucid dreaming, embraces vast impermanence as the boundless intimacy of total reality, and viscerally receives the transmission of being dreamed within the momentary flashing of a vast Oneness that has no coming or going.

When you embody core-Self while compassionately entangling with the transparent functioning of your ego-self and thinking mind, you will come to know beyond all doubt that your peaceful life of vast impermanence, your Way of loving and being loved with beginner's heartmind, and your visceral transmission of being dreamed with all beings and things are continuously intertwining to authenticate your basic goodness, your boundless intimacy, and your limitless interdependency. To somatically confirm your life of basic goodness, boundless intimacy, and limitless interdependency is to conscientiously and compassionately entangle with your daily activities, affairs, and relationships without grasping or pushing away. To compassionately entangle with everyday life without grasping or pushing away is to somatically arrive as a radical human being who cherishes the surprising arrival of ungraspable enlightenment in each passing moment. This is the Way we embody the lamp of core-Self, viscerally enjoy our sensual exuberance in everyday life, confidently entangle with ego-self and thinking mind, passionately delight in the basic goodness of our beginner's heartmind, and joyfully include all human beings in the completion and fulfillment of our radical humanness.

Turning The Wheel Karma

As we embody the lamp of core-Self, enjoy our vast Oneness with total reality, confidently express the power of our lucid dreaming, and gratefully take refuge in being dreamed with all beings and things, we do not push away the pragmatic application of logic, reasoning, and the gathering of knowledge. This means that we do not ignore the importance of thinking, labeling, analyzing, remembering, and learning. Nor do we ignore the karmic law of cause and effect, our responsibility and accountability in society, our mental capacity to refine the clarity and soundness of our thinking and doing, and our commitment to insure the precise, factual, and upright use of language. When we pay careful attention to the karmic law of cause and effect, refine the healthy functioning of our ego-self and thinking mind, and all the while live through the still paradox of our core-Self, we are able to actualize our everyday dreams with the exuberance of beginner's heartmind while blending those dreams with the boundless intimacy of total reality.

In our mirrored Way of shikantaza and zazen-only, we endlessly awaken to the still discernment of our core-Self, lucidly and tenderly entangle with our ego-self and thinking mind, passionately align all our goals, activities, behaviors, and relationships with the still wholeness and vast Oneness of total reality, and continuously embody deep gratitude for being dreamed in limitless interdependency with all beings and things. When you practice your everyday life just like this, know that there will be times when you inadvertently fall asleep in your dreamy inner chatter, your behavioral reactiveness, your emotional defensiveness, and your mental drivenness. When this happens, viscerally accept that you have been turned under by the karmic wheel of cause and effect, gently come back to your abdominal breathing, sink into the sensuality of your hara, and anchor in your somatic center-point of gravity. Once you reestablish intimacy with your core-Self, silently illuminate how you got caught-up in the tension, aggravation, and stress that overtook your body. Honestly investigate the insubstantial ego-self prison of your armoring, defending, denying, withdrawing, projecting, and blaming. Examine how your feelings of inadequacy, helplessness, and dissatisfaction began to arise. Clarify how you caused yourself and others to suffer by speaking, thinking, and behaving from your fear, ignorance, aggression, and delusion. Study how your egoself-centricity breeds false pride, obsessive pity, dishonesty, separation, isolation, and a deep sense of human incompleteness. When you investigate all of this from the still discernment of your core-Self, know that you are embodying the truth with ancient buddhas, genuinely honoring the treasury of Katto, and somatically recovering the visceral integrity and completion of your radical humanness.

Remember, just as there is the time of falling asleep, the time of yearning for awakening and liberation, and the time of longing for bodily ease, emotional intimacy, and deep caring, there is also the time to honor the truth as a friend, the time to molt off all dishonesty and armoring, the time to embody beginner's humility, the time to accept yourself just as you are, and the time to honorably begin again. When the time intimately arrives to begin again, compassionately turn the wheel of karma toward your basic goodness, your noble sincerity, your honorable practice, and your originally enlightened nature. As you turn the wheel of karma in this Way, you will somatically clarify that boundless intimacy, vast Oneness, and ungraspable enlightenment are always being viscerally transmitted as the radical birthright of all human beings without a hair's gap between falling asleep and endless awakening.

Realization And Liberation

All human beings without exception are viscerally called from their core-Self to refine the healthy functioning of their ego-self and thinking mind, to brilliantly turn the wheel of cause and effect for the benefit of all sentient beings, to tenderly entangle with sensuality, suffering, joy, pain, and vast impermanence, to practice the Way of loving and being loved beyond deception and manipulation, to embody the humility and wonder of their beginner's heartmind, to realize their boundless intimacy and limitless interdependency with each other, and to always hold themselves accountable to the vast Oneness of total reality. This visceral calling of core-Self germinates at birth, tenderly whispers during our early childhood development, becomes increasingly louder during our teenage years, and continues to echo and resonate throughout the passage of our adult life. When the time intimately arrives to heed the calling of core-Self, I encourage you to spread the wings of shikantaza and zazen-only, gratefully embody the still paradox of total reality, empathically entangle with all beings and things, receive the visceral transmission of your radical humanness, and somatically express the treasury of Katto by daily intertwining with your realization and liberation.

By "realization," I mean visceral realization that all of core-Self is freely transmitting the still paradox of core-Self far beneath our cerebral thinking. To viscerally embody the still paradox of core-Self far beneath our thinking is to somatically confirm that core-Self is the still flashing of vast impermanence and the timeless stillness of total reality. As we viscerally live from the still paradox of core-Self, we compassionately entangle with ego-self and thinking mind, spontaneously bow to express our life of boundless intimacy, gratefully practice the Way of loving and being loved with beginner's heartmind, and passionately enjoy the sensual exuberance and timeless freshness of our radical humanness. Always remember that the visceral realization of core-Self is somatically verified and confirmed in our mirrored Way of shikantaza and zazen-only. This means that all of realization and liberation, as well as their organic intertwinement in everyday life, is always somatic and visceral and never cerebral. We can never embody the still paradox of core-Self, somatically verify the intertwinement of realization and liberation, nor experientially confirm the treasury of Katto through any reading, studying, thinking, and figuring.

When I speak of "liberation," I mean liberation from our egoself-centricity with its grasping and pushing away, its drivenness and defensiveness, and its reactiveness and automaticity. This is liberation from an ego-self that falls fast asleep in its given name, its separateness, its endless drama, its dreamy mental chatter, and its dualistic way of thinking and knowing. Liberation is awakening to the still discernment of core-Self, silently illuminating the dysfunctional nature of greed, ignorance, and hatred, and all the while bowing to the interdependent equality of all beings and things. Liberation is living from our radical humanness, compassionately seeing all beings and things just as they are, dreaming and actualizing everyday dreams with beginner's heartmind, and passionately blending all our dreams with the still essence and vast Oneness of total reality.

Liberation is freedom from the insatiable nature of ego-self dissatisfaction. This means that one is no longer driven by an ego-self that constantly seeks to gain, profit, and attain solely to advance and uphold its virtual existence, its social status, and its personal identity. Even so, our Way is not to extinguish our ego-self, still our mental chatter, remove ourselves from society and its material abundance, avoid our difficult feelings and emotions, or turn our face away from loving and being loved. Rather, we tenderly entangle with ego-self and thinking mind, intertwine with society and its material abundance, practice intimacy with all our feelings and emotions, gratefully practice the Way of loving and being loved, unfold ungraspable enlightenment with all beings and things, and embody the still paradox of core-Self for its own sake.

When we are constantly driven to uphold our ego-self, attach to our endless mental chatter, and advance cerebral control over beings and things, we cultivate a vast field of isolation, separation, ignorance, and suffering. On the other hand, when we respectfully approach all beings and things from the still integrity of our core-Self, all beings and things come forth to unfold our everyday life as ungraspable enlightenment itself. In this Way we cultivate a vast field of limitless interdependency, wholehearted caring, unconditional equality, still entanglement, and boundless intimacy. All this is how we embody the treasury of Katto while viscerally intertwining with realization and liberation in the mirrored Way of shikantaza and zazen-only.

The Sword of Just One Flower

As we throw our whole life force into living the mirrored Way of shikantaza and zazen-only, we experience the treasury of Katto as visceral embodiment of core-Self, visceral entanglement with lucid dreaming, visceral completion of our radical humanness, and visceral transmission of being dreamed in vast Oneness with all beings and things. When we embody the treasury of Katto in this visceral Way, we hold up the sword of just one flower with Shakyamuni Buddha and spontaneously smile with monk Mahakasyapa. This is the Way we somatically verify that Shakyamuni Buddha held up a flower to simply share IT while Mahakasyapa smiled just to reflect IT. As Shakyamuni Buddha, we do not own IT, withhold IT, hide IT, or transmit IT. As monk Mahakasyapa, we do not grasp IT, attain IT, or gain IT. This is the Way we honor the still paradox of total reality while always birthing a beginner who viscerally meets IT as core-Self in shikantaza and zazen-only.

All of core-Self in shikantaza and zazen-only is Shakyamuni Buddha's sword of just one flower that cuts off all separateness while emitting the still fragrance of boundless intimacy and limitless interdependency at the surface and depth of total reality. Similarly, all of core-Self in shikantaza and zazen-only is the moon glow smile of Mahakasyapa that silently illuminates the completion of our radical humanness and the basic goodness of our beginner's heartmind. To hold up the sword of just one flower with Old Shakyamuni and smile with monk Mahakasyapa is to gratefully molt off our greed, aggression, and ignorance while tenderly cultivating a limitless field of health, love, wisdom, compassion, and healing in everyday life. To do just this is to continuously realize our total completion and fulfillment as a radical human being who lives the Way of loving and being loved as ungraspable enlightenment itself.

To live the Way of loving and being loved as ungraspable enlightenment itself is to freely entangle with daily affairs and relationships while silently illuminating the dysfunctional nature of any behaviors that are motivated by egoself-centric guilt, manipulation, control, shame, narcissism, and deceit. When we silently illuminate all of this while raising the sword of just one flower, we sever the chains of our karmic bondage to egoself-centricity, liberate the humility and basic goodness of our beginner's heartmind, and viscerally confirm that our interdependent life of upright wholeness is deepening our radical humanness just as we are. This is how we come to experientially realize that the sword of just one flower cuts off all delusion, isolation, separation, and ignorance while somatically confirming a beginner's Way of remaining truly accountable to the vast Oneness of total reality.

Honorable Caretakers

Shakyamuni Buddha held up one flower to silently express the still fragrance of core-Self and share the basic goodness of his beginner's heartmind. In his beginner's uninhibited Way, he revealed beyond all hiddenness that core-Self is the still paradox of total reality, the visceral taproot of our radical humanness, the lamp of silent illumination, and the vast Oneness and limitless interdependency of our original nature. Seeing a flower raised beyond figuring, intending, or thinking, Mahakasyapa smiled to mirror the basic goodness of beginner's heartmind, to viscerally acknowledge the lamp of silent illumination, and to somatically express his boundless intimacy with Shakyamuni Buddha. In this Way, Old Shakyamuni and monk Mahakasyapa intertwined within the visceral silence of a timeless moment to mutually reflect the basic goodness of beginner's heartmind while the still fragrance of core-Self elicited the moon-glow smile of core-Self in the vast Oneness of total reality. This is how the lamp of core-Self was originally transmitted far beyond transmission with the basic goodness of beginner's heartmind.

The visceral lamp of ancient buddhas has been passed down with somatic impeccability by Zen teachers and Zen students who tenderly embody the still fragrance of core-Self with the authenticity and humility of beginner's heartmind. As all Zen practitioners somatically mirror each other in the embodiment of shikantaza and zazen-only, they continuously awaken to core-Self in lucid dreaming, hold up the sword of just one flower with Shakyamuni Buddha, smile with monk Mahakasyapa in limitless interdependency, and lift up their hearts in endless gratitude for being dreamed in vast Oneness as a radical human being with not one thing lacking. This is how all Zen practitioners become honorable caretakers of the authentic Buddha seal that is the lamp of core-Self in silent illumination. This is the Way that they continue to revitalize the treasury of Katto while viscerally intertwining with all beings and things in shikantaza and zazen-only.

As Zen teachers and Zen students continue to embody the still fragrance of core-Self with the basic goodness of beginner's heartmind, they somatically transmit Shakyamuni's upheld flower and Mahakasyapa's smile to all future generations. This is how our Soto Zen school honorably invigorates the treasury of Katto, passionately advances the Buddha seal of silent illumination, and respectfully acknowledges all Zen practitioners as buddhas midwifing buddhas, ancients birthing ancients, and lucid dreamers awakening lucid dreamers to the somatic realization of being dreamed within the vast Oneness and boundless intimacy of total reality.

Beyond Mind Transmission

The first interpersonal Zen transmission of ungraspable enlightenment was fundamentally a visceral transmission between the core-Self of Shakyamuni Buddha and the core-Self of monk Mahakasyapa. To speak of the first Zen transmission between Shakyamuni Buddha and monk Mahakasyapa as a mind-to-mind transmission is to speak incorrectly. To think of Old Shakyamuni mentally transmitting ungraspable enlightenment to monk Mahakasyapa is far off the mark. Similarly, to think of monk Mahakasyapa mentally receiving ungraspable enlightenment from Shakyamuni Buddha also misses the mark. Such erroneous views cause sincere Zen practitioners to miss the still flowering of core-Self that viscerally transmits the fragrance of boundless intimacy, vast Oneness, and ungraspable enlightenment far beneath the cerebral functioning of mindfulness and mind. This is why I encourage you to somatically study and investigate the original visceral nature of Zen transmission by wholeheartedly sitting as core-Self inside of just sitting while daily arising to passionately embody core-Self inside of just living. As you continuously study and investigate in this mirrored Way, you will somatically verify beyond all doubt that the first interpersonal Zen transmission between Old Shakyamuni and monk Mahakasyapa was entirely visceral and far beyond the erroneous view of mind-to-mind transmission.

When Zen practitioners mistake the transmission between Shakyamuni Buddha and monk Mahakasyapa as a mental transmission between two minds, they become misdirected in their practice of shikantaza and zazen-only. They wrongly assume that awakening, liberation, and realization are all dependent on the one-pointed concentration of their cerebral mind. This one-pointed concentration of cerebral mind is historically known in India, China, and Japan as the power of "samadhi mind." Many people spend hours a day in seated meditation to cerebrally generate this one-pointedness of samadhi mind. As they strengthen their willpower and intensify the focus and concentration of their samadhi mind, misguided Zen practitioners patiently wait in seated stillness to mentally awaken to their true nature, to mentally realize perfect wisdom, and to mentally grasp enlightenment itself. They think that to cerebrally generate the power of samadhi mind is to drop off all entanglement with society, to subjugate the body in stillness, to extinguish the functioning of ego-self and personality, to transcend a daily life of responsibility and accountability, to detach from the challenges of loving and being loved, and to go far beyond a beginner's humility and confident Way of not-knowing. Seeking to experience voidness, emptiness, and egolessness, they detach from worldly affairs and intensify their training in the fixed stillness of zazen-only. Their deepest longing is to accomplish the samadhi mind of great liberation, awaken to the vast Oneness of total reality, and actualize their boundless intimacy with ancient buddhas and venerable ancestors. However, all their misdirected views keeps them from experiencing the still brilliance of their core-Self that encourages liberated entanglement with ego-self and thinking mind, compassionate entanglement with social activities, responsibilities, and affairs, tender entanglement in the Way of loving and being loved, accountable entanglement with the vast Oneness of total reality, and awakened entanglement with lucid dreaming and the Way of being dreamed in boundless intimacy with all beings and things.

Misguided by teachings that focus on mind-to-mind transmission and a mentally graspable enlightenment, Zen practitioners willfully concentrate the power of their samadhi mind, push away entanglement with ego-self and its dualistic way of thinking and knowing, attach to mental stillness, voidness, and emptiness, and all the while practice a cerebrally generated mindfulness in everyday life. As Zen practitioners are motivated and guided by incorrect teachings, they neglect the still discernment of their core-Self, blindly accept Zen schools that inflate the value of mind-to-mind transmission, put ancient buddhas and patriarchs on illusory pedestals, idealize their Zen teachers far beyond accountability, and sit through pain in zazen-only to intensify the one-pointed concentration of samadhi mind. They do not know that the cerebral power of samadhi mind only removes them from the unborn silence and birthless stillness of core-Self. They do not realize that ignoring the arising of tingling, numbness, and pain is tantamount to ignoring the still brilliance of core-Self that viscerally transmits the ancient Way of living in boundless intimacy, vast Oneness, and ungraspable enlightenment with all beings and things.

When Zen practitioners drop off the erroneous view of mind-to-mind transmission and a mentally graspable enlightenment, they will no longer exert nor excessively employ their cerebral power to achieve the intense one-pointed concentration of samadhi mind. As they will no longer exert their cerebral power in shikantaza and zazen-only, they are liberated to sink into the sensuality of their hara and the still vibrancy of their core-Self. As they completely end the mental subjugation of their bodies, they will linger with ease and joy in the stillness of zazen-only far beyond the force of discipline and the exertion of patience. They will finally liberate themselves from false views that perpetuate enslavement to immobility, ignorance of physical discomfort and pain, and bondage to the cerebral arousal of mindfulness and samadhi mind. Meeting the treasury of Katto in shikantaza and zazen-only, they will simply enjoy the sensuality of their hara, light the lamp of silent illumination, awaken to the power of lucid dreaming, tenderly entangle with ego-self and thinking mind, confidently actualize dreams with beginner's heartmind, delight in the wonder of not-knowing, openly practice the Way of boundless intimacy, and gratefully bow to the vast Oneness of being dreamed with all beings and things.

Treasure Beginners Way

When we just sit as core-Self inside of zazen-only, we do not seek or desire the power of samadhi mind. We do not try to cerebrally push through the barrier of duality, extinguish our ego-self and thinking mind, destroy our karmic hindrances and obstructions, sever the muddy roots of human intimacy, break into the storehouse of perfect wisdom, gouge out a cave of light to banish the darkness, penetrate the mystery of vast emptiness and nothing holy, and all the while foolishly think that all this is the path of ungraspable enlightenment itself. This is not our Way.

Our Way is far beyond extinguishing, forcing, pushing, penetrating, and grasping. We simply embody core-Self with the tenderness of beginner's heartmind for its own sake. We do not practice being core-Self in shikantaza and zazen-only without the humility, gentleness, and receptivity of beginner's heartmind. The enlightened Way of Shakyamuni Buddha is never removed from a beginner's sincerity, authenticity, and curiosity. In our Way, we never go beyond beginner's heartmind that earnestly studies how we fall asleep in ego-self and thinking mind, how we awaken to core-Self and the power of lucid dreaming, how we compassionately embrace the muddy roots of our life, how we tenderly cultivate the lotus of human intimacy, how we gratefully bow in limitless interdependency, how we experience completion as a radical human being, and how we take refuge in the vast Oneness of being dreamed with all beings and things.

Anyone who embodies core-Self with the tenderness of beginner's heartmind is exactly Shakyamuni Buddha holding up just one flower. When you see a beginner sitting inside the stillness of zazen-only with beginner's heartmind, whether they are male or female, young or old, know that you are seeing Shakyamuni Buddha viscerally awakening to the vast Oneness of total reality while compassionately embodying our radical humanness at the ever fresh crossroads of life and death. To know just this is to bow to all beginners who are simply abiding in the traceless fulfillment and formless completion of core-Self inside of just sitting. This is the Way we honor all beginners who practice core-Self within the timeless wholeness and boundless intimacy of shikantaza and zazen-only. This is the Way we encourage all beginners to viscerally confirm their core-Self, somatically verify their basic goodness, faithfully embody the treasury of Katto, and unfold the Way of ungraspable enlightenment within the ordinariness of everyday life.

Thank you.

Then there is the great awakening
after which we shall know that this life
was a great dream. All the while people think
they are awake, busily and brightly assuming they
understand things, calling this man ruler, that one a
herdsman…. And when I say you are dreaming,
I am dreaming, too. These words may
seem very strange to you….

Chuang Tzu
Chinese Taoist Sage
369 B.C. 286 B.C.

"You need to know that the
principle being recognized here is
completely clear; namely, that giving
expression all day long to a dream in a
dream is simply giving expression to a
dream from within a dream. This is why
Shakyamuni Buddha once said, 'I now,
for you, am giving expression to the
dream within a dream. All buddhas,
of past, present, and future taught
a dream within a dream. The first
six Chinese ancestors of the Way
also taught a dream in a dream.'
You should clearly study these
words. Holding up just one
flower with twinkling eyes
is openly teaching the
dream within a
dream."

Dogen Zenji,
Muchū Setsumu
(A Dream Within A Dream)

"There are inner dreams,
dream expressions, expressions
of dreams, and dreams inside. Without
being within a dream, there is no expression
of dreams. Without expressing dreams, there is
no being within a dream. Without expressing
dreams, there are no buddhas. Without being
within a dream, buddhas do not emerge and
turn the wondrous Dharma wheel. This
Dharma wheel is none other than a
buddha together with a buddha,
and a dream expressed
within a dream."

Dogen Zenji,
Muchū Setsumu
(A Dream Within A Dream)

PART IV

CULTIVATION

"There is no need
to have a deep understanding
of Zen. Even though you read much Zen
literature, you must read each sentence with
a fresh mind. You should not say, "I know what
Zen is," or "I have attained enlightenment." This
is also the real secret of the arts: always be a
beginner.... If you start to practice zazen, you
will begin to appreciate your beginner's
mind. It is the true secret of
our Zen practice."

Shunryu Suzuki-roshi
Zen Mind, Beginner's Mind

CHAPTER 8

Beginner's Heartmind

Have Faith in Yourself,
Honor the Truth
as a Friend,
Live Compassion
for Self and Others.

"Truly, you need
to recognize that a beginner's
zazen-only is the first time of doing
zazen-only, and that one's first time in
zazen-only is the first instance of
being a seated buddha."

Dogen Zenji,
Zazen-Shin
(Needle of Zazen-Only)

Shoshin

The Japanese word "shoshin" is translated by many Zen teachers as "beginner's mind." Although this is not incorrect, it is not a complete view. "Shoshin," is more accurately translated as "beginner's heartmind." "Sho" means original or beginning. "Shin" comes from the ancient Chinese ideogram "Xin" pronounced "sheen." The ideogram "Xin," written in Chinese and Japanese just like this, (心) refers to both heart and mind simultaneously. The Chinese sages used the ideogram "Xin" to express the original wholeness and oneness of our beginner's heartmind. The pristine oneness of beginner's heartmind is not the way we experience heart and mind through our ego-self functioning. Our ego-self functioning views mind and heart as totally separate ways of knowing and being in the body. This ego-self experience of heart and mind functioning separately from each other distances us from the original simplicity and undefiled unity of our beginner's heartmind. Shoshin is our original heartmind that precedes the cerebral development of our ego-self and our word thinking mind. Shoshin is before the childhood dawning of language and the genesis of "I, me, and mine."

As very young children we somatically enjoyed the pristine joy and wonder of beginner's heartmind before we knew our given name, before we understood any words, and before we could use words to talk to others. When we just sit as core-Self inside of zazen-only, we somatically recover the simplicity, spontaneity, and ever fresh exuberance of beginner's heartmind. The spontaneous exuberance of beginner's heartmind is akin to the playful wildness of spinning dolphins and the jubilant leaps of breaching whales.

In our mirrored Way of shikantaza and zazen-only, we somatically verify the undefiled unity and basic goodness of our beginner's heartmind like a flower verifies its own blooming, like a morning bird verifies the sounding of its song, and like a fish verifies the fluid softness of water.   To embody core-Self and recover the pristine functioning of beginner's heartmind is to somatically confirm that shoshin is the "enlightened heartmind" of all radical human beings. This is why venerable sages and buddha ancestors have always honored beginner's heartmind as immeasurably deep, everlastingly fresh, and endlessly profound.

Noble Completion

The Way of shoshin was honored by Shakyamuni Buddha who held up one flower beyond words, by Mahakasyapa who affectionately smiled without inhibition, by Shunryu Suzuki who advanced the practice of beginner's heartmind, and by Dogen Zenji who encouraged all beginners to confidently embody shikantaza and zazen-only in noble completion. In our Way, anyone who viscerally embodies core-Self with the undefiled humility and unfabricated sincerity of beginner's heartmind wholly soaks in the traceless fulfillment and formless completion of ungraspable enlightenment with not one thing lacking. This means that all beginners who wholeheartedly embody core-Self in shikantaza and zazen-only are in noble completion and total fulfillment just as they are.

An endless beginner who embodies shikantaza and zazen-only with the noble completion of beginner's heartmind gratefully lives the Way of core-Self for its own sake. This is why endless beginners do not seek or strive beyond their core-Self and the noble completion of their beginner's heartmind. When endless beginners do not seek or strive beyond this, they somatically arrive as radical human beings who simply live ungraspable enlightenment by expressing their basic goodness, their undefiled wholeness, their noble completion, their spontaneous playfulness, their brilliance beyond words, and their wholeheartedness that gives and receives affection without inhibition.

Way-Seeking

We cultivate the Way of shoshin as an endless beginner by continuously honoring the abdominal refuge of our breathing, by taking care of our body with kindness, wakefulness, and tenderness, by enjoying the wholesome sensuality of our hara, by faithfully abiding in our core-Self, by extending love and receiving love beyond resistance and fear, and by daily practicing our boundless intimacy with all beings and things. When we cultivate the Way of shoshin in shikantaza and zazen-only, our beginner's heartmind entangles with the birthless stillness of core-Self to meet the limitless interdependency and wholeness of total reality. As beginner's heartmind meets the limitless interdependency and wholeness of total reality, it somatically listens and viscerally yields to vast Oneness like an infant somatically listens and viscerally yields to the comforting touch of its mother. We call this somatic listening and visceral yielding the Way-seeking goodness of our beginner's heartmind. This Way-seeking goodness of beginner's heartmind is far beyond ego-self grasping and pushing away. When we embody core-Self while devotedly Way-seeking with our beginner's heartmind, we brilliantly unfold ungraspable enlightenment in the activities, affairs, and relationships of everyday life.

As we practice our beginner's Way-seeking heartmind and steadfastly entrust the passage of our everyday life to the vast Oneness and bright wisdoming of total reality, we do not attach to doubting thoughts or judgements that may arise from our ego-self functioning or the ego-self functioning of others. We just continue to enjoy the sensuality of our hara, anchor in the birthless stillness of our core-Self, take refuge in the completion and fulfillment of our radical humanness, live in compassionate interdependency with total reality, delight in the ordinariness of ungraspable enlightenment itself, and forget all thoughts of gain or attainment even as we daily experience visceral realization and somatic confirmation. This is how we live our exquisite life of boundless intimacy and limitless interdependency while confidently embodying our core-Self and the Way-seeking goodness of beginner's heartmind.

Awe And Wonder

When we practice the embodiment of shikantaza and zazen-only, we viscerally confirm the unborn silence and birthless stillness of our core-Self, the completion of our radical humanness with not one thing lacking, and the basic goodness of our beginner's heartmind that practices Way-seeking before speaking, figuring, and thinking. As beginner's heartmind practices Way-seeking while entangling with the birthless stillness of core-Self, it extends its non-interfering curiosity to an unbounded moment of timelessness that instantly flashes everywhere while happening as a particular instant right here and now. To remain curiously attentive to this only moment of unbounded timelessness with beginner's heartmind is to gratefully embody wonder and awe in the simplicity and ordinariness of linear time. To embody the wonder and awe of beginner's heartmind while entangling with the birthless stillness of core-Self is to somatically comprehend that core-Self is exactly this only moment of timelessness that flashes everywhere without coming or going. As each timeless and unbounded moment of core-Self is happening everywhere without coming or going, our beginner's heartmind cherishes core-Self as the still essence and vast Oneness of total reality.

A timeless moment of core-Self can happen during the passage of linear time as a moment of joy, a moment of sadness, a moment of pain, a moment of love, a moment of anger, a moment of suffering, or a moment of ecstasy. Whatever timeless moment of core-Self arises during the passage of linear time, we faithfully take refuge in the vital flow of our breath, the sensual and rhythmic movement of our lower abdomen, the Way-seeking goodness of our beginner's heartmind, and the boundless intimacy and limitless interdependency of all beings and things. This is how we abide in the noble completion of our radical humanness while being the awe and wonder of beginner's heartmind in each timeless moment of core-Self that flashes everywhere at the surface and depth of total reality.

The Surprising Journey

As we embody each timeless moment of core-Self with the awe and wonder of beginner's heartmind, we devotedly practice Way-seeking to naturally unfold our journey of life and death within the boundless intimacy and limitless interdependency of total reality. In our Way, we do not use the cerebral power of our ego-self and thinking mind to manipulate, control, or predetermine the entire unfolding of our life journey. We do not journey through life in such a contrived, premeditated, and interfering way. Rather, we entrust our whole journey through life and death to the still guidance of core-Self and the Way-seeking goodness of beginner's heartmind. However, as we journey through life in this non-interfering Way, we still apply the healthy functioning of our ego-self and thinking mind to responsibly and wholeheartedly navigate our daily activities, affairs, goals, and relationships. As we unfold the ever surprising journey of our life in this balanced Way, we do not attach to dualistic social views that distinguish the lesser from the superior, the higher from the lower, the special from the ordinary, and the successful from the unsuccessful.

When we live through the still guidance of our core-Self while devotedly Way-seeking with beginner's heartmind, our life journey creatively unfolds in the vast Oneness of total reality far beneath the conscious thinking and knowing of our ego-self. As our journey unfolds beneath the interfering thinking and knowing of our ego-self, we cannot comprehend where we are going nor see into our distant future even as it continues to surprisingly arrive. Likewise, our ego-self cannot mentally grasp that our life journey is unfolding in ungraspable enlightenment itself. Although it is hard to know where we are going, see our evolving future, and mentally grasp the ungraspable, we faithfully embody the still guidance of our core-Self, diligently practice Way-seeking with beginner's heartmind, and continuously enjoy this only moment of vast Oneness as our true nature and our true home. When we viscerally embody core-Self in shikantaza and zazen-only with beginner's Way-seeking heartmind, we somatically discern all this and more far beneath the doubt and skepticism of ego-self and thinking mind.

In our Way, we do not view our life journey heading toward some distant future that will bring us happiness, completion, and fulfillment. We journey through the daily adventure of our everyday life in total completion and fulfillment just as we are. We experience noble completion and honorable fulfillment as we continue to embody core-Self with beginner's heartmind. This is how we somatically realize completion and total fulfillment with every step we take, and in everything we do. This is how we journey through life and death as a radical human being who courageously embodies the still flashing of core-Self, who tenderly expresses love and gratefully receives love with beginner's heartmind, and who practices daily accountability to the vast Oneness of total reality. This is the Way we unfold our life journey in ungraspable enlightenment while exemplifying a realizable future where all radical human beings live in boundless intimacy and limitless interdependency with not one thing lacking.

Our Pristine Way

We practice our mirrored Way of shikantaza and zazen-only from the time we open our eyes in the morning until we close our eyes at night. Each morning when we awaken, we sink into the sensuality of our hara and the visceral center-point of our lower abdomen. We do this to prepare for our daily embodiment of core-Self in shikantaza and zazen-only. When we sit down each morning to viscerally embody our core-Self inside of zazen-only, we do so with the humility and wonder of beginner's heartmind. As we arise from zazen-only to practice shikantaza in our everyday life, we continue to viscerally embody our core-Self with a beginner's Way-seeking heartmind. This is how we cultivate our pristine and timeless Way in shikantaza and zazen-only. This is how we start each day to live in the boundless intimacy of core-Self while our beginner's heartmind enjoys Way-seeking as ungraspable enlightenment itself.

As we embody the pristine Way of core-Self and gratefully practice Way-seeking with beginner's heartmind, we experience no need to take narcotics or other street drugs to heighten our bright and vivid wakefulness, to augment the brilliance of our lucid dreaming, to further validate that we are being dreamed with all beings and things, or to confirm the somatic realization of living in boundless intimacy with not one thing lacking. We have no desire to take psychedelic substances to deepen the radical completion and fulfillment of our original humanness, to enhance the natural exuberance and spontaneity of our beginner's heartmind, or to go beyond the birthless stillness and unborn silence of our core-Self.

As not one thing is lacking in the embodiment of core-Self and the Way-seeking goodness of beginner's heartmind, there is no need to transport a cerebrally generated consciousness to illusory worlds that are far removed from the sensual, wondrous, and mysterious world that we live in right here and now. Human beings can never come to viscerally know the pristine Way that naturally exists within themselves until they inwardly entrust their life and death to the pristine Way itself. This is why we discourage the social and recreational use of organic psychotropics in everyday life. This is why we do not encourage cultural norms that traditionally ritualize the ingestion of hallucinogens to advance spiritual realization, to promote mystical and religious experiences, or to foster insights during ceremonial life passages. We passionately exemplify and viscerally transmit the pristine Way of core-Self so that all human beings can somatically realize the radical completion and total fulfillment of their original nature that is far beyond lacking, desiring, grasping, and pushing away.

Nothing Holy

As we practice living in the pristine Way of core-Self with the basic goodness of beginner's heartmind, we do not seek out or attach to a religious faith or spiritual belief. This does not mean that we do not embody faith as a Way of life. We confidently experience faith in the still illumination of our core-Self, the Way-seeking goodness of our beginner's heartmind, and the vast Oneness of total reality. However, our Way of confidently living the body of faith is viscerally engendered and somatically grounded in our hara. This means that our visceral embodiment of faith is not generated or perpetuated by our thinking mind. Our visceral experience of faith is not dependent on any mental or emotional attachment to a collectively cherished or historically venerated religious belief. This is why we confidently embody faith beyond all atheistic and religious views that are cerebrally upheld and defended by ego-self and thinking mind. This is how we somatically advance the liberation of our radical humanness while wholly enjoying the magnanimous openness of our beginner's heartmind in shikantaza and zazen-only.

As we confidently embody faith and somatically advance the liberation of our radical humanness, we viscerally realize that the still flashing of core-Self is fundamentally empty and that vast Oneness is Nothing holy. However, this does not mean that our visceral embodiment of faith is devoid of any feelings associated with holiness or sacredness. Quite the opposite. We viscerally experience core-Self and vast Oneness as a still sacredness, an awe inspiring emptiness, and a holy Nothingness. To viscerally embody core-Self and vast Oneness in this precious Way is to somatically verify beyond all doubt that the still emptiness and vast wholeness of total reality is eternally refreshing the boundless intimacy and limitless interdependency of all beings and things. Thus, when I speak of core-Self as fundamentally empty and vast Oneness as Nothing holy, I am really saying that core-Self and vast Oneness are exactly the still sacredness and unbounded holiness of total reality. This is completely in accord with Zen Master Bodhidharma who taught us to viscerally transmit Zen as the Way of vast emptiness and Nothing holy. This is why an endless beginner passionately embodies the trustworthy emptiness of core-Self while wholeheartedly bowing to Nothing holy at the surface and depth of total reality.

Satiating The Root

Now, if someone was looking at us just sitting as core-Self with beginner's heartmind inside of zazen-only, they may think that we are wasting our time by not doing anything productive. However, inside of just sitting is where we experience the still sacredness of our core-Self and the vast holiness of total reality. Inside of just sitting is where the total dynamic functioning of ungraspable enlightenment is being viscerally transmitted as the boundless intimacy and limitless interdependency of all beings and things. Inside of just sitting is where we are silently illuminating the surface and depth of total reality, tenderly molting off our ego-self and thinking mind, completely satiating all our desires with not one thing lacking, and all the while somatically listening with the wondrous curiosity of our beginner's heartmind.

The satiation of all our desires that takes place inside the behavioral stillness of zazen-only is our somatic and visceral reference point for wholeheartedly living the body of shikantaza with clarity, peace, settledness, and uprightness. In our Soto Zen school, we chant a vow that reminds us to extinguish all our desires in shikantaza and zazen-only. When we chant our precious vow, we say, "Desires are inexhaustible; I vow to put an end to them." This is something that sounds overwhelming and impossible. Some people try to fulfill this vow by getting rid of all material goods and monetary wealth. Others try to ignore or repress thoughts and feelings that arouse desires. Still others attach to monastic environments that curtail the stimulation and satiation of wanting and desiring. Then there are those who think that ending desires would extinguish the fundamental essence of being human. However, all these are mistaken views held by those who do not understand the deep meaning and true blessing of our Zen vow.

When we practice our mirrored Way in everyday life, we do not push away material goods or monetary gain. We do not repress thoughts and feelings that may stir desires. Nor do we cling to monastic environments even as we gratefully entangle with them. We do not negate the natural arising of human desires nor their honorable and moderate satiation. However, as we compassionately entangle with our needs and desires within a material world, we daily take time to extinguish inexhaustible desires and wholly fulfill our Zen vow. We do this by totally satiating the root of desiring itself. We satiate the root of desiring through the still emptiness of our core-Self inside of zazen-only. Satiating the root of desiring is very different from going around trying to satisfy one desire after another. We satiate the root of desiring by embodying the still emptiness of our core-Self where desires no longer arise. To embody the still emptiness of core-Self where desires no longer arise is to viscerally experience the completion and fulfillment of our radical humanness far beyond lacking, wanting, or desiring. When we satiate the root of desiring inside of zazen-only, we come to somatically realize a beginner's Way of living shikantaza from the "zazen seal of total satiation." To live shikantaza from the zazen seal of total satiation is to continuously nurture a life of simplicity, serenity, composure, and moderation. Our beginner's Way of living shikantaza from the zazen seal of total satiation is very different from an ego-self that is constantly driven by an insatiable dissatisfaction to gratify inexhaustible desires.

Although we wholly fulfill our precious Zen vow by daily satiating the root of desiring inside of zazen-only, this does not mean that desires stop arising during the passage of our everyday life. We still have arising desires just like everyone else does. We clearly see how our emerging desires tend to propel us toward a transient and ever fleeting satiation. However, we entangle with arising desires from the still emptiness of our core-Self that satiates the root of desiring itself. When we entangle with desires from the still emptiness of our core-Self and the noble completion of our beginner's heartmind, desires do not immediately propel us toward an ever fleeting satiation. We do not experience bondage to an ego-self drivenness that seeks instant gratification for every desire that arises. We viscerally know that no amount of transient satiation will ever bring us the deep spiritual fulfillment and completion that we daily experience by simply satiating the root of desiring itself. This is why an endless beginner takes time each day to embody the still emptiness of core-Self that gratifies inexhaustible desires by satiating the root of desiring itself.

Enduring Dissatisfaction

When we daily embody our mirrored Way of shikantaza and zazen-only, we lucidly and compassionately entangle with our arising needs and desires from the still emptiness of our core-Self and our beginner's Way-seeking heartmind. We gratefully live from our core-Self and our beginner's heartmind because together they help us navigate our basic needs and arising desires with simplicity, clarity, delight, and moderation. Our Way is to live as an ordinary human being who compassionately satisfies basic human needs while healthfully curbing and sensibly gratifying human desires as they arise. However, we also know that human beings inadvertently attach to their egoself-centricity, confuse their basic needs with arising desires, get lost in incessant craving and coveting, and persistently suffer bondage to transient satiation and inexhaustible desiring.

When human beings get caught up in the daily round of needing, desiring, wanting, and satiating, they somatically experience a growing dissatisfaction with their everyday life and relationships. This growing dissatisfaction is really the visceral calling of vast Oneness that somatically urges all human beings to live from the birthless stillness of their core-Self, the Way-seeking goodness of their beginner's heartmind, and the boundless intimacy and limitless interdependency of their radical humanness. Confused by their inner bondage to the round of needing, desiring, craving, and satiating, human beings unwittingly focus their embodied consciousness on the outside world to find a gratifying and enduring liberation from the suffering of dissatisfaction. This outward searching keeps human beings from viscerally realizing their deep root of dissatisfaction, their innocent yearning for boundless intimacy and limitless interdependency, and their original longing to live in vast Oneness with all beings and things.

When human beings do not viscerally discern that the somatic language of suffering and dissatisfaction is exactly the visceral calling of vast Oneness, they seek to embody a satisfactory relief by habitually engaging in social relationships, by obsessively overworking, by emotionally overeating, by multitasking here and there, by micromanaging their life and the life of others, by having extramarital affairs, by numbing themselves with drugs, sex, and alcohol, by becoming dependent on the secretion of adrenaline, by losing themselves in technological devices, by creating needless drama in their everyday life, by constantly grasping at wealth, social status, and political power, and by rigidly adhering to collectively valued goals, agendas, views and beliefs. However, all these misdirected behavioral strategies do not address the visceral calling of vast Oneness that somatically urges us to embody the still emptiness of our core-Self, to liberate the authenticity and basic goodness of our beginner's heartmind, and to experientially arrive as radical human beings who cherish boundless intimacy, vast Oneness, and limitless interdependency far beneath the functioning of I, me, and mine.

Turning the Light Inward

Society reinforces our outward searching and daily distracts us from the visceral calling of vast Oneness by excessively commercializing our needs and desires, by continuously stimulating the round of grasping, craving, and satiating, and by associating the pursuit of happiness with the acquisition of wealth, power, fame, status, and goods. This social distraction from the deep visceral root of our discontent and the constant reinforcement of our outward searching keeps us in bondage to the round of desiring, craving, and satiating while perpetuating the suffering of dissatisfaction.

Our Way is to daily take time away from society, stop all our outward searching, turn the light of our embodied awareness inward, heed the visceral calling of vast Oneness, and silently illuminate things just as they are. When we silently Illuminate things just as they are, we clearly discern that the social idealization of happiness and the constant reinforcement of its outward pursuit spreads across all cultures, subcultures, genders, and age groups. In our Way, we meet the commercialization of our needs and desires, the pervasive social idealization of happiness, and the reinforcement of its outward pursuit with the still emptiness of our core-Self and the Way-seeking goodness of our beginner's heartmind. Instead of trying to achieve a socially idealized state of happiness by satiating one commercialized need and desire after another, we simply turn the light of our embodied awareness inward, sink into the still composure of our core-Self, soak in the pristine exuberance of our beginner's heartmind, and all the while enjoy the completion and total fulfillment of our radical humanness that is far beyond the suffering of dissatisfaction.

The driven pace of our busy society does not encourage us to come to a dead stop, take time to turn the light of our embodied awareness inward, silently sink into the birthless stillness of our core-Self, realize our radical humanness and our boundless intimacy with all beings and things, and recover the Way-seeking goodness of our beginner's heartmind. This is why we create a special time and a true place to daily remove ourselves from the unrelenting pace and drivenness of society. This time and place is where we temporarily disengage from the dynamic interpersonal web of social relationships and honor the integrity of our aloneness. To honor the integrity of our aloneness is to turn the light of our embodied awareness inward, come to a dead stop in the timelessness of zazen-only, sink into the still emptiness of our core-Self, and silently illuminate the surface and depth of total reality.

When we turn the light of our embodied awareness inward, sink into the sensuality of our hara, linger in our core-Self with not one thing lacking, and somatically enjoy the noble completion of our beginner's heartmind, we viscerally discern the exquisite refuge of shikantaza and zazen-only. To viscerally discern the exquisite refuge of shikantaza and zazen-only is to see through the prevalent idealization of happiness, the social reinforcement of its outward pursuit, the commercialization of needs and desires, and the monetary exploitation of drivenness and dissatisfaction. Even as we clearly see things just as they are, we continue to tenderly entangle with our needs and desires during the passage of our everyday life. As needs and desires arise, we practice making sensible choices by effortlessly yielding to restraint, renunciation, and moderation while wholly delighting in the simplicity of satiation without grasping or regret. We unhesitatingly yield to restraint, renunciation, and moderation because we deeply value the still vibrancy of our core-Self, the vital exuberance of our beginner's heartmind, and the healthy sensual radiance of this Only Moment Body. To compassionately entangle with our needs and desires in this lucid and awakened Way is to continuously live our life of ungraspable enlightenment even as we wholeheartedly enjoy and gratefully appreciate transient satiation.

Saving Sentient Beings

When we meet all our arising needs and desires with a generous attentiveness, a wholehearted acceptance, and a compassionate discernment, we are simply practicing our precious Zen vow to save all sentient beings. When we chant our Zen vow, we say, "Sentient beings are numberless; I vow to save them." This means that we vow to save all sentient beings without exception. Our vow to save all sentient beings without exception is not just about saving people. It also includes saving our own needs, feelings, emotions, thoughts, and desires, as well as all the beings, things, and events that arise within the experiential field of our everyday life.

We practice our Zen vow by respectfully engaging all sentient beings from the still composure of our core-Self, by lucidly and compassionately seeing and meeting them just as they are, by spontaneously bowing to their unique wholeness and their great functioning in everyday life, by acknowledging their vast Oneness with total reality, and by attentively caring for them with the basic goodness of our beginner's heartmind. This is the Way we save our passing thoughts and feelings, our needs and desires, and all the people, things, and events that come forth to engage our core-Self in the dance of vast Oneness and limitless interdependency.

When we attentively and tenderly demonstrate a deep visceral interconnectedness with all sentient beings during the passage of our everyday life, we cultivate a vast field of boundless intimacy, effortlessly molt off separation, drivenness, and dissatisfaction, cut off the inflation and advancement of egoself-centricity, save our own health and well-being, and gratefully enjoy the continuous arrival of ungraspable enlightenment itself. However, if we ignore and trivialize all the sentient beings that support our everyday life, we cultivate a vast field of ignorance and delusion, promote the advancement of our egoself-centricity, obsessively work on our goals and agendas, inadvertently diminish our health and well-being, and all the while perpetuate our bondage to separation, drivenness, and dissatisfaction.

As we include people in our Zen vow to save all sentient beings, we do not try to save them from an originally sinful human nature or deliver them to a deified Buddha. We do not teach them to gain redemption, salvation, or enlightenment by willfully suppressing their sensuality or transcending their human feelings, needs, emotions, and desires. This is not our Way. We do not think about "saving or delivering people" in the same way that others do. We save and deliver people to their highest potential and their true greatness. We deliver them to the visceral integrity of their core-Self, the basic goodness of their beginner's heartmind, the completion and fulfillment of their radical humanness, and the honorable Way of blending their everyday life with the vast Oneness of total reality.

When we chant our Zen vow, we are vocally expressing our deep commitment to acknowledge the interdependent equality of all sentient beings from the still composure of our core-Self and the original wholeness of our beginner's heartmind. As we daily embody and practice our Zen vow, we do not judge any sentient being as insignificant, trivial, or unimportant. All sentient beings that arise in our daily life mean everything to us. They are like precious friends that support our body's vibrant sensual aliveness and our boundless intimacy with total reality. When we do not show up with visceral attentiveness and wholehearted caring for all sentient beings, we maintain a cerebral distance and separation from our whole life, diminish the vibrant sensual aliveness of our body, and foolishly miss the opportunity to somatically verify the fulfillment and completion of our radical humanness.

In our Way, saving and being saved are intimately one. When we save all sentient beings by attentively meeting them from the still composure of our core-Self and the pristine freshness of our beginner's heartmind, we completely save ourselves. To save ourselves by tenderly and attentively taking care of our everyday life and relationships is to save all sentient beings. We save ourselves and all sentient beings when we continuously embody our core-Self with beginner's heartmind in shikantaza and zazen-only. When we do just this, we instantly birth a future where all radical human beings live together far beyond grasping, lacking, and drivenness. This is how we passionately fulfill our Zen vow of "saving and being saved" within the boundless intimacy and vast Oneness of total reality.

Endless Reawakening

Sometimes, in the midst of our daily practice of shikantaza, we may inadvertently fall asleep in thinking mind, drift in the drama and drivenness of ego-self, and start ignoring all sentient beings that graciously come forth to engage core-Self in the dance of boundless intimacy and limitless interdependency. When this happens, we do not meet beings and things with the attentive tenderness and magnanimous openness of beginner's heartmind. At those times, we find ourselves ignoring the interdependent equality of all beings and things. We go from one being and thing to another without being grateful for their presence. We forget to appreciate who they are, what they are teaching us, what we are doing with them, what they are doing for us, and what they are showing us about our accountability to the vast Oneness of total reality.

When we do not show up to meet all beings and things from the still composure of our core-Self and the Way-seeking goodness of our beginner's heartmind, we begin to spatially and temporally project our ego-self and thinking mind ahead of our body, split our attention between what we are doing and what we are going to do in a future moment, forget where we have been or what we really did, leave cabinets opened or slam doors shut, knock things over, hurt ourselves unnecessarily, withdraw further into our cerebral chatter, and totally ignore the bright wisdoming of vast Oneness in our everyday life. Such behaviors keep us in bondage to drivenness and dissatisfaction, illuminate our preoccupation with the drama and drivenness of ego-self, and clearly reveal our ingratitude and lack of appreciation for all sentient beings that come forth to engage our core-Self and our beginner's heartmind in the interdependent dance of ungraspable enlightenment itself.

Whether you are a beginner or a veteran practitioner of shikantaza and zazen-only, there will always be a time when you unwittingly fall asleep in ego-self and thinking mind, disregard your vow to save all sentient beings, forget to practice your beginner's Way-seeking heartmind, neglect your visceral intimacy with core-Self, and ignore the vast Oneness and limitless interdependency of total reality. As those times, you will find yourself concentrating on a specific goal, a problem, a concern, a project, a relationship, or multiple tasks. You will begin to ignore your interdependency and boundless intimacy with all beings and things. You will forget to show up from the still composure of your core-Self and the basic goodness of your beginner's heartmind. You will begin to feel more isolated in your heady ego-self-centricity, feel increasingly driven to control each situation, event, and relationship, experience needless tension, agitation, worry, distress, and frustration, and see all this as your conscientious way of taking good care of your everyday life.

When you find yourself ill at ease, unwittingly asleep in your ego-self and cerebral thinking, and entirely distracted from your core-Self and your beginner's heartmind, just remember that your deep sincerity and devotion to the daily practice of shikantaza and zazen-only will continue to advance your reawakening, help you to see the ignorance of your distraction, and present the true Way to compassionately begin again. At the intimate arrival of reawakening, you will realize that you have been ignoring the profound depth of all beings and things, disregarding your unconditional intimacy with the vast Oneness of total reality, and losing touch with the completion and fulfillment of your radical humanness. You will see that all this is happening because you have forgotten the refuge of core-Self, the power of lucid dreaming, and the Way of being dreamed in vast Oneness with all beings and things. When you reawaken to all of this, arouse your vow to save all sentient beings, come back to the flow of your breath, sink into the center-point of your lower abdomen, begin to easefully embody the still composure of your core-Self, tenderly arouse your beginner's Way-seeking heartmind, and simply enjoy your boundless intimacy and limitless interdependency with total reality.

Beyond Fixed Identity

As we compassionately reawaken to our core-Self in shikantaza and zazen-only, we devotedly practice our Zen vow to save all sentient beings without exception. To sincerely advance our Zen vow with a beginner's Way-seeking heartmind is to somatically verify that we cannot mentally establish a fixed personal identity for our core-Self nor speak of core-Self as a socially identifiable being. To viscerally embody the still unfixed identity of core-Self is to simply be boundless intimacy and limitless interdependency at the surface and depth of total reality. As we embody the still unfixed identity of our core-Self with beginner's Way-seeking heartmind, we courageously live far beneath the knowing and thinking of our ego-self functioning. To faithfully live far beneath the knowing and thinking of our ego-self functioning is to honorably accept that we do not mentally grasp who we are as a still unfixed identity. To honorably accept not knowing who we are with the unfabricated humility and magnanimous openness of our beginner's heartmind is to passionately live the Way of ungraspable enlightenment itself.

This Way of confidently living from the still unfixed identity of our core-Self with the magnanimous openness of our beginner's heartmind may seem strange and unfamiliar to you. We have grown accustom to mentally knowing who we are as a fixed ego-self identity that has a distinct name and an individual personality. It is difficult for us to see how we can mentally uphold and socially validate our fixed ego-self identity if we do not have a name and an individual personality that we can share with others. We uphold our familiar ego-self identity by constantly thinking about ourselves, by chattering about our likes and dislikes, by mentally focusing only on ourselves when talking with others, and by telling ourselves repetitive stories about how great we are, how inadequate we are, how we are mistreated, or how things never go our way. All this egoself-centricity is driven by fear. We fear that if we do not uphold and advance our fixed ego-self identity, we will no longer exist to ourselves or to others. This is why we guardedly protect and rigidly defend our fixed set of ideas about who we are and what we believe in. This is why we expend a great deal of our life force just to uphold the fixed identity of our ego-self. All this ego-self expenditure of our life force creates needless tension and stress while depleting and exhausting us over time. However, all this ego-self depletion of our life force can be substantially diminished by courageously living from the still unfixed identity of our core-Self and the magnanimous openness of our beginner's heartmind.

In our Way, we do not negate mentally knowing who we are as a developed ego-self that has a personal history, special life memories, and a unique personality. For example, if people ask me who I am, I would answer just like everyone else does, "I am so and so who was born here and now lives in this place, who writes and teaches about these things, who loves his wife and cherishes his growing family, who practices yoga and exercises daily, who dances with sensual abandonment, and who teaches, educates, and counsels people worldwide." However, if they ask me to personally or socially share my still unfixed identity as core-Self, I would have no-answer to give them. The only verbal answer that I could honestly and confidently give them with my beginner's heartmind is, "I don't know."

This simple and honest Way of answering, "I don't know," was originally verbalized by Zen Master Bodhidharma. As you might remember, Bodhidharma was the famous monk from India who transmitted the Zen Body of the Buddha to China. He is considered the first Chinese patriarch of Zen. In 520 A.D., Master Bodhidharma was invited to share his Zen teachings with Chinese Emperor Wu. Emperor Wu asked Bodhidharma many questions about the Buddha Way. However, the emperor became upset by Bodhidharma's perplexing Zen answers. Finally, in his frustration and confusion, Emperor Wu asked, "Who are you to speak to me in this way? Bodhidharma confidently said, "Your majesty, I do not know." People generally do not understand the fulfillment, completion, and liberation that Bodhidharma compassionately shared by simply and honestly saying, "I do not know."

Many of us have become deeply attached to our fixed ego-self identity. So much so that we vehemently uphold, defend, and protect it well into the later years of our life. Some hold so tightly to their fixed ego-self with its rigid pride and judgements that they will not extend love and forgiveness to others even when facing their own death. We may think that we know who we are, what we believe in, what reality is, and what is always true for us. We may think that we do not need to see our world or ourselves anew. However, when we hold on tightly to a fixed ego-self identity, we impede our mental, emotional, and spiritual growth over our limited lifetime. When we are not willing to see the insubstantial and transparent nature of our ego-self pride and fixed identity, we begin to lose touch with the ever fresh impermanence of our life force and the pristine sensual vibrancy of our whole body. This makes it difficult for us to viscerally experience the still unfixed identity of our core-Self, enjoy the noble completion of our beginner's heartmind, always see things anew as they really are, and continue to grow as a radical human being who unfolds ungraspable enlightenment within the ordinariness of everyday life.

When we expend so much energy upholding and defending our fixed ego-self identity at any cost, we advance unhealthy stress in our body, cultivate delusion, ignorance, and tension in our everyday life, hinder the realization of sincerity and authenticity in our relationships, and obstruct the completion and fulfillment of our radical humanness. When we are deeply attached to a fixed ego-self identity and a static view of our personality, we cannot live in the boundless intimacy and vast Oneness of our core-Self. Nor can we liberate the unfabricated humility and noble completion of our beginner's heartmind. Our Way is to viscerally embody our still unfixed identity, confidently accept the brilliance of not knowing who we are, enjoy our boundless intimacy and limitless interdependency, daily fulfill our Zen vow to save all sentient beings, and live ungraspable enlightenment with the basic goodness of our beginner's heartmind.

Healthy Functioning

As we viscerally embody our core-Self with beginner's Way-seeking heartmind in shikantaza and zazen-only, we silently illuminate that our ego-self identity is really a dynamic set of cerebral functions that empower us to linguistically label, intellectually comprehend, behaviorally test, emotionally process, mentally recollect, and interpersonally share our embodied experience of everyday life. At the same time, we silently illuminate that our personality is a cerebrally organized pattern of stable characteristics that include our individual way of thinking, feeling, perceiving, emoting, relating, and doing. Our cerebral ego-self functions and the stable characteristics of our individual personality are both there to assist us in navigating the outer lawful world of material reality, the inner world of our passing thoughts, feelings, needs, and desires, and the daily interpersonal world of our familial and social relationships. As our ego-self and our personality assist us in navigating these three worlds of our everyday life, we ground the total dynamic functioning of both in the still illumination of our core-Self and the Way-seeking goodness of our beginner's heartmind. Then, we wholeheartedly practice not being mentally rigid and narrow, emotionally protective and defensive, and behaviorally reactive and aggressive. When we sincerely do just this from the birthless stillness of our core-Self and the magnanimous openness of our beginner's heartmind, we experience no urgency to uphold the fixed existence of our ego-self, no pressing desire to advance our individual personality, and no reactive instinct to behaviorally defend either one at any cost.

When we navigate the three worlds of our everyday life, we do not adhere to a fixed ego-self identity or a rigid view of our individual personality. Here, I am not saying that we should not have a clear idea of who we are as a person and a unique individual in society. I am not saying that we should negate our early childhood memories or the memories of our lived experience over time. I am not saying that we need to cut ourselves off from the developmental continuity of our ego-self or the coherent integration of our individual personality. It is perfectly natural to celebrate and enjoy our individual personality while taking care of the practical matters of everyday life with our cerebral ego-self functioning. However, it is also important to consistently refine and sustain the healthy functioning of our ego-self and our individual personality from the still brilliance of our core-Self and the magnanimous openness of our beginner's heartmind.

As we practice our mirrored Way of shikantaza and zazen-only, we honor our cerebral ego-self functions and the stable characteristics of our personality. We are grateful for the healthy and transparent functioning of our ego-self identity, the ongoing transformation and refinement of our individual personality, the still composure of our core-Self that allows us to honestly and compassionately process traumatic life experiences, and the pristine exuberance of our beginner's heartmind that always revitalizes the vigorous freshness of our radical humanness and the emotional vitality and richness of our personal life memories. We know that our cerebrally generated ego-self consciousness and our individual personality help us to coherently integrate our past memories with our present moment of aliveness while connecting our present moment of aliveness with the ever fresh embodiment of our future. If we only experienced the still timeless flashing of core-Self without having a cerebrally fixed ego-self consciousness in linear time, we could not intelligently connect the passing moments of our embodied existence nor weave them into a rich emotional tapestry of life memories.

In our Way, we compassionately integrate our past with our present while wholeheartedly trusting the organic unfolding of ungraspable enlightenment that is always intimately arriving as our surprising future in this only moment we call here and now. We accept the gracious functioning of our ego-self and our individual personality even as we heal, transform, and refine both from the still composure of our core-Self and the magnanimous openness of our beginner's heartmind. This is how we continuously protect ourselves from sticking to a rigidly fixed ego-self identity or inadvertently grasping at an unchanging, static, and dogmatic personality. When we embody our core-Self in this healthy and inclusive Way, we somatically flourish as radical human beings who viscerally enjoy the ordinariness of everyday life while somatically blooming in boundless intimacy and ungraspable enlightenment itself.

Beginner's Nobility

Some of you who are just beginning to practice shikantaza and zazen-only may feel that you will never accomplish the completion and fulfillment of your radical humanness. You may think that you will never be able to viscerally embody your boundless intimacy and limitless interdependency with all beings and things. You may falsely assume that ungraspable enlightenment cannot be lived amidst the challenges, difficulties, and distractions of everyday life. You may even think that viscerally awakening to the lamp of core-Self, somatically realizing the power of lucid dreaming, envisioning and actualizing your personal dreams, and blending those dreams with the vast Oneness of total reality are all far beyond your capacity as a beginner. You may wish to go far beyond a beginner's mind of not-knowing. You may want to exceed the romantic and passionate heart of a beginner. You may seek to be a professional who confidently knows everything about Zen enlightenment and the mature and dispassionate Way of living shikantaza and zazen-only.

If you are a beginner who grasps at being a professional, you may become inadvertently attached to arising doubts and expectations. You may become disheartened when you do not immediately experience the sensuality of your hara and the still vibrancy of your core-Self. You may begin to doubt the magnanimous openness of your beginner's heartmind. You might feel overwhelmed by the seeming discrepancy between who you are and who you would like to be. For those of you who may feel like this, I hope that I have clarified just how special you are as a genuine beginner in our Way. I hope that I have shown you the infinite value that we place on your beginner's heartmind. When we see your beginner's mind of not-knowing and the expression of your unfabricated humility and wonder, we see the true completion of our Way. When we see your passionate heart beating with devotion, sincerity, and faithfulness even in the midst of your struggle, we see the total accomplishment of our Way. Never forget that every beginner is an honorable model and a noble exemplar in our Soto Zen school. This is a very important point to understand.

Some of you who have been practicing Zen for many years may see yourselves as highly skilled and proficient in shikantaza and zazen-only. You may think that you are far beyond a beginner who graciously embodies the mind of not-knowing. You may feel that you are more mature than a beginner whose fervent heart engages shikantaza and zazen-only with romantic zeal and exuberance. You may feel that you have more experience and spiritual maturity than a beginner who is unaccomplished in our Way. To those of you who assume that you are far beyond a beginner, I hope that I have clearly revealed just how important it is to keep your beginner's heartmind that endlessly romances shikantaza and zazen-only with humility, sincerity, freshness, and wonder.

As you practice shikantaza and zazen-only, whether you are alone or with others, always remember that the nobility of your beginner's heartmind is absolutely respected and honored in our Way. Know beyond all doubt that you are living the completion and total fulfillment of your radical humanness when you devotedly practice our mirrored Way for its own sake. To be a noble beginner who practices our mirrored Way for its own sake is to accept the brilliance of not-knowing who you are and the freedom of not-wanting anything else. Not-wanting anything else means that you are an endless beginner who is not trying to become a buddha, gain perfect wisdom, advance an idealized view of yourself, transcend your physical body, escape the difficulties of your life, or attain a graspable enlightenment. To accept the brilliance of not-knowing who you are means that you are an endless beginner who viscerally embodies the still unfixed identity of core-Self while silently illuminating the surface and depth of total reality. When you sincerely practice the Way of an endless beginner just like this, you will somatically arrive in boundless intimacy, vast Oneness, and limitless interdependency far beneath the knowing of your ego-self and thinking mind.

Visceral Learning

As you continue to embody the still composure of core-Self with the magnanimous openness and exuberant curiosity of beginner's heartmind, you will always be studying and learning how to passionately live the ordinariness of everyday life as ungraspable enlightenment itself. You will not be studying and learning by reading books, going to school, ingesting psychotropic drugs, spending time with shamans and gurus, or googling information on your smartphones or laptops. You will be studying and learning through the still intelligence of your core-Self and the brilliant wholeness of your beginner's heartmind. This is how we viscerally study and somatically learn in our mirrored Way of shikantaza and zazen-only. Most people have not been exposed to this somatic and visceral Way of studying and learning. Many do not realize how important our mirrored Way is to their personal growth and spiritual development, their interpersonal synergy and human fulfillment, their emotional healing and physical well-being, their creative, productive, and efficient way of living, and their ongoing arrival as radical human beings who embody boundless intimacy with not one thing lacking.

Our visceral and somatic Way of studying and learning happens far beneath the cerebral thinking and knowing of our ego-self. However, we do not get rid of words, stop reading and thinking, or push away the use of science and technology. We read, learn from words, think logically, and use twenty-first century science and technology with gratitude, curiosity, and wonder. We use language and social media to speak and communicate with honesty, openness, and uprightness. However, we also value and deeply respect our somatic and visceral Way of studying and learning in shikantaza and zazen-only. We passionately study and learn with our whole body about the great matter of life and death, the still unbounded essence of total reality, the radical and transpersonal nature of all human beings, the Way of loving and being loved with beginner's heartmind, the timeless refuge and vast impermance of our core-Self, the ever surprising and wondrous unfolding of ungraspable enlightenment, and the refreshing and healing embodiment of boundless intimacy, vast Oneness, and limitless interdependency.

Always Begin Again

Whether you are a beginner or a veteran practitioner who is somatically studying and viscerally learning in the mirrored Way of shikantaza and zazen-only, remember that you are not trying to extinguish your ego-self, still your passing thoughts, cut off your logical thinking, get rid of your painful memories, willfully arouse your mindfulness and mental concentration, or eliminate your individual personality. This is not our Way. We passionately study and learn by nourishing intimacy with our abdominal breathing, by gratefully experiencing the sensuality of our hara, by wakefully sustaining our easeful and upright posture, by viscerally anchoring in the still composure of our core-Self, and by meeting all beings and things with the tenderness and magnanimous openness of our beginner's heartmind. When you study and practice in this lucid and straightforward Way, you will somatically discover beyond all doubt that your core-Self unconditionally transmits the vast Oneness of total reality, compassionately refines the healthy functioning of your ego-self and thinking mind, and graciously refreshes the spontaneity, wholeness, and exuberance of your beginner's heartmind.

As you somatically study and viscerally learn in shikantaza and zazen-only, always take refuge in the pristine clarity, original nobility, and basic goodness of your beginner's heartmind. Do not get caught up in mentally idealized standards that perpetuate a false duality and an unhealthy tension between where you are and where you would like to be. Do not be swayed into thinking that you are far removed from ungraspable enlightenment or the completion and fulfillment of your radical humanness. Do not give way into thinking that you will never be good enough just as you are. Simply honor your bright sincerity, your wholehearted determination to always begin again, and your commendable devotion to daily practice shikantaza and zazen-only for their own sake. Always remember that an endless beginner is deeply respected and treasured in our mirrored Way. We never ask you to achieve a human completion or to attain a spiritual evolution that is far removed from the simplicity, humility, authenticity, and naturalness of beginner's heartmind. We do not ask you to become a professional who knows everything about shikantaza and zazen-only. We simply ask you to become the original beginner and radical human being that you already are.

When you practice the embodiment of core-Self with the basic goodness of beginner's heartmind, you faithfully exemplify the total completion and fulfillment of our Way while inspiring others to live ungraspable enlightenment within the ordinariness of everyday life. Whether you have been sitting for one day or for fifty years, I encourage you to always nourish and sustain the wonder, exuberance, and curiosity of your beginner's heartmind. All Zen teachers and Zen practitioners, no matter how long they have been practicing, are continually facing the truth of having to begin again as a beginner. So do not focus on comparing yourself to an idealized view of Zen practice or Zen realization. There will be countless times that you will have to begin again as a beginner, but this does not mean that you are incompetent or a failure. Simply accept yourself as an endless beginner, embrace your inner struggle that clearly demonstrates your honorable sincerity, courageously sink into the still emptiness of your core-Self, and begin again to practice the Way of boundless intimacy and limitless interdependency. When you continuously do just this, I know beyond all doubt that you will viscerally realize the completion and fulfillment of your radical humanness, somatically affirm the magnanimous nobility of your beginner's heartmind, and experientially verify that core-Self gratefully places the monarch's crown of ungraspable enlightenment on the vast Oneness of total reality.

Thank You

"The pursuit of truth and beauty
is a sphere of activity in which
we are permitted to remain
children all our lives."

Albert Einstein

Honoring His Beginner's Way

"The most difficult thing is to keep beginner's heartmind in our practice. So if you can keep your beginner's heartmind forever, you are Buddha. In this point, our practice should be constant. We should always practice our Way with beginner's heartmind."

Shunryu Suzuki-roshi

"The important thing is not to stop
questioning. Curiosity has its own reason
for existing. One cannot help but be in awe
when contemplating the mysteries of eternity,
of life, of the marvelous structure of reality. It
is enough if one tries merely to comprehend
a little of this mystery every day....
never lose a holy curiosity."

Albert Einstein

"Dogen Zenji
always emphasized
"beginner's heartmind." We
should always remain in beginner's
heartmind. It means our experience
should always be refreshed and renewed.
It means always have the joy of discovering
something. The same joy as children
discovering something new."

Suzuki-roshi

PART V

INSTRUCTION

"A person of the Way fundamentally
does not dwell anywhere. The white clouds are
fascinated with the green mountain's foundation.
The bright moon cherishes being carried along with
the flowing water. The clouds part and the mountain
appears. The moon sets and the water is cool. Each
bit of autumn contains vast interpenetration without
bounds. Every dust is whole without reaching
me; the ten thousand changes are stilled
without shaking me. If you can sit
here with stability, then you can
freely step across and engage
the world with energy. There
is an excellent saying that the
six sense doors are not veiled, the
highways in all directions have no
footprints. Always arriving everywhere
without being confused, gentle without
hesitation, the perfected person
always knows where to go."

Chinese Zen Master Hongzhi
(1091 AD–1157 AD)

CHAPTER 9

Daily Home Training

Take Refuge in
Vast Silence,
Embrace Peace
as your True Nature.

"Bit by bit, moment to moment, Ango, becomes the crown of the skull. Even though this is so, don't take [Ango] as the start of your training; don't take it as going beyond. Even if you see it as the start, kick over the starting. Even if you see it as going beyond, stamp-out going beyond. Already having attained this thing, how do we not get caught-up in starting or going beyond?"

Eihei Koroku
(Dogen's Extensive Record)

The Way of Ango

The Japanese word Ango (pronounced 'on-go') means "peaceful dwelling." Ango refers to a three-month practice period that is held once or twice a year at many Zen centers and Zen temples. The daily round of Ango includes a morning Zen service with chanting, meal meditations known as "oryoki," several periods of zazen-only, slow walking meditations known as "kinhin," silent work activities known as "samu," study groups and formal lectures, and personal meetings with the Zen teacher. During the training period of Ango, Zen practitioners honor the Buddha by embodying core-Self inside of zazen-only, honor the Dharma by Way-listening to vast Oneness with beginner's heartmind, and honor the Sangha by living in boundless intimacy with total reality.

The spirit of Ango is not meant to be practiced exclusively at a Zen temple or a Zen center for a set period of linear time. Ango is fundamentally an unobstructed Way of being peacefully embodied in the timeless stillness of each moment. We give life to the true spirit of Ango by living from the still composure of our core-Self and the magnanimous openness of our beginner's heartmind. To passionately live in the unobstructed spirit of Ango is to daily journey in the ever surprising Way of ungraspable enlightenment itself. When we sincerely practice the spirit of Ango with the basic goodness of our beginner's heartmind, this only moment is continuously realized as the noble crown of total reality. To viscerally realize the noble crown of total reality is to embody core-Self as Buddha, to embody vast Oneness as Dharma, and to embody limitless interdependency as Sangha.

Detailed Instructions

In this supplemental chapter, I will show you how to create a Zen home training dojo, give you step-by-step instructions on how to embody the ancient seal of zazen-only, and teach you how to peacefully dwell in your core-Self far beneath thinking. As you train in your Zen home dojo, I encourage you to study, investigate, and diligently apply all my instructions with the sincerity, curiosity, and openness of your beginner's heartmind. Always remember that your daily practice of zazen-only is the somatic and visceral foundation for continuously embodying core-Self in the practice of shikantaza. When you endlessly return as a noble beginner to embody core-Self inside of shikantaza and zazen-only, you will organically bloom in ungraspable enlightenment and somatically seal your boundless intimacy with total reality far beyond doubt.

I present my instructions in forty-six steps that anyone can easily follow. As you read these forty-six steps, you will notice that I point you to multiple photos that act as visual aids. You can access these visual aids at the very end of my verbal instructions. These forty-six steps and their visual aids provide all human beings with true guidance for faithfully embodying the still brilliance of core-Self within the vast Oneness of total reality. If you are a beginner, do not get caught-up in a beginner's false assumption of being far removed from the total fulfillment and completion of our Way. On the other hand, if you are a veteran practitioner of Zen, do not get caught-up in the false assumption of being far beyond a beginner's ever fresh practice and truthful Way of not-knowing.

I encourage all beginners to have deep visceral confidence that their ever fresh embodiment of shikantaza and zazen-only is exactly the total completion of our Way and the true unfolding of ungraspable enlightenment far beyond ego-self thinking and knowing. If you are a veteran practitioner of Zen, I encourage you to romance the ever fresh embodiment of shikantaza and zazen-only and never go beyond just this. Remember that the total somatic completion of our Way is always at the new and ever fresh beginning. This new and ever fresh beginning of our endless practice is always the total fulfillment of our radical humanness and the visceral confirmation that our everyday life is ungraspable enlightenment itself.

Never assume that you have mastered these forty-six steps and their visual aids. Do not take your starting as insignificant; do not think that you are a practitioner who has gone far beyond the beginning. If you begin to think that your starting is without significance, kick over insignificance with the brilliant nobility of beginner's heartmind. If thoughts of significance and going beyond arise, stamp-out going beyond by remembering that a radical human being is constantly learning in the kindergarten of everyday life. To stamp-out going beyond in this Way is to bow to the magnanimous humility of beginner's heartmind. To kick over insignificance with the brilliant nobility of beginner's heartmind is to joyfully return to the root of your profound simplicity. To return to the root of your profound simplicity is to courageously embody the ungraspable nature of your core-Self and wholeheartedly place the monarch's crown on the still essence of total reality.

"Our life at this very moment is the true Self
in operation, and the operating of our true
Self is our life that is this only moment."

Eihei Dogen,
(1200 AD to 1253 AD)

Instructions For Daily Home Practice
How To Touch The Still Brilliance Of Total Reality

1) Acting upon your decision to wholeheartedly sit as core-Self inside of zazen-only, choose a room in your home or apartment that will be relatively quiet, secluded, and free from disturbances. Know that this room will be your Zen meditation dojo during the time of practice. You can use most any room you want, including your bedroom, hall, or front-room. Your Zen dojo should be neither too hot nor too cold; neither too bright nor too dark. If you practice in the late evening or before the break of dawn, illuminate your Zen meditation dojo with the same glow as subtle moonlight.

2) Select a special area in your Zen dojo room where you will sit quietly in zazen-only. Pick your Zen meditation area with the intuitive devotion and romantic exuberance of your beginner's heartmind. This meditation area is where you will practice the ancient seal of zazen-only on a cushion, a bench, or a simple chair. Remember that this area of practice is where you will embody core-Self in boundless intimacy with total reality.

3) I also recommend that you create a Zen meditation altar in your home dojo. *(photo 1)*. This training altar will inspire and encourage your daily embodiment of core-Self inside of shikantaza and zazen-only. Again, trust the intuitive devotion and romantic exuberance of your beginner's heartmind when you create your altar. You can decorate your Zen training altar with a small flower vase, a rock or crystal, a candle, a picture, a statue, an incense burner, or any arrangement of

these objects together. Always keep your home dojo and training altar harmoniously organized, aesthetically pleasing, and free from dirt and dust. This is the Way you will train yourself to practice tender caring and compassion for all beings and things. If you use incense, do not use heavy or sweet smells. I use only Japanese incense that has very subtle earthy aromas. If you practice in a small room, use only a three to four inch incense stick. I recommend that you place your incense stick upright in a small container filled with clean sand.

4) Once you have created your training altar and established the true place where you will practice zazen-only, choose a time during the day that will be relatively quiet and free from interruptions. If you have a family life or live with others, schedule your embodied training in the early morning before anyone wakes-up. You can also practice zazen-only in the evening after everyone has gone to bed. The early morning between 4:30 AM and 6:30 AM is recommended. When you sit in the early morning, know that you establish a clear and bright Way of being in your body that will continuously inspire and encourage your practice of shikantaza in everyday life. Pick a specific amount of time that you will sit in zazen-only. I recommend that you use a timer for training. You can use an oven timer, a microwave timer, or any small digital timer that operates quietly. In this way, you will train yourself not to think of time even as you liberate your embodied practice from the passage of time.

5) Do not make your training time too short or too long. If you are just starting out, 10 to 15 minutes is fine. As you get more comfortable with just sitting in the physical stillness and silence of zazen-only, I encourage you to naturally stretch the time of your seated practice. Do not stretch your daily sitting by more than five minutes at a time. For example, do not go from ten minutes to twenty minutes. Take your time to stretch into a longer period of just sitting inside of just sitting. When you sense that you can linger longer in zazen-only without forcing yourself, gently and compassionately stretch your daily time by five minutes. Don't try to willfully or forcefully extend your time. Only extend your sitting when your body has become very comfortable with your previously scheduled time. Wait until you are naturally drawn to linger in the sensuality of your hara and the

still vibrancy of your core-Self. The maximum time that I recommend for anyone to sit in zazen-only is sixty minutes. Remember that it is not the amount of time that is important. What is important is how you honestly throw your whole life force into each moment of sitting. What is important is your genuine intimacy with each breath, your sensual and sincere embodiment of core-Self, your deep appreciation for the pristine freshness of beginner's heartmind, and your felt visceral confidence that all this is the expression of your radical humanness that has not one thing lacking.

6) If you sit early in the morning do not take coffee or caffeinated tea before you sit. Wait until after your sitting. If you sit in the evening, make sure that you eat moderately and avoid any kind of alcoholic drinks during or after your dinner. Do not use psychotropic drugs (including marijuana) anytime before, during, or after your formal training in zazen-only. Also, never use any kind of organic or artificial mind altering substances throughout your daily embodiment of shikantaza.

7) Always allow at least one hour after a moderate meal before you sit in zazen-only. If you eat just before sitting, your body may feel sluggish and heavy. It may also be difficult for you to maintain a peak state of embodied alertness during digestion. If you get up in the early morning, prepare yourself for zazen-only by washing your face, brushing your teeth, and combing your hair. In the evening rinse your face with water and arrange your appearance. I recommend that you set aside specific garments to wear during Zen meditation. These can be wide pants or skirts, a loose top, a half or full Japanese kimono, or any other comfortable garment. When you choose your clothing for zazen-only, pick garments that have subdued earth tone colors. You can use black or white clothing, but do not use garments with bright colors.

8) Set up a simple training schedule so that you are ready to practice zazen-only at least once a day (twice if you can). Be consistent, devoted, and totally committed to your training schedule. I encourage you to view your everyday life as a wheel that has many spokes. Each spoke represents a part of your daily life where you use a certain amount of physical, mental, emotional, and spiritual energy. It is important to remember that your practice of zazen-only is not just another spoke

that you are trying to add to your life wheel. Your practice of zazen-only should be the very center or hub of your life. When the wheel of your everyday life does not have a hub or center-point of gravity, it tends to wobble, stray from the Way, and fall. When zazen-only is the hub or true center-point of gravity for the wheel of your life, all the spokes naturally turn together in harmony, align to the peace and balance of our Way, and rotate lucidly and uprightly in ungraspable enlightenment itself.

9) However, making your practice of zazen-only the hub of your everyday life does not mean that you should be rigidly following your schedule come hell or high water. Be honest and compassionate with yourself. Allow space to sleep-in when feeling ill or exhausted. There may be times in everyday life when your loving family relations need to be set as a priority or work activities need to be lucidly and compassionately finished. During these times, remember that our Way is to tenderly practice shikantaza right in the midst of our daily challenges and ever changing life circumstances. On the other hand, it is important to keep in mind that your practice of shikantaza in everyday life needs to be grounded in the consistent and daily embodiment of zazen-only. Just be thoroughly clear regarding your physical condition, your work involvement, and your precious family time. Again, the important point is to balance all of this with honesty and integrity while not making your practice of zazen-only just another spoke in your everyday life.

10) You can practice zazen-only in one of four ways *(photos 28, 31, 41, & 44)*. You can sit on a cushion in cross-legged posture, sit kneeling with a cushion between your thighs, kneel on a low bench with heels tucked back, or just sit upright on a comfortable chair. If you sit cross-legged on the floor, use a small sitting cushion or a folded pillow that raises your sit bones about four to six inches off the ground. If you choose to sit on a round meditation cushion, rest your sit bones on the middle half of the pillow so that a third of the pillow can be seen protruding from the back of your seated position. In the kneeling position, your sit bones should be raised about the same height. If you are sitting on a chair, sit on the front half of the seat with both feet placed flat on the ground and about a foot

apart. Keep your own posture and do not lean into the back support of the chair. If you have back pain or are physically unable to maintain your own upright posture, use a support pillow between your back and the back support of the chair. Do not lean completely into the pillow for support. On the other hand, do not hesitate to feel intimately and tenderly supported by the pillow.

11) When you are ready to implement your daily Zen training schedule, arouse your beginner's heartmind to endlessly start with utmost sincerity, vitality, and devotion. Set your intention to let go of all your agendas, expectations, and concerns from the moment you wake up to implement your training. Remember that you are going to simply embody core-Self inside of zazen-only for its own sake.

12) When you wake up in the morning, go to the bathroom, wash your face, comb your hair, brush your teeth, and put on your meditation clothing. Make yourself presentable to yourself. As you prepare yourself in this Way, surrender your habitual labeling, comparing, thinking, and judging. Openly experience and compassionately witness your felt sensations, your passing thoughts, and your arising feelings. Give up your tendency to grasp or push away this only moment. Yield up your constant drivenness to know things only through your thinking mind. Be ready to throw your whole life force into just sitting as core-Self inside of zazen-only.

13) Approach the entry of your meditation dojo with dignity. Stop at the threshold and begin to breathe through your nose with your lips gently touching each other. Slowly raising the flat palms of your open hands, bring them together at a level between your heart and your chin. The fingers should be together and naturally upright (photo 5). This upright Way of palms touching together is called the hand mudra of "gassho." As your palms meet, gently drop your embodied awareness into the center-point of your lower abdomen. Sense the sensuality of your hara and the still vibrancy of your core-Self.

14) Having established the hand mudra of gassho, take a breath and bring your opened eyes to a forty-five degree angle. As you express gassho with eyes

gently lowered to a forty-five degree angle, bow at the waist and completely sense the visceral meaning of just this *(photo 6)*. Sense the tranquillity and peace that arises in your body. As you bow at the threshold of your dojo room, know that you are entering a special training place where you will embody core-Self inside of zazen-only. When you bow in gassho, do not willfully intend to bow. Just trust the profound nature of bowing and viscerally surrender to being bowed beyond thinking.

15) After you bow, you will slowly bring your hands into the mudra of "shashu." You will do this by first bringing your left hand downward toward your lower abdomen. As you do just this, tuck your thumb inside your four fingers and make a very soft fist. *(photo 2)*. This should feel like your four fingers are gently embracing the thumb. The fingers that wrap around your thumb should be gently touching your lower abdomen just below your belly button. I call this part of the shashu mudra, "Embracing the infant." Now take your right palm and cover your left fist. You should feel like you are cradling your left fist with your right hand *(photo 3)*. I call this part of the shashu mudra, "Holding the precious treasure." I encourage you to always embody the precious mudra of shashu with the tender attentiveness and openhearted devotion of beginner's heartmind.

16) Now that you are in shashu, continue to keep your eyes at a forty-five degree angle. Gently tilt your head ever so slightly toward the floor. Don't bend your neck too far nor hold it back stiffly. As you tilt your head, keep it aligned with your upright and easeful posture. Enter your dojo by walking slowly in half-step kinhin *(photo 7)*. Kinhin is a slow and meditative Way of walking in shikantaza *(photos 51 & 52)*. You will use the hand mudra of shashu and the walking form of kinhin whenever you train in your home dojo.

17) Walk into your training dojo with a beginner's humility, nobility, and dignity. Be aware of your whole body as you move with each step. Allow your feet to meet the floor with tender caring and awareness. During your meditative walking, sense your upright posture and its relationship to gravity. Be intimately aware of each step that you take in kinhin. As you walk with a tender attentiveness, sense

the still vibrancy of your core-Self that is within and beyond the movement of walking itself.

18) Approach the front of your training altar. When you are about four to six feet away from your meditation altar, come to gassho position and bow at the waist. As you bow, you are honoring the training altar of your everyday life. *(photos 47 & 48)*. Move towards the altar and light your candle and incense. After you open your training altar, step back about two feet and bow in gassho. Then bring your hands back into the shashu hand mudra.

19) While in shashu walk slowly and wholeheartedly toward your true place of sitting. As you walk in shashu, keep your embodied awareness in the felt visceral center-point of your lower abdomen. When you are directly in front of your sitting area, bring your hands to gassho and bow at the waist toward your chair or cushion *(photos 8, 9, 12, & 13)*. This is called, "Bowing and being bowed we surrender our ego-self to meet the boundless intimacy and vast Oneness of total reality."

20) After you bow toward your meditation mat and cushion, remain in gassho, turn clockwise 180 degrees, and bow outward in the direction away from your chair or mat *(photos 10,11,14, &15)*. This is called, "Bowing outward, we include all sentient beings in this very body." This is our Way of inviting all beings and things to sit with us in the vast Oneness and boundless intimacy of total reality.

21) After bowing outward, take a step back and sit down on your chair or cushion. Your sit bones should be on the front half of your cushion or chair *(photo 30, 42, & 43)*. Half of the meditation cushion that is behind you will tilt upward slightly in the rear. In a wholehearted and deliberate manner, take a hold of your right foot, bring it towards your body, and tuck in the heel toward your groin. Likewise, take your left foot, bring it toward your body, and tuck the heel in the arch made by the curvature of your right foot. Both heels will be almost directly in line with each other *(photos 16, 17, & 24)*. When you cross your legs in this Way, your knees and the base of your spine will form a pyramid-like stability for the whole body.

This is called, "Laying the foundation for the sublime posture of tranquillity and repose."

22) Once you have your legs tucked comfortably together, scan your body for any uncomfortable pressure in the area of your sit bones and folded legs. Make physical adjustments as needed. Carefully and neatly arrange your clothing so it does not pull or bind anywhere around your body. Any somatic tightness or pressure created by your clothing, the horizontal misalignment of your sit bones, or the vertical misalignment of your posture can hinder blood circulation, diminish neural transmission, and cause tingling and numbness. This is why I encourage you to wear loose and comfortable clothing. This is why I tell you to always check and scan your whole body for alignment and balance before you completely let go into the physical stillness of zazen-only.

23) After you have scanned your whole body and arranged your clothing, relax your lower belly and start tilting your pelvis slightly foreword. When you do this, notice how effortlessly your torso unfolds into its natural spinal uprightness. The small of your back just above your hips will naturally curve forward toward your belly button. Do not strain this natural forward thrust of your belly and small curvature of your lower spine as it will create undue tension and muscular tightness in your mid-back. When your spine straightens into its curved uprightness, your lower abdomen will protrude slightly downward at a forty-five degree angle. As you tilt your pelvis forward, gently allow your shoulders to extend to either side and let your chest naturally open without thrusting it forward. Your shoulders should be in a relaxed and natural position, neither drooping forward nor thrusting backward. Your ears should be parallel with your shoulders; the tip of your nose should be directly over your navel; and your chin should be slightly tucked in *(photos 25, 26, 29, & 33)*.

24) After tilting your pelvis and establishing your natural posture, bring your left hand toward your lower abdomen with palm facing upward. Gently hold the blade of your little finger against your lower abdomen, about two and a half inches below your navel. Then bring your right hand with palm upward and place it underneath your left hand. Allow only the fingers of both hands to overlap each other. Bring

the tips of your thumbs gently together so that your hands and thumbs form a beautiful oval at the center of your hara *(photos 22, 23, & 24).* The point where your thumbs touch together should be directly in front of your navel. Make sure that your thumbs are lightly touching each other. If you place too much pressure on the meeting of the thumbs, you will create undue tension in your arms and hands. However, if you do not keep just enough tension in the meeting of the thumbs you will not be able to keep them together to form a straight horizontal line with the floor. This hand mudra is called the "cosmic mudra" (hokkai-join). You should keep this hand mudra in zazen-only with great care and tenderness. When you form the cosmic mudra, we say that you are holding "Nothing holy and everything sacred right here and now." The oval of the cosmic mudra should not be too wide or too narrow. If I were to take my forefinger and point into the middle of your hand mudra, my finger would touch the center of your hara where visceral intimacy with your core-Self arises *(photos 37 & 38).* As you will remember, this area is known as the tanden and is located about two and a half inches directly below your navel.

25) Once you have placed your hands in the cosmic mudra for zazen-only, sway the upper torso slowly to the left and to the right so that the waist, hip muscles, rib cage, and neck muscles are stretched on both sides *(photos 18 & 19).* After stretching each side once, sway your torso slowly and gently from side to side with decreasing motion towards the center. When your swaying comes to rest at your true center, your back should be naturally and easefully upright.

26) Allow your head to effortlessly rise toward heaven. Let it naturally rest on the top vertebra of your spine. Inhaling through your nose with lips closed, breathe into any muscular tension or tightness. Then tenderly release the muscular tension or tightness with an exhalation through your pursed lips. You can do this several times until you feel physically at ease in the ancient seal of zazen-only.

27) Once you have naturally settled into your upright posture and established ease in your whole body, allow your eyes to remain half open with eyelids slightly lowered. The eyes in this half open position are "just seeing" and reflecting reality just as it is. They are neither straining to see nor drooping closed *(photos 20 &*

21). Rather than looking straight ahead, they should be gently and comfortably lowered at a forty-five degree angle. When you do just this, you will be naturally seeing the floor about four to five feet in front of you. Do not concentrate or focus your eyes on any particular area or object. Just allow them to remain in an easeful, alert, and soft mirror-like gaze. Let them crisply reflect everything that exists within the natural field of your vision.

28) By keeping our eyes open, we remain intimate with the world of cause and effect. We do not close our eyes, withdraw into an inner world, or leave our body. This is a very important point in our practice. We treasure just seeing things as they are even as we embrace all beings and things just as IT is. Seeing things as they are means that we brilliantly shine all our senses outward while enjoying the still composure of our core-Self. Embracing all beings and things just as IT is means that we honor the vast Oneness and boundless intimacy of total reality. Our eyes are a mirror of seeing, our nose is a mirror of smelling, our skin is a mirror of touch, our ears are a mirror of sound, and our tongue is a mirror of taste. As mirrors they intimately reflect the pristine nature of our physical world before the interference of ego-self and thinking mind. This is the Way we return to the root of profound simplicity, recover the brilliance of our beginner's heartmind, embody the great round mirror of boundless intimacy, and viscerally anchor in our core-Self that silently illuminates the vast Oneness of total reality.

29) Once you have established your naturally upright posture, your mirror like gaze, and your cosmic mudra, gently touch your lips together to close your mouth. Rest your tongue comfortably against the roof of your mouth. The tip of your tongue should be gently touching your upper front teeth. Your breathing should now continue only through your nostrils. Relinquish your mental tendency to keep track of linear time. Dwell in the timelessness of total reality and simply wait forever for nothing to happen. To dwell in timelessness is to linger in the still essence of core-Self with nothing extra. To linger as core-Self with nothing extra is to faithfully and confidently surrender all your desires and expectations to have something happen.

30) Become aware of each inhalation and exhalation. Feel the air coming into the nostrils and exiting the nostrils. Allow yourself to also embody the immediate experience of your ever fresh impermanence. Sense the delicate thread upon which your life hangs with each breath and heartbeat. Clarify how each inhalation nourishes your ever fresh aliveness and revitalizes your passion for life. Investigate how each exhalation releases life beyond grasping while intimately nurturing your faithful entrustment into death and dying.

31) Once you are intimately aware that breathing is the Way of life and death, begin to slowly breathe into your belly. When you belly breathe, you are using your diaphragm instead of your chest muscles to expand your lungs. The diaphragm itself is a dome-shaped sheet of muscle that separates the chest cavity from the abdominal cavity. When you belly breathe, your chest should stay relatively motionless while your belly naturally fills up like a balloon *(photos 35 & 36)*. As you begin to belly breathe, don't try to force your belly outward. Belly breathing happens naturally and easefully. Just remember that this is the Way we all started out breathing as infants. All of us have a cellular memory of belly breathing that is always there for us. Gently and tenderly breathe into your belly without judging yourself. Sense each inhalation as it enters your nostrils, passes down your throat, moves through your chest, and slowly expands your belly. With each inhalation, let your embodied awareness naturally sink away from your head and drift downward into your expanding belly. You should feel your belly gently expanding forward with complete ease and without force. If you find that you are creating tension and frustration in your body, let go of belly breathing for the time being and simply pay attention to the natural rhythm and flow of your breath.

32) As you feel your belly gently expand directly forward, you will notice that your lower abdomen, just below your belly button, is tilting and extending downward at a forty-five degree angle *(photos 35 & 38)*. You will also notice a slight tautness in your lower abdomen that accentuates its downward extension toward the floor. Don't force this downward extension of your lower abdomen. It naturally happens as the belly fully extends forward. Sense how the skin of your lower abdomen stretches and turns downward into a forty-five degree angle toward the floor. Be

aware that this stretching and angling happens naturally at the end of each inhalation. If you ever so slightly tense your lower abdominal muscle at the end of inhalation, you will experience a true visceral sensation of the downward forty-five degree angle.

33) Notice that your cosmic hand mudra is gently touching, compassionately outlining, and tenderly emphasizing the great functioning of your stretched lower abdomen. As your lower abdomen becomes stretched and slightly taut, intimately sense the center-point of the tautness. Be aware of felt sensations that arise from the visceral center-point of your lower abdomen about two inches beneath the skin. You may feel a sensual warmth, a pleasureful tingling, or a felt groundedness emanating from this area. Always sense your visceral core deeply and inwardly. Just let yourself enjoy the felt sensations as they arise. To linger in the felt sensations that arise within your deep somatic center is to viscerally embody your core-Self while generating, containing, and extending Ki energy throughout your whole body.

34) Once you become intimate with the felt sensations that arise from the visceral core of your whole body, ever so slightly begin to keep a very gentle pressure or subtle tension in your hara or lower abdomen. Keep this subtle tension present during each inhalation and exhalation. You should feel a tender and gentle tautness in your hara without any pushing or tensing of your belly. This felt tautness in your lower abdomen will help you to remain continuously aware of your core-Self that arises from the visceral center-point of your hara. Remember that the slight tensing of your hara should be very soft, gentle, and extremely subtle. Relax inwardly. Have compassion for yourself. Practice beyond the comparing and judging of your inner critic. Take refuge in the humility, nobility, and openness of your beginner's heartmind. Remember, we are all endless beginners in the practice of shikantaza and zazen-only. You do not need to be a professional. Just be a tender and noble beginner who has the true power to begin again at the ever fresh beginning. Know that each precious moment of your sincere and compassionate practice is ungraspable enlightenment itself.

35) As you sit in zazen-only, do not be concerned about the passage of endless thoughts. Do not try to still your mind. Do not follow your thoughts nor try to stop them. Your brain functions much like a gland that secretes hormones. However, instead of hormones, your brain naturally secretes thoughts. Sometimes your brain secretes thoughts rapidly one after another. At other times, thoughts may be secreted in a very slow succession. Whether you are practicing shikantaza or zazen-only, diligently investigate how your thoughts arise without a thinker. Study the difference between your heady experience of thinking, your chasing after thoughts, your thoughts just happening, your mind trying to stop itself, and the still essence of your core-Self that is totally unaffected by the passage of your thoughts and the movement of your thinking.

36) If you let a thought distract your visceral embodiment of core-Self, then you are engaged in chasing after thoughts or thinking. On the other hand, if you are embodying your visceral sensuality while silently illuminating your passing thoughts from the still brilliance of your core-Self, then you are expressing the intelligent discernment of non-thinking. To express the intelligent discernment of non-thinking during zazen-only does not mean that the mind is necessarily empty or devoid of thoughts. Nor does it mean that the thinking mind has stopped the movement of thinking mind. The intelligent discernment of non-thinking means that the still brilliance of core-Self is silently illuminating, compassionately witnessing, and effortlessly renouncing passing thoughts and thinking mind. Our Way of renouncing passing thoughts and thinking mind is not based on mental discipline or asserting our conscious will. We continuously renounce passing thoughts and thinking mind in zazen-only because we are deeply drawn to somatically abide in the sensuality of our hara and the still vibrancy of our core-Self.

37) Always remember that when you become somatically intimate with the innocent sensuality of your hara, you will begin to experience a vibrant stillness and tranquil silence just beneath the visceral center-point of sensuality itself. To somatically experience this vibrant stillness and tranquil silence is to viscerally

realize that core-Self is transmitting core-Self in boundless intimacy, vast Oneness, and limitless interdependency.

38) When you begin to viscerally experience the vital sensuality, vibrant stillness, and tranquil silence of your core-Self, you will be less apt to identify with your thinking, unlikely to chase after passing thoughts, and less inclined to use your thinking mind to still your thinking mind. However, if you find yourself distracted by passing thoughts, asleep in ego-self, or attached to the mental process of thinking, bring your embodied awareness back to your breathing, gently sink away from your headiness, follow the next inhalation into the visceral center-point of your lower abdomen, somatically experience the vital sensuality of your hara, and take refuge in the vibrant stillness and tranquil silence of your core-Self. This is how you endlessly reawaken from your sleep in ego-self and thinking mind, instantly return to the still brilliance of non-thinking, and gratefully recover the pristine wonder of your beginner's heartmind.

39) Whether you are a beginner or veteran practitioner of zazen-only, confidently trust that you are totally embodying the Way of ungraspable enlightenment by compassionately keeping your seat of stillness, by anchoring in the felt sensuality of your hara, by remaining viscerally awake to your core-Self, and by somatically enjoying your beginner's heartmind. However, know that there will be times when you fall fast asleep in passing thoughts and thinking. During those times, do not become disheartened. Simply reawaken to core-Self with the sincerity and nobility of beginner's heartmind. On the other hand, if you remain continuously awake to your core-Self inside of zazen-only, gratefully accept the ordinariness of your embodiment without exaltation. When you neither become disheartened nor exalted, you are embodying the Way of zazen-only as ungraspable enlightenment itself. This is a very important point in our practice.

40) Keep physically still during zazen-only, but do so with a caring and tender attitude toward your body. Never force yourself to sit absolutely still through physical discomfort and arising pain. Ignoring the early signals of physical discomfort and arising pain is tantamount to perpetuating ignorance. We cannot establish or create the still essence of core-Self by willfully holding ourselves

absolutely still in zazen-only. When we willfully force our body to sit absolutely still through physical discomfort and arising pain, we are inadvertently attached to an illusory view. This illusory view falsely assumes that the still essence of core-Self is dependent on our will power, our mental concentration, and our cerebral mindfulness in zazen-only. Our Way is to embody the still essence of core-Self that inherently exists before our will power, our mental concentration, and our cerebral mindfulness. This is exactly so because core-Self is the still essence of total reality. To think that the still essence of total reality is created or established by our willpower, our mental concentration, or our cerebral mindfulness is to cultivate a vast field of ignorance and arrogance.

41) If you experience increasing somatic discomfort or arising pain in zazen-only, trust the intelligent non-thinking discernment and compassion of your core-Self. Let your core-Self guide you to reestablish the body of ease and joy. Make subtle physical adjustments that nourish and sustain a relaxed alertness and a composed wakefulness in the body of zazen-only. Let the adjustments all begin from the visceral and sensual integrity of your core-Self. Do not make adjustments that are initiated by your heady ego-self and thinking mind. The adjustments might be very subtle shifts in specific areas of your musculature, your spinal column, your joints, or your skeletal structure. For example, if your right leg below your knee begins to tingle or go numb, you might first try to gently tighten and relax your calf muscle. If that doesn't work, keep your formal hand mudra, mirror gaze, somatic intimacy with breath, and grounded visceral core-Self awareness while slowly bending your torso forward at the waist. This will lift your sit bones off the meditation cushion and release pressure on any nerve or vessel that was causing the leg to tingle or go numb. You can also tighten and relax your lifted butt muscles several times. This also helps to recover blood flow and nerve transmission to your calf muscle. If all this still doesn't work, slowly and tenderly release your right hand from the cosmic mudra to help extend your right leg and stretch it out. Remember to stay true to your mirror gaze, your breath, and your visceral core-Self awareness as you move. After you stretch out your leg, bring your right hand back underneath your left hand to complete the cosmic mudra and continue to sit as core-Self inside of just sitting. After the

numbness and tingling subside, slowly bring your leg back into cross-legged position and return to the ancient seal of zazen-only. This is the Way we realize the boundless compassion of buddhas and ancestors while verifying that the still essence of core-Self is not dependent on our physical stillness nor hindered by any of our tender and caring movements.

42) If you need to respond to increasing pain in zazen-only, make sure that all your movements reflect the meditative Way of ancient sages and buddha ancestors. If you need to make some movements to diminish pain and bring ease to your body, do so in a very slow, dignified, and wholehearted manner. Let all movements arise from the still discernment of your core-Self. Do not start any movement from your ego-self or thinking mind. Never move in a heedless, careless, or casual manner when responding to pain in zazen-only. As you move, keep true to your mirror gaze, your postural integrity, your slow rhythmic breathing, and your visceral intimacy with core-Self.

43) At the end of your timeless sitting in zazen-only, disengage your hands from the cosmic mudra, slowly bring them to gassho position, and wholeheartedly bow from the waist *(photos 39, 40, 45, & 46)*. When you bow in this Way, you sanctify the vast Oneness of total reality, honor the vast impermanence of each moment, bless your boundless intimacy with all beings and things, and consecrate the still essence of core-Self far beyond thinking.

44) Continuing to embody the sincerity and felt integrity of your core-Self, place your hands on your thighs and gently sway your torso side to side. If you are sitting on a cushion, unloosen your legs and stretch them out. Then, bring your legs back close to your torso with knees pointed toward the ceiling. Bracing yourself firmly with your hands, come to a standing position. Remember not to stand up abruptly. Give your leg muscles, knees, and ankles a chance to adjust. After you stand, bring your hands into shashu mudra. Turn around to face your sitting chair or cushion. Take one step back, release your shashu mudra, and come to gassho. Now bow once at the waist to honor the true place where you sat in ungraspable enlightenment and boundless intimacy with buddhas and ancestors *(photos 9 & 13)*.

45) After you bow in gassho toward your sitting place, come to shashu, keep eyes at a forty-five degree angle, and slowly step sideways away from your chair or mat. Once you have cleared your chair or mat, walk in kinhin with dignity toward your meditation altar. Come to gassho just in front of the altar and bow at the waist *(photos 47 & 48)*. If you have a candle on the altar, blow it out. After you close your training altar, come to shashu, and step back three to six feet. Then bring your hands into the gassho mudra and bow at the waist. This is the way we honor the training altar of everyday life.

46) After you bow toward your training altar, come to shashu and walk slowly toward the room entrance in slow, half-step kinhin. Once you are at the threshold of your home dojo, stop and bow in gassho *(photos 53 & 54)*. As you make this final gassho to honor the closure of your training dojo, arouse your sincere intention to live your everyday life by just sitting as core-Self inside of just living. Then, simply walk through your dojo threshold and continue to embody the Way of shikantaza in all your activities and relationships. After you walk through the threshold of your home dojo, the room turns back into its normal daily function. You can walk in and out without having to bow. However, you can walk in and bow to your altar or sitting area any time you wish. You can do this to somatically encourage your daily practice of shikantaza and viscerally recall your embodiment of core-Self inside of zazen-only.

Final Reminder And Encouragement

If you are a longtime practitioner of Zen, I encourage you to somatically study, viscerally refine, and experientially integrate these forty-six steps into your daily embodiment of shikantaza and zazen-only. Approach each step with the magnanimous openness of beginner's heartmind. Do not get caught-up in thinking you are more than a beginner. Do not resist or disparage reentering at the endless beginning. Do not attach to thoughts of having gone far beyond your starting. When you honorably accept yourself as an endless beginner, you are the upheld flower of our mirrored Way that openly transmits the fragrance of boundless intimacy, vast Oneness, and limitless interdependency.

Always remember that what truly prevails in our Way is the sincerity and humility of beginner's heartmind. Whether you are a beginner or veteran practitioner, do not doubt the basic goodness of your sincerity nor belittle the integrity of your inner struggle to honorably embody shikantaza and zazen-only. Do not ignore the original clarity of your beginner's heartmind or leave the refuge of your core-Self to wander about in vain. If you do not take refuge in your core-Self right here and now, you will miss the timeless opportunity to somatically realize the completion and fulfillment of your radical humanness while viscerally confirming your life of boundless intimacy and ungraspable enlightenment far beyond doubt.

Just know that I have deep confidence in your ability to somatically study and viscerally learn all my instructions and teachings on your own. Although I wholeheartedly trust that you can study and practice alone, I encourage you to seek out fellowship with other practitioners. Try to find a Zen center or a spiritual meditation group that has a deep visceral affinity with the teachings and instructions in this book. If you cannot find such a group, I recommend that you join my global online community where you will be able to study, investigate, and share my teachings with other spiritual practitioners around the world. There, you will have open access to my audio talks, my globally published articles, and my wide variety of collected inspirational videos. You can freely access and join my spiritual life community by going to my internet web-portal at Zendoctor.Com.

Finally, if you feel viscerally called by vast Oneness to start a small Zen meditation group in your home, I want you to know that I wholeheartedly support your genuine spiritual endeavor. You can ask people to study one or two pages of this book each week, tell them to investigate and put into practice what they have studied, meet one evening to sit together in the silence of zazen-only, and then freely and openly discuss the studied teachings and their practical application. Whichever way you choose to engage in heartfelt fellowship and camaraderie, know that I am always with you in the boundless intimacy and limitless interdependency of total reality.

If you need my support, I am readily available by telephone or webcam
to teach, mentor, and counsel both individuals and groups.
You can contact me by email at drb@zendoctor.com

"Each moment of zazen-only
is equally wholeness of practice,
equally wholeness of realization. This
is not only practice while sitting, it is
like a hammer striking emptiness:
before and after, its exquisite peal
permeates everywhere. How
can it be limited to just this
moment [of sitting]?"

Dogen Zenji

Visual Aids For Zen Embodiment

Bendowa
(Practicing the Way)

"Thinking
that practice
and enlightenment
are not one is no more
than a view that is outside
the Way. In the Buddha Way,
practice and enlightenment are
one and the same. Because it is the
practice of enlightenment, a beginner's
wholehearted practice of the Way is exactly
the totality of original enlightenment itself.
For this reason, in conveying the essential
attitude for practice, it is taught not
to wait for enlightenment
outside of practice."

Dogen Zenji

[1]
Zen Meditation Altar

[2]
Shashu (a)
Embracing the Infant

[3]
Shashu (b)
Holding the Precious Treasure

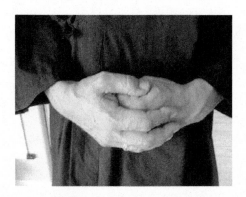

[4]
Dojo Threshold In Shashu

[5]
Dojo Threshold In Gassho

[6]
Bowing in at Threshold

[7]
Walking Into Dojo in Shashu

[8]   [9]

Bowing To The Place Where You Surrender Your Ego-Self

[10]   [11]

Bowing Outward To Include All Human Beings Through Your Body

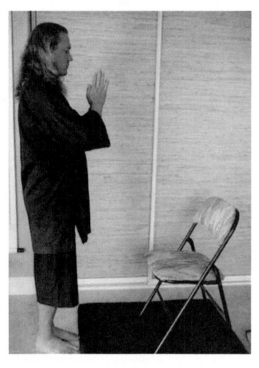 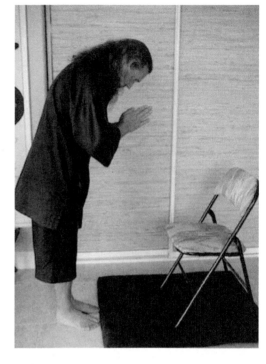

[14]   [15]

[16]

Tucking Legs Together In Burmese Style

[17]

[18]
Sway to Establish Your True Alignment To Gravity

[19]

[20]
Zazen Eyes Slightly Open During
Sitting And Walking In Shashu
45 Degree Angle

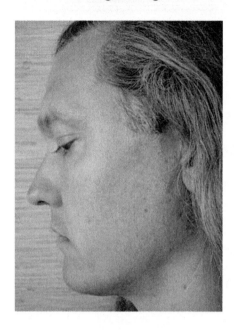

[21]

[22]
Cosmic Hand Mudra Held Gently
Against Your Lower Abdomen

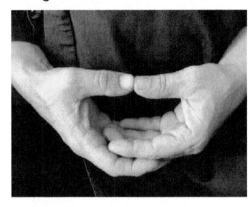

[23]

[24]

[25]

[26]

[27]

[28]

[29]

[30]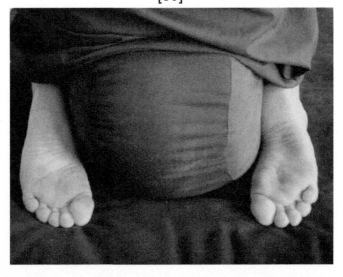

[31]

[32]

[33]

[34]

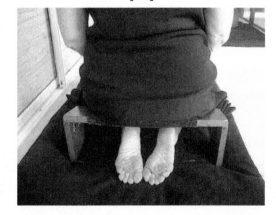

[35]
Inhalation

[36]
Exhalation

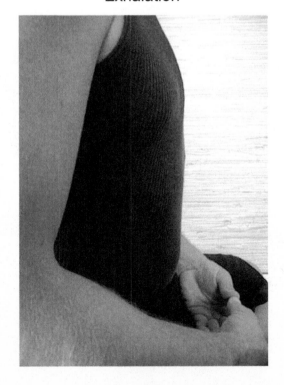

[37]

[38]

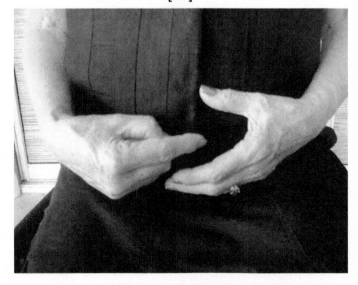

[39]

[40]

[41]

[42]

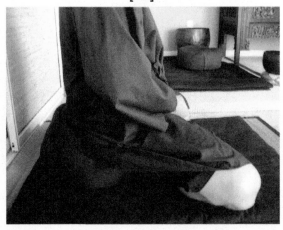

[43]

[44]

[45]

[46]

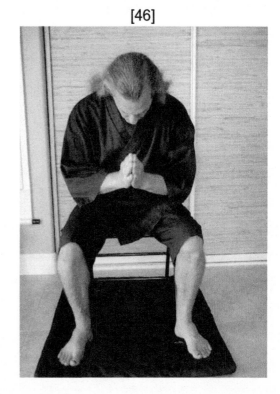

[47]

[48]

[49]

[50]

[51] Slow Half-Step Kinhin [52]

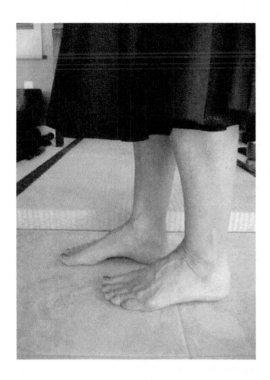 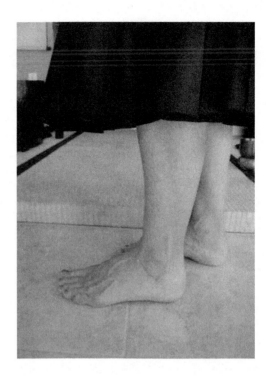

[53] Exiting Dojo [54]

Being Core-Self In This Only Moment Body

Honoring The Sacredness Of Total Reality

Bowing To All Beings And Things Beyond Thinking

Offering Our Whole Life As An Endless Beginner

Transmitting The Way Of Boundless Intimacy

Do Not Wait!

"Instantly sink into the felt sensuality of your hara, inwardly touch the visceral center-point of gravity, and viscerally rest in the still arising of core-Self. Practice the Way of loving and being loved with the tenderness, wholeness, and authenticity of beginner's heartmind. Gratefully meet vast impermanence as the ever fresh blooming of total reality. Dream of your vocation and your true calling. Envision and actualize your dreams while blending them with the vast Oneness of being dreamed in boundless intimacy and limitless interdependency with all beings and things. Then, simply live your everyday life from the still flower of awakening, the blooming of lucid dreaming, and the fragrance of ungraspable enlightenment with not one thing lacking."

Shugyo Daijo-roshi
(Dr. Bonnici)

EPILOGUE

• This Only Moment •

THIS ONLY MOMENT

May we cherish this day with deep gratitude, for we may never see tomorrow. Each breath and heartbeat intimately arrives to be the first and last moment of our life right here and now. The precious dependability of our days is constantly subject to the winds of change, randomness, and uncertainty. Our everyday life is like a shimmering dewdrop being warmed by the sun of vast impermanence.

Although our future is not yet, it is unfolding in the present through the behaviors and intentions of our body, speech, and mind. Even though our past is gone by, it is entering the present moment to influence who we are right here and now.

Each moment is the crossroads of life and death. In this only moment of life and death we can choose liberation and freedom from greed, aggression, and ignorance while passionately creating a loving, caring, and peaceful future together.

As each moment together may be our last, the infinite value of practicing kindness, clarity, truthfulness, and consideration is far beyond any worldly measure of fame, success, accomplishment, or gain.

May we choose to live this only moment wisely, for in its fleetingness, the chance to embody our radical humanness together and realize a brilliantly enlightened world may be completely lost.

Let us practice life together with an integrity, honesty, and humility that is far beyond the empty pride, righteousness, and defensiveness of our ego-self with its partial views of who is right and who is wrong.

Let us see our true Self reflected in each other so that we may forever take refuge in our vast Oneness, our boundless intimacy, and our limitless interdependency that is our guiding light.

Let us remember that the blessing of being alive and all our small and great accomplishments could never be realized without the bright wisdoming of total reality.

May we practice each moment of our everyday life as a sacred prayer that all human beings will finally live from the still composure of their core-Self, faithfully take refuge in the still essence of total reality, passionately express the magnanimous openness of their beginner's heartmind, and continuously arrive in boundless intimacy and ungraspable enlightenment with all beings and things.

Shugyo Daijo-roshi
(Dr. Bonnici)

CPSIA information can be obtained
at www.ICGtesting.com
Printed in the USA
LVOW05s1114151215
466715LV00033B/2453/P